ABOUT THE AUTHOR

Born and raised in Iceland, Arnfríður Guðmundsdóttir is Professor of Systematic Theology at the Faculty of Theology and Religious Studies of the University of Iceland and an ordained pastor within the Evangelical Lutheran Church of Iceland. She received her Ph.D. from the Lutheran School of Theology at Chicago in 1996. She has taught courses in Systematic Theology, Feminist Theology, and Religion and Film at the University of Iceland. This is the author's first book published in English.

D1319824

Meeting God on the Cross

AMERICAN ACADEMY OF RELIGION

ACADEMY SERIES

SERIES EDITOR
Kimberly Rae Connor, University of San Francisco

A Publication Series of
The American Academy of Religion
and
Oxford University Press

THE ETHICS OF ANIMAL EXPERIMENTATION
A Critical Analysis and Constructive Christian Proposal
Donna Yarri

PAUL IN ISRAEL'S STORY
Self and Community at the Cross
John L. Meech

CROSSING THE ETHNIC DIVIDE
The Multiethnic Church on a Mission
Kathleen Garces-Foley

GOD AND THE VICTIM
Traumatic Intrusions on Grace and Freedom
Jennifer Erin Beste

THE CREATIVE SUFFERING OF THE TRIUNE GOD
An Evolutionary Theology
Gloria L. Schaab

A THEOLOGY OF CRITICISM
Balthasar, Postmodernism, and the Catholic Imagination
Michael P. Murphy

DISABILITY AND CHRISTIAN THEOLOGY
Embodied Limits and Constructive Possibilities
Deborah Beth Creamer

MEETING GOD ON THE CROSS
Christ, the Cross, and the Feminist Critique
Arnfríður Guðmundsdóttir

AMERICAN ACADEMY OF RELIGION

Meeting God on the Cross

Christ, the Cross, and the Feminist Critique

ARNFRÍÐUR GUÐMUNDSDÓTTIR

UNIVERSITY PRESS

2010

OXFORD

UNIVERSITY PRESS

Oxford University Press, Inc., publishes works that further
Oxford University's objective of excellence
in research, scholarship, and education.

Oxford   New York
Auckland   Cape Town   Dar es Salaam   Hong Kong   Karachi
Kuala Lumpur   Madrid   Melbourne   Mexico City   Nairobi
New Delhi   Shanghai   Taipei   Toronto

With offices in
Argentina   Austria   Brazil   Chile   Czech Republic   France   Greece
Guatemala   Hungary   Italy   Japan   Poland   Portugal   Singapore
South Korea   Switzerland   Thailand   Turkey   Ukraine   Vietnam

Published by Oxford University Press, Inc.
198 Madison Avenue, New York, New York 10016

www.oup.com

Oxford is a registered trademark of Oxford University Press

Library of Congress Cataloging-in-Publication Data
Arnfríður Guðmundsdóttir.
Meeting God on the cross : Christ, the cross, and the feminist
critique / Arnfríður Guðmundsdóttir.
p. cm.
Includes bibliographical references and index.
ISBN 978-0-19-539796-3
1. Jesus Christ—Crucifixion. 2. Theology of the cross. 3. Feminist
theology. I. Title.
BT453.A76   2010
232'.401—dc22   2009038202

9 8 7 6 5 4 3 2 1

Printed in the United States of America
on acid-free paper

In memory of my brother, Jón Eiður Guðmundsson
1964–1990

Acknowledgments

Writing a book is in many ways similar to being pregnant. Pregnancy is an extraordinary time; a time mixed with hard work, exhaustion, excitement, worry, yearning, and hope. Having three children myself means that I have survived the joy as well as the turmoils of pregnancy three times. Of course the underlying sentiment during pregnancy is the great hope to eventually hold a baby, a new being that has been a part of yourself and is finally ready to live a life of its own. The moment of birth, preceeded frequently by unbelievable pain, together with screaming, yelling, crying, panting, and whatever it takes to get your baby out of your own body and into this world, is truly a moment of total bliss. There is nothing to compare and indeed no words can even start to describe the experience of a birth of a new being. It can only be characterized as a moment of true grace. Just to make sure, I am not implying that my book is in any way as important and valuable to me as my children. By no means. Nevertheless, during a long and often painful writing process, at times I could not help thinking about the comparison between being pregnant with a child and writing a book. This book began as a dissertation and has for an extended period of time been revised and enlarged, and then revised and enlarged all over again. Thus, the questions and issues of this book have stayed with me for quite a while and will for sure continue to do so when this book finally has a life of its own.

Like during my three pregnancies, I have enjoyed the support and the extended care and compassion of not only one but a whole crowd of midwives from the time that the idea of the book was conceived to the moment of birth. They have given me good and helpful advise, read me the rites when needed, but most important created a context in which different parts and pieces of the process could take place. Without them this book would never have been finished.

Special thanks to my good friend, teacher, and later collegue, Einar Sigurbjörnsson, professor of systematic theology, at the University of Iceland, who first introduced me to the exciting field of systematic theology. My advisor at the Lutheran School of Theology at Chicago, Carl Braaten, convinced me that I had to pick a topic for my dissertation that was close to my heart and would help me stay motivated to the end. I am grateful for his advising, as well as his support during the first part of the writing process. Other Chicago-people played an important role in the initial stage, amongst them Reinhard Hütter and the late Anne Carr, greatly missed and inspiring theologian and teacher. Last but not least I owe big thanks to Vitor Westhelle, whose support has been invaluable, for nominating this project to the American Academy of Religion Series at Oxford University Press. I am very grateful to the Theological Department at the University of Iceland for granting me a time off from teaching for the academic year of 2003–2004 and again in the spring of 2008. I am also grateful for the Fulbright Reasearch Grant I received for the academic year of 2003–2004 and to Professor Mary Elizabeth More, director of Program for Women in Theology and Ministry, Candler School of Theology, Emory University, for inviting me as a visiting Fulbright Scholar during that year.

An amazing group of friends within the vicinity of Hyde Park in Chicago became our extended family while we lived so far from our family and friends in Iceland for so long. BIG thanks to them all. I will not be able to mention every single one of them, but amongst them were: Joy Ann McDougall, Steffan Lösel, Hilda Koster, Jan Henrik Pranger, Claudia Santosa, Guðrún Guðmundsdóttir, Rúnar Helgi Vignisson, Lois Malcolm, Julie Dennison, Sarita Tamayo, Monica Melanchton, Rebecca Miles, and Damayanthi Niles. Other dear friends who have been supportive during the writing process of this book are: Anna Carter Florence, David Florence, Alexandra Brown, Anne-Louise Ericsson, and Wendy Farley. Carol Breimeier and Nína Leósdóttir did a marvelous job in trems of editing, proofreading, and formating, a job greatly appreciated. Special thanks to Jill Carter, for inviting my family to her home and creating a working space for me in her beautiful "pink house" in Annesquam, Massachusetts, in the summer of 2008. And last but not least, a great appreciation to Kimberly Connor and Cynthia Read, my editors at the OUP, who have been absolutely wonderful, supportive, understanding, and patient through it all.

Two of my friends have been particularly important to me during the writing process, two living proofs of invaluable feminist sisterhood. I owe more thanks to both of them than I will ever be able to express. My friend Joy Ann McDougall and I have been a fellow travellers on our theological pilgrimage for more than twenty years. Thank you, Joy, for your support, encouragement, prompting, and inspiration. It has been an exciting and adventurous journey, and I look forward to journeying with you for many more years to come. My friend Anna Carter Florence, whom I got to know at the soccerfield (where we were watching and admiring our sons) during my Fulbright year in Atlanta, has been a great source of strength, comfort, and insight. Thank you, Anna, for being my friend, and thank you for inviting me and my Anna Run to your home in the summer of 2008, providing a much appreciated space for me to work on the last chapter of this book.

I owe a big thank-you to my parents, Margrét María Jónsdóttir and Guðmundur Jónasson who have always been there for me, and so has my older brother Jónas and his wife Anh-Dao Tran, as well as my in-laws, Jóhanna Pálmadóttir and Matthías Einarsson. My kids, Guðmundur Már, Anna Rún, and Margrét Tekla, continue to be my greatest inspiration as well as an endless source of joy. They have been there on the sideline, cheering me on, eager to see me finish, hoping we can spend more time together once the book is done. I truly hope that will be the case. And finally my biggest supporter through it all has been my husband and closest friend, Gunnar, who has made it possible for me to take the time I needed to get the job done. To him I owe the greatest thanks. Above all, I give thanks to God for all these wonderful people and for all the good gifts of life.

I have dedicated this book to the memory of my younger brother, Jón Eiður. His suffering and pain and finally his death made me painfully aware of how important it is for us to take the human experiencec of suffering and pain seriously in our theological work. To watch so closely somebody in his early adulthood fight for his life, against all odds, is beyond words. His experience has heavily influenced my ongoing struggle with the meaning of the cross of Christ, in our God-given yet broken world.

Contents

Meeting God on the Cross

Introduction

Christ, the Cross, and the Feminist Critique

The important task of theologians (literally: those who talk about God) is to figure out how we can continue to talk about God in our rapidly changing world. Who said it was an easy task? Constantly faced with new challenges, theologians need to be aware of their context and the time and space they live in. Before they can even start their talk about God they need to listen to the people and know their questions. After the second world war the great challenge of European theologians was to figure out how, if at all possible, to continue to talk about God after all the horror that had taken place right there in their backyard. Too often theologians and churchbodies had simply remained silent during the war, or their responses had been totally inadequate and out of touch with what was happening.

Theologians who were left in the remains of the war needed to decide if it was at all possible to talk about a living and loving God in light of what had happened. The need to change the focus of the theological discourse was pressing. The revitalization of a theology of the cross was an attempt to respond to the situation of suffering and pain, as well as the hopelessness of those who had survived, by talking about a suffering God who is right there with those who suffer. A theology of the cross presents the cross as the locus of our knowledge of God, where God is found revealed and yet paradoxically hidden in that revelation. By presenting God known through suffering and dying, the theology of the cross reveals how the crucified and hidden God is the God whose strength lies hidden behind apparent weakness, and whose wisdom lies hidden behind apparent folly.

The cross of Christ has proven to be no less of a "stumbling block" or "foolishness" for Christians living in the end of the twentieth century and the beginning of the twenty first, than was the case back in the first century when the newly established community of friends and followers of Jesus Christ were trying to define the basics of their faith over against the harsh criticism of Jews and Greeks. In the writings of the first Christians their struggle to make sense of their belief in someone who had not only died in the presence of so many eyewitnesses, but had also been condemned as a criminal to the worst possible execution, is apparent. The growing awareness of abuses of the cross, where Christ's cross has been used by the more powerful to justify or excuse their abusive and oppressive behavior toward those with less power, has called into question all theologization of the cross. To some, the only legitimate response is to eliminate the cross from all theological discourse and shift the focus to Jesus' life and his message, instead of his death on the cross. To others, the abuse does not call for an end to all cross-centered theology, but rather a critical retrieval of the meaning and importance of the cross and a clear stop to all abuse that continues to take place in the name of Christ. This book is meant to respond to the question if a feminist theology of the cross is indeed a viable option.

Written from a feminist-lutheran perspective, this book presents a theological response to the feminists' challenge to classical Christology, particularly the meaning of the cross, by means of an explicit feminist retrieval and reconstruction of a theology of the cross. It is argued that a feminist theology of the cross can serve a dual purpose for feminist Christology: to show the patriarchal distortion of traditional Christology and to reveal lost dimensions in the understanding of the person and work of Jesus Christ. Although the feminist critique of christological doctrines is seen as an indispensable element of contemporary Christology, the argument is made that there is a redemptive message in the cross of Christ that is retrievable for women today. Despite its potential for abuse and indeed its well-documented history of misuse in the past, a feminist theology of the cross proclaims Jesus as a divine co-sufferer who brings good news to the poor and oppressed and as such can be a source of healing and empowerment for suffering people. The constructive task of this book is to show how a theology of the cross can be retrieved as a theology of hope today, offering meaning and strength from a God who takes human form and enters redemptively into their situations of suffering.

The procedure of the argument is as follows: The first chapter explores three major issues of feminist theology, namely, the role of women's experience, the patriarchal bias of the Christian tradition, and the sexism of our

God-language. This chapter serves as an introduction to the typology of feminist reconstructions of Christology presented in chapter 2. Christology has been an important theme in feminist theology for the last two decades, and this typology offers helpful categorizing of feminist viewpoints on reconstructing the doctrine of the person and work of Jesus Christ. It includes three different types of a feminist Christology: the post-Christian perspective (Daphne Hampson), the limitation of Jesus' significance to a moral example (Carter Heyward), and the attempt at feminist reconstruction of classical Christology (Elizabeth Johnson). Chapters 3 and 4 proceed with a feminist reconstruction of Christology by means of a critical retrieval of a theology of the cross. Chapter 3 lays the groundwork for this reconstruction with an exploration of the understanding of God's passibility within the Christian tradition, focusing on, among others, Martin Luther's groundbreaking work within the field of theology of the cross and the twentieth century's retrieval of this doctrine in the work of Jürgen Moltmann. In the fourth, and last, chapter, the aim is to show how a theology of the cross can become an important hermeneutical tool, when appropriated to unveil the distortion of patriarchal Christology, and how an understanding of the crucified and hidden God provides an inherent critique of any abuse of power. Here the importance of the double function, the *passive* and the *active* aspects of the cross, becomes apparent: the passive aspect demonstrated in Jesus' solidarity with women in their suffering and the active aspect as it is found in his empowerment of women in their struggle for liberation. Thus, a theology of the cross becomes a theology of hope for those who find meaning and strength in their discernment of Jesus, not simply as a moral example, but as a God who becomes human, fully participating in their human predicament.

Acknowledging the fact that the symbol of the cross cannot be recovered by women without a recognition of its *abuse*, I nevertheless maintain that a lot of this criticism has not recognized the difference between abuse of the cross and an essentially abusive theology of the cross. Fed by the unrealistic vision of the human ability to erase all sources of evil and pain, the danger has been to lose sight of the hope women have seen, and still do, in Jesus the co-sufferer. Here I find the writings of womanist theologians, as well as women outside the Western world, particularly helpful, as they help us remember the significance of the cross of Christ, as a source of hope, courage, and strength, for women in hopeless situations past and present. Immersed in a world full of suffering and pain, sometimes so severe that it threatens to destroy the ground and meaning of our lives, the need for a hopeful theology of the cross is evident. This book aims to construct a feminist theology of the cross, giving hope to those who are searching for courage and strength, amidst suffering and pain.

I

An Introduction to the Feminist Critique of the Christian Tradition

The beginning of the feminist movement in the 1960s signifies a radical shift in human history, at least within the Western part of the world. This movement certainly did not occur without any historical precursors. A feminist critical reading of history identifies a good number of women who were able to pinpoint the injustices of patriarchy. Women often directed their criticism toward the Bible and its influence on women's secondary status within a patriarchal society.[1] But even if women were able to recognize the oppressive character of the patriarchal system, they were not always able to stimulate changes, as their situation was often considered to be part of God's order of creation. The Enlightenment, with its criticism of authority and tradition and its emphasis on autonomy and reason, became an important factor in raising women's self-consciousness and the forming of the women's rights movement in the middle of the nineteenth century. A clear indication of the effects of this movement within the church and theology was Elizabeth Cady Stanton's *Woman's Bible*, first published in 1895. Feminist theology, written since the 1970s, can therefore, on one hand, be seen as a continuation of women's striving to make their voice heard within the church of the past. On the other hand, it can be seen as an offspring of the Enlightenment and the women's liberation movements in the nineteenth and twentieth centuries. Feminist theologians recognize the importance of the relationship between the liberation of women in society and the liberation of women in the church.[2] Thus, women's experience of oppression, whether inside or outside of the church, has always been a prevalent issue for feminist theology.

The Role and Meaning of Experience

It is certainly true that women's experiences of oppression are not all the same; ethnicity and social status, among other factors, contribute to this diversity. Beneath this diversity of individual experiences lies the common denominator of a social structure that systematically oppresses women. Elisabeth Moltmann-Wendel described the situation of women in the following way in 1989:

> The world of women today is also the world in which physical violence, rape and incest are suffered far more than we suspect, where the powers of state and industry keep women in the lower-income groups, make them redundant more quickly than men, drive them on to the streets as prostitutes to earn their daily bread, making them goods which have to sell themselves. It is the world of silent humiliation, in which women are second-class citizens and helpers for men, with the result that many remain dependent all their lives and are treated like children. It is the world of solitude and isolation, in which many have to bring up their children by themselves, while the lifestyle of marriage and family is encouraged by society and expected by the churches. It is the world in which women nowadays are fighting all over the world and in very different ways for their views of life, for daily water and daily bread, and for self-determination and responsibility for themselves.[3]

According to *WHO Multi-country Study on Women's Health and Domestic Violence against Women* from 2005, the situation is as bleak as ever.[4] It is exactly this common experience of oppression—the experience of physical violence, humiliation, dependence, and isolation, as well as the experience of struggle for self-determination and responsibilities for themselves—that plays a key role for women doing theology from a feminist perspective. Women have pointed out the contradiction that exists between the gospel of Christ and women's experience of exclusion and denigration within the church as well as out in society. They argue that in this sense women's experience within the church mirrors their daily experience in patriarchal society. Furthermore, feminist theologians have drawn critical attention to the fact that women have been excluded, both *explicitly* and *implicitly*, from theological doctrines. When the question of gender has been raised explicitly within the theological tradition—for example, in theological anthropology—it has been raised to women's disfavor.

In Scriptures, as well as in the whole Judeo-Christian tradition, we are faced with two distinct ideas of the female body. One idea defines the female body as impure, corrupt, the site of offensive discharges (the foremost of which being blood), a threat to masculinity, a source of moral and physical contamination, or, as Tertullian put it, "the devil's gateway."[5] The other idea exalts the same body as beneficent, sacred, pure, asexual, and nourishing.[6] The images of Eve and Mary respectively have been used to represent these two ideas. But, while Mary is seen as mother, she is also the virgin, fulfilling two roles other women are unable to combine.

The dominant attitude within the Western church toward women, sexuality, and marriage has been shaped to a large extent by Augustine, bishop of Hippo (354–430), and Thomas Aquinas (1225–1274).[7] Both were influenced by negative attitudes toward the flesh, drawn, for example, from Greek philosophy. Theologians frequently discussed whether or not women had a soul and whether they were made in God's image. Most theologians, including Augustine and Aquinas, affirmed women's humanity but rejected women's equality to men. For both Augustine and Aquinas, the male human being was assumed to be the norm; in comparison, the female human being appeared to be deficient. Aquinas found in Aristotle's idea of woman as a "defective male" a convenient explanation of her inferiority, which for Aquinas was then further magnified by sin. Aquinas was convinced that even though women's status worsened through sin, inequality was already a fact in the original created state. Only because of women's role in procreation, Aquinas explained, would God have created anything defective.[8]

Women doing theology from a feminist standpoint are not only addressing the question of what theologians of the past have said explicitly about women but also applying a hermeneutic of suspicion to those theologians who did not explicitly address the issue of gender. Hence, they are questioning the gender bias in such writings, by asking whether past theologians have been "androcentric" in only taking *male* experience into account in their writings. In her now classic book on the anthropology presented in the writings of Reinhold Niebuhr and Paul Tillich on the doctrines on sin and grace, Judith Plaskow insists that neither Niebuhr nor Tillich addresses properly the situation of women in Western society.[9] Plaskow maintains that Niebuhr and Tillich fail both in dealing with "women's sin" of self-abnegation and in explaining the role of grace in reconstituting the self-denying self. Behind Plaskow's criticism is her differentiation between men's and women's sin: women's sin being "self-abnegation," or the "failure to turn toward the self," while men's sin agrees with the traditional understanding of sin as self-exaltation. As oppressed and subordinated, women have not been able to develop a self separate from their husbands, children, or any others in their care. Therefore, women's sin cannot be defined in the classical terms of "turning toward the self," since indeed they don't have an independent self. At the same time, grace for women cannot be "a response to the sin of pride," as it is for Niebuhr, since this view, Plaskow contends, "does not address the self which may spend its life in service to others but which cannot meet them as subjects because it has not become a subject itself."[10] Plaskow finds Tillich's emphasis on the self, which must simply accept the fact that it is accepted, also an inappropriate response to the self "whose sin is the failure to act, the failure to become a self."[11]

I raise Plaskow as an example of how a wider group of feminist theologians have critically exposed the exclusion of women's experience from the formulation of theological doctrines within the Christian tradition. Mary Daly, a pioneer in the field of feminist theology, has called this exclusion "the power of naming" that has been robbed from women. In her groundbreaking book, *Beyond God the Father: Toward a Philosophy of Women's Liberation* Daly argues that women have not had the freedom to use their own power to name themselves, the world, or God.[12] She maintains that, under patriarchy, women's questions have been excluded to the extent that even women are deaf to questions based on their own experiences. In Daly's words, this means "women have been unable even to experience our own experiences."[13]

Having been formed within a patriarchal society, Christianity has, according to Daly, not only excluded women's experience, but also become damaging for women. For Daly, there is a fundamental incompatibility between feminism and Christianity.[14] Given this perceived incompatibility, Daly rejects Christianity as a viable option for women committed to feminism. Although not all draw Daly's radical conclusion, a growing number of women from all over the world are asking why they should believe or adhere to a theological tradition "that either fosters women's second class status, or, at the very least is content to permit that second-class status as the norm."[15] This response is based on women's experience of "lived oppression," the contradiction they experience "between the suffering caused by sexism and the *humanum* of women, between the crushing on the one hand and women's own dignity on the other."[16] At stake here, feminist theologians contend, is women's affirmation of the equivalence of maleness and femaleness as being *imago dei*, created in the image of God. It is exactly this affirmation of both women and men being created in the image of God that has been obscured by the tendency to correlate femaleness with the lower part of human nature in a hierarchical scheme of mind over body, reason over passions.[17]

In order to expose and correct the patriarchal bias of the Christian tradition, feminist theologians have argued on the basis of Scripture and the sacraments for the full humanity of women. The baptismal formula in Galatians 3:27–28 has proved significant here, where it says:

> Baptized into union with him, you have put on Christ as a garment.
> There is no such thing as Jew and Greek, slave and freeman, male
> and female for you are all one person in Jesus Christ.

Elizabeth Johnson talks about the "fundamental egalitarianism of the baptismal and martyrdom traditions" that continues today in the baptismal and funeral liturgies. She writes:

> Both coming into and going out of the historical community are
> celebrated with the same texts and rituals whether the individual
> involved is woman or man; for the theological character of their
> being in Christ is identical. Created women, baptized women,
> persecuted women, martyred women, sinful and redeemed women
> of all varieties—all are genuinely *imago Dei, imago Christi.*[18]

Within the feminist theological discussion itself there has also been an important internal critique of how white feminists have falsely universalized their experience as representative of women's experience. Just as Daly and other white feminists have criticized men for stealing the "power of naming their own experience" away from women, nonwhite women have turned the same argument against white and privileged women. For example, in her book *White Women's Christ and Black Women's Jesus,* Jacquelyn Grant shows the inadequacies of feminist theology's appeals to experience because of its Eurocentrism, Anglocentrism, and its racist ideology.[19] Grant insists that even "if some individual feminists are not racists, the movement has been so structured, and therefore takes on a racist character." And she continues:

> In a racist society, the oppressor assumes the power of definition and
> control while the oppressed is objectified and perceived as a thing. As
> such, White women have defined the movement and presumed to do
> so not only for themselves but also for non-White women.[20]

Therefore, Grant concludes, if white women's analyses were adequate, they would be more conscious about identifying the experience they are writing about as their own experience, instead of presuming to name or define the experiences of others.[21]

In an effort to respond to this critique, many feminist theologians have stressed the diversity of women's experience, arguing, like Rosemary Radford

Ruether, that their own theology is *a* feminist theology and not *the* feminist theology. It implies that there is no final and absolute feminist theology, which represents all human experience, criticizes sexism, and retrieves what is usable within all historical tradition.[22] This has resulted in a widespread recognition among feminist theologians of the danger "of absolutizing any particular set of experiences or any single interpretation as *the* experience of women,"[23] thus, the strong emphasis on the diversity of women's experience within feminist theology. Even if I fully agree with those who argue for this danger, I still think there are important reasons not to give up all universal claims as part of the feminist critique of the tradition. Therefore, I agree with Pamela Dickey Young who, in her book *Feminist Theology / Christian Theology*, argues for "certain shared characteristics" of all human experience, although she admits that "the experiences of women and men in terms of reflected experience are in many ways vastly different."[24] Young sees women's experience playing a crucial part in the interpretation of the common religious experience of faith and hope.[25] She stresses the role of women's "feminist experience" in particular, as it "exposes a patriarchal theology for what it is, half a theology, and judges it accordingly."[26] Young understands this as the normative function of women's experience, but she also sees it providing "the material for making half a theology a whole theology."[27]

It is the "conscious appeal" to women's experience, and not simply its use of human experience as a resource for doing theology, that is most distinctive for the feminist approach to theology.[28] What is distinctive about the use of human experience in feminist theology is that feminist theologians acknowledge the perspectival character of their work. According to Pamela Dickey Young, this is indeed what gives feminist theology

> the opportunity to judge theologies that claim to have no particular point of view, that claim to be totally objective. Women's experience provides a shared authority, a communal criterion, not just an individualistic one, for judging Christian theology. This helps to guard against both individualism and elitism in theology.[29]

By appealing to women's experience there is therefore a communal and not just an individualistic criterion of truth in theology.

Besides providing a "communal criterion," the appeal to women's experience in feminist theology is particular in its identification of "the lived experience" of women as constitutive to the theological task. Recognizing the diversity of women in the concrete, Elizabeth Johnson admits that there is no "stereotypical norm" to be found in women's experience. Nevertheless, she argues that there is identifiable shared experience: "living within patriarchal systems does forge among women recognizable experiences of suffering along with typical patterns of coping and victoriously resisting, strategies that enable women to survive."[30] In sum, theologians such as Johnson and Young maintain that despite the admitted diversity among women's experiences, there are definable commonalities.

While most feminist theologians agree on the crucial role of women's experience of oppression in theology, there are important differences about the role to be assigned to women's experience in the actual making of the theological discourse. Although most feminist theologians agree on the corruption of patriarchy, the pluralism within feminist theology becomes obvious when questions of norms and criteria are raised. Rosemary Radford Ruether, for example, defines the *critical principle* of feminist theology as "promotion of the full humanity of women."[31] On the basis of this principle, Ruether argues that "whatever diminishes or denies the full humanity of women must be presumed not to reflect the divine or an authentic relation to the divine, or to reflect the authentic nature of things, or to be the message or work of an authentic redeemer or a community of redemption."[32]

Elisabeth Schüssler Fiorenza, like Ruether, looks for a "critical principle" within women's experience. Yet, for Fiorenza, the only adequate *norm* for feminist theology is the one that upholds and assures the overcoming of women's oppression and at the same time encourages women's religious quest for self-affirmation and self-determination. Unlike Ruether, Fiorenza rejects the possibility that one can derive the norm "for theological evaluation of biblical androcentric traditions and their subsequent interpretations" from the Bible itself. It can only be formulated, according to Fiorenza, "in and through women's struggle for liberation from all patriarchal oppression."[33] Thus, Fiorenza looks for a norm for her theological position outside of Scripture and within women's experience for liberation.

But, whatever role is assigned to women's experience in feminist theology, most feminist theologians acknowledge women's experience as a hermeneutical place (starting point) that shapes both their understanding and their interpretation of God's revelation in past and present.[34] Its importance is stressed in the argument that states that eventually "the question, *whose* experience counts in theological reflection turns into a question that is more than methodological, for it addresses the understanding of salvation, revelation and truth."[35] In other words, whether women's experience is taken into account or not has to do with the inclusive intent of the Christian doctrines.

Because our experience affects our understanding of Christ, and, furthermore, because women's experience has been excluded or misinterpreted within traditional Christology, it is necessary to reconsider specifically the role that experience plays in our interpretation of Jesus Christ. One need not accept Mary Daly's negative conclusion on the compatibility of feminism and Christology in order to see her point about women's inability to "name their own experience" in the past. While I think it is important to recognize the issue of diversity in naming women's experience, I side with those who argue for basic commonalities in human experience in general and more specifically in women's experience.[36]A helpful example of the universal aspect of suffering is, for example, given by the womanist theologian M. Shawn Copeland. In her chapter "'Wading through Many Sorrows': Toward a Theology of Suffering in Womanist Perspective," Copeland writes:

> Suffering is universal, an inescapable fact of the human condition; it defies immunities of all kinds. Suffering despoils women and men irrespective of race or tongue, wealth or poverty, learning or virtue; disregards merit or demerit, reward or punishment, honor or corruption. Like sun and rain, suffering comes unbidden to the just and the unjust alike.[37]

The experience of suffering is certainly basic to all human experience. Thus, despite different social and cultural situations, there are not only differences but also similarities in women's universal experiences of suffering.[38] The commonalities are, among other things, based on social structures of patriarchy that transcend racial and cultural differences. The common experience of suffering can serve a critical function in feminist theology by presenting a common point of critique as well as an important reference point to Jesus' truly human experience.

The Christian Tradition and Its Patriarchal Bias

The reconsideration of the role and meaning of experience provides the methodological backdrop to the feminist critique of the patriarchal character of Scripture and the Christian tradition. While most feminist theologians agree on the "patriarchalization" of the tradition, they do not all agree on its "redeemability." Some feminists consider the whole Christian tradition to be so intrinsically patriarchal and androcentric[39] that it is able to function only as a continued source of women's oppression and should therefore be dismissed. Others see it as still a source of revelation, arguing that the "source of our oppression is also the source of our power." Hence, Elisabeth Schüssler Fiorenza insists that reclaiming the Bible "as a feminist heritage and resource is only possible because it has not functioned only to legitimate the oppression of *all* women" but has also inspired and "continues to inspire countless women to speak out and to struggle against injustice, exploitation, and stereotyping."[40] Katie Cannon gives an example of how the Bible has functioned as a source of power for black women, as she writes:

> In its [i.e., the Bible] pages, Black women have learned how to refute the stereotypes that depict Black people as minstrels or vindictive militants, mere ciphers who react only to omnipresent racial oppression. Knowing the Jesus stories of the New Testament helps Black women be aware of the bad housing, overworked mothers, underworked fathers, functional illiteracy and malnutrition that continue to prevail in the Black community. . . .[41]

Consequently, what is needed is a critical rereading of the Bible and the entire Christian tradition from a feminist perspective. A key to such feminist rereading is not only a critique of the patriarchal bias but also a retrieval of "lost traditions," including new dimensions of biblical symbols and theological interpretations. In the following, I will look at three feminist approaches for engaging in a hermeneutical retrieval of the Christian tradition.

Since the publication of her groundbreaking work, *In Memory of Her: A Feminist Theological Reconstruction of Christian Origins*, Elisabeth Schüssler Fiorenza, a pioneer in the field of feminist biblical interpretation, has argued consistently for a "critical evaluation as well as structural and creative transformation"[42] of the Bible. Such a feminist critical interpretation is necessary, according to Fiorenza, since the Bible is still today functioning as a "religious justification and ideological legitimization of patriarchy."[43] In order to make a feminist critical interpretation possible, feminist biblical scholars need "a shift in paradigm" and a hermeneutical criterion for their interpretation. For Fiorenza, "a shift in paradigm" means a shift from understanding the Bible as a *mythical archetype* to understanding it as a *historical prototype*. As a mythical archetype the Bible is given a normative authority for all time and cultures, apart from its own historical circumstances. This happens when historically limited experiences and texts are given universal meaning. Fiorenza insists that as an archetype the Bible has to be either accepted or rejected and therefore does not allow for any critical evaluation.[44]

Fiorenza thinks the Bible–as an alternative to a timeless archetype–should be taken as a historical prototype, or as a "formative root-model of biblical faith and life," in which women can experience solidarity with women in biblical religion in their struggle for liberation.[45] The critical feminist interpretation, as presented by Fiorenza, takes women's experience of struggling for liberation as its hermeneutical criterion. This is why Fiorenza finds the locus of divine revelation and grace in neither the Bible nor the tradition of a patriarchal church, but in the *ekklesia of women* (the women-church). She explains:

> The hermeneutical center of feminist biblical interpretation is the women-church (*ekklesia gynaikon*), the movement of self-identified women and women-identified men in biblical religion. The *ekklesia* of women is part of the wider women's movement in society and in religion that conceives itself not just as a civil rights movement but as a women's liberation movement.[46]

What the women-church is striving for is nothing less than a full liberation of women from alienation, marginalization, and oppression caused by patriarchal forces.

Because the biblical writings contain male-made traditions, written in androcentric language and reflecting patriarchal culture and religion, feminist theologians find critical interpretations of the Bible absolutely necessary. Fiorenza maintains that the task of critical feminist interpretations is to "break" the silences about women's participation and interrupt the invisibility of women. In order to accomplish this task Fiorenza proposes a feminist model of critical interpretation, beginning with *a hermeneutic of suspicion*, which takes as its starting point the assumption that biblical texts and their interpretations are androcentric and serve patriarchal functions. Hermeneutic of suspicion is supposed to clear away androcentric mistranslations, patriarchal interpretations, and one-sided reconstructions. When this has been done, it becomes the task of *a hermeneutic of proclamation* to assess the theological significance and power of the Bible for the community of faith. A hermeneutic of proclamation is to point out those texts that transcend their patriarchal contexts and articulate a liberating vision of human freedom and wholeness in order to give them their proper place in liturgy and teaching of the churches. To serve as a balance to the hermeneutic of proclamation, and to bring forth positive results from the hermeneutic of suspicion, *a hermeneutic of remembrance* is meant to recover all biblical traditions by reaching beyond the androcentric text to the history of women in biblical religion. Through the "remembered past," the suffering and hopes of women in the biblical past are kept alive, while at the same time a universal solidarity among women of the past, present, and future is made possible. The task of the hermeneutic of remembrance is to keep alive this *memoria passionis* of biblical women and to reclaim the biblical heritage, not just as a remembrance of patriarchal oppression, but also as the story of the leadership, struggle for liberation, and life of these women. The fourth and last element in Fiorenza's feminist model of biblical interpretation is *a hermeneutic of creative actualization*. Its purpose is to urge women to use tools—such as historical imagination, artistic recreation, and liturgical ritualization—in order to enter the biblical stories. By including a hermeneutic of creative actualization,

Fiorenza wants to demonstrate that she is considering a feminist biblical interpretation not as just a critical interpretation but also as a constructive one, oriented not only toward the past but also toward the future.[47]

Elisabeth Schüssler Fiorenza has proposed her feminist model of biblical interpretation as an "alternative option" to Rosemary Radford Ruether's *method of correlation*.[48] Ruether's correlation takes place between women's experience and Scripture or, more precisely, between a *feminist-critical principle* and a *biblical-critical principle*. Ruether maintains that the critique of sexism implies a fundamental principle of judgment, which is the "affirmation of and promotion of the full humanity of women."[49] What is unique about the use of this principle within feminist hermeneutics is, according to Ruether, neither the category of experience as a context of interpretation nor the critical principle of "full humanity." The unique element is rather the appeal to women's experience, which has been "shut out of hermeneutics and theological reflection in the past,"[50] along with the fact that women are claiming the principle of full humanity for themselves.

A key to Ruether's method of correlation is the conviction that the Bible can be appropriated as a "source of liberating paradigms" only if there is a correlation between biblical-critical and feminist-critical principles. She contends such a correlation can be drawn on the basis of the biblical-critical principle as that which can be drawn from the *prophetic-messianic tradition*. Ruether understands the prophetic-messianic tradition as

> a critical perspective and process through which the biblical tradition
> constantly reevaluates, in new contexts, what is truly the liberating Word
> of God, over against both the sinful deformations of contemporary
> society and also the limitations of past biblical traditions, which saw
> in part and understood in part, and whose partiality may have even
> become a source of sinful justice and idolatry.[51]

In order for the prophetic-messianic tradition to remain the source for the prophetic-critical perspective, which again brings out the liberating message from the Bible, Ruether maintains it has to be in a constant state of revision.[52]

Letty Russell agrees with Ruether about the liberating tradition present within the biblical "prophetic-messianic" message of ongoing self-critique. Russell finds the evidence for a message of liberation for women within the Bible, not in particular stories about women, but in "God's intention for the mending of all creation."[53] In spite of "its ancient and patriarchal worldviews, in spite of its inconsistencies and mixed messages," Russell contends, "the story of God's love affair with the world leads me to a vision of New Creation that impels my life."[54] It is this focus on the New Creation, and the Bible as "the memory of the future," that distinguishes Russell's way of interpreting the Bible from other feminist theologians. Thus, her method differs from, for example, Fiorenza's, as Russell treats the Bible not only as a prototype but also as a place where God's work in history can be anticipated. Besides being future-oriented, Russell's method of interpretation is clearly focused on action, more particularly on God's partnership at work with those who are striving for the liberation of all the oppressed.[55]

Like Fiorenza, Russell calls for a shift in paradigm. In Russell's case, the shift is from the paradigm of "authority as domination" to that of "authority as partnership." Characteristic of the latter is that reality is no longer seen in the form of a hierarchy, or pyramid, but is "interpreted in the form of a circle of interdependence."[56] This particular understanding of authority then becomes important for Russell's interpretation of the pluralism that exists within feminism. She insists that within "the community paradigm of authority," there is no need for competition between different feminist principles. While each feminist theologian works out of her own particular context—life experience and expertise included—the most important thing is that all share a common commitment to the full liberation of women. This is why, Russell argues, she and Ruether are more likely to use theological principles of interpretation than to appeal to historical-critical reconstruction, simply because they are theologians and not New Testament scholars such as, for example, Fiorenza.

Russell believes that the shift in feminist interpretive framework to a paradigm of "authority as partnership" reveals the dichotomy between feminist experience and biblical witness to be unnecessary. With her paradigm, she contends, "the dilemma of choice between faithfulness to the teaching of Scripture or to our own integrity as human beings" is eliminated. Based on different experiences, some will stress one aspect of the biblical witness while others will stress something else:

> But together we will continue to find our way through the thickets of patriarchal ideas and structures that challenges us to abandon the "hope that is in" us (1 Peter 3:15) for which we seek to give account.[57]

Hence, Russell's argument for the plurality of feminist interpretations of Scripture is based on her recognition of the diversity within women's experience. If Russell is right that Scripture is still, despite its patriarchal bias, able to communicate the Word of God to women in their particular contexts, the next question must be about the language that is appropriate to communicate this Word of God today.

The Christian tradition, as the written and lived witness of the Christian church,[58] provides the sources for Christology, while the patriarchal bias of the tradition calls for its feminist-critical reinterpretation.[59] But it is not only what is said that can be harmful but also what is left unsaid. This is why Elizabeth Cady Stanton, in her *Woman's Bible*, wanted to revise not only those biblical texts and chapters that talked about women but also those "in which women are made prominent by exclusion."[60] Another example of a "silent" misrepresentation of the tradition is how the texts that talk about women, about Jesus and women, and about what women have said about Jesus have been left unnoticed. This is why the work of those who are looking for the "lost tradition" is so important, as it helps to correct the distortion that the tradition has suffered for so long.

An important example of this search for the "lost tradition" is found in the so-called Jesus-was-a-feminist writings of the early 1970s, which we will return to in the following chapter. Those writings are particularly helpful to show how Jesus' life, his works, and his words (and not only his death and resurrection) witness to the radical nature of the kingdom of God. They also unveil how the Gospels' portrayal of Jesus contradicts the patriarchal character of Jesus' own society as well as our society today. A second example of the search for lost traditions is the rediscovery of the writings of the medieval women mystics. Their female-images of different persons of the Trinity have been an important reminder of how the Christian tradition provides for a much richer God-language than the all-male, "disembodied imagery and arguments of the tradition."[61] A third example is the preaching tradition of Christian women, an important reminder of the significant contribution women have made to the interpretation of the Christian message in the past, so far scarcely recognized.[62]

Religious Language and Sexism

Closely related to, or rather a crucial part of, the feminist critique of the Christian tradition is its critique of the patriarchal character of all language, religious language included. Together with other theologians, such as liberation theologians from South America, feminists are arguing that "talk is not just talk,"[63] but rather an ideological weapon often used by those in power against the powerless. Hence, feminist theologians are arguing that the exclusive maleness of traditional God-talk has become not simply meaningless to them but also harmful. The maleness of God has indeed caused some feminists to reject the Christian God, basing their rejection, like Daly, on the assumption that "if God is male, then the male is God."[64] An appealing alternative to many of the feminists is to revive "the Goddess of antiquity as an alternative manifestation of the divine."[65] For those who have opted to stay within the Christian tradition, the issue of religious language has become one of the most challenging and controversial issues, particularly the question of the exclusive use of masculine language for God.

An important part of the feminist critique of religious language is the warning against the propensity to literalize metaphors and to forget about the dissimilarity in every analogy. Many feminist theologians use the image of "idolatry" to describe what happens when the analogical character of all God-talk is forgotten and a literal meaning is ascribed to the metaphor—i.e., when the metaphor has been turned into an "idol." Ruether, for example, stresses the importance of extending the proscription of idolatry to verbal pictures. Ruether takes the example of the word "Father," arguing that when the word is taken literally to mean "God is male and not female, represented by males and not females,"[66] then this word has truly become an idol. The contention that the patriarchal model has not only become idolatrous but also is harmful to women has underscored women's critique of the traditional God-language.

Some feminist theologians have argued that what happened to the model of God as Father within the Christian tradition was that instead of pointing in the direction of benevolent parent, the "parent became the patriarch."[67] For this reason, the "official language" for God, having become exclusively male, pictures God as authoritarian, as judge, as king, as lord, as master. As the social hierarchy within a patriarchal society has frequently resulted in what has been called "male monotheism," Ruether describes the relationship between what she calls "male monotheism" and the social hierarchy of patriarchal rule in the following way:

> God is modeled after the patriarchal ruling class and is seen as addressing this class of males directly, adopting them as his "sons." They are his representatives, the responsible partners of the covenant with him. Women as wives now become symbolically repressed as the dependent servant class. Wives, along with children and servants, represent those ruled over and owned by the patriarchal class. They relate to man as he related to God. A symbolic hierarchy is set up: God-male-female. Women no longer stand in direct relation to God, they are connected to God secondarily, through the male.[68]

Because of the dominating power of this symbolic hierarchy of God-male-female, both in the Old Testament and New Testament as well as in Judeo-Christian culture, it has often been accepted as reality itself, and therefore its ideological character not been recognized.

By exposing the relationship between the patriarchal hierarchy and *androcentrism*, feminist theologians are uncovering the oppressive character of traditional God-language. In androcentric thinking-patterns, the male is treated as the normative human being, while the female is seen as inferior, defective, and less than fully human. Likewise, men represent the spirit, while women represent the lower, material nature. This is how "gender becomes a primary symbol for the dualism of transcendence and immanence, spirit and matter."[69] Hence, those who believe that Christianity is intrinsically patriarchal and androcentric have consequently decided that Christianity cannot be anything else than harmful for women, while those who have opted to remain within the Christian tradition are looking for alternatives to the traditional male-language for God.

There are some Christian feminists who find a solution to the problem of God-talk in an androgynous God or the female aspect of the Trinity, but there are others who do not. Ruether belongs to the group of feminists who think something more has to be done. She writes:

> We need to get beyond the ideal of a "feminine side" of God, whether to be identified with the Spirit or even with the *Sophia*-Spirit together, and question the assumption that the highest symbol of divine sovereignty still remains exclusively male.[70]

Drawing her conclusion from the definition of idolatry and the analogical character of God-language, Ruether insists that the "male language for the divine must lose its privileged place."[71] Instead of "adding" a feminine side to the male God, Ruether thinks both female and male metaphors should be used for God.

Still the question remains: If the ultimate goal of feminism is to free women from the patriarchal oppression they have suffered for centuries, is there any hope to be found in a tradition that has not only played a significant role in this oppression but also presented a male figure from the past as a savior for women? Ever since Mary Daly reached her eminent conclusion, that "if God is male, then the male is God,"[72] the question of the compatibility of feminism and Christianity has been prevalent within feminist theology. Feminist theologians have tried to answer what it means for women that God became human as a male. In 1981, Ruether argued that Christology is the doctrine of the Christian tradition most frequently used against women, thus, her frequently quoted question: "Can a male saviour save women?"[73] As a historical religion grounded in God's self-revelation in a particular individual, Christianity cannot dismiss the significance of Jesus' concrete humanity, in a masculine body, for his divinity.[74]

While many feminist theologians maintain that the story of Jesus Christ—both his words and deeds—shows that his maleness is not necessarily oppressive for women, they nevertheless have to respond to the question whether his sexuality should be considered strictly contingent (so that the work could have been done by a woman, i.e., by Jesa Christa instead of by Jesus Christ) or whether his maleness is essential to this particular time and place in history. Those who have not found Jesus' maleness innately oppressive for women often experience in Jesus' message and praxis an important support of the feminist critique of the Christian tradition and the patriarchal social structure within the church as well as in society. Given the feminist evaluation of the role and meaning of experience, as well as the patriarchal bias of the Christian tradition and God-language, feminist theologians have emphasized the need for a feminist reconstruction also of that part of the Christian tradition devoted to the person and work of Jesus Christ. Still others have deemed the christological doctrines irretrievable because of their patriarchal bias. The next chapter provides a typology of feminist christological proposals, in which the focus it set on three different answers to questions regarding Jesus' question: Who do you say that I am?[75]

NOTES

1. In her book, *The Creation of Feminist Consciousness*, Gerda Lerner argues for a long tradition ("one thousand years") of feminist Bible criticism, insisting "there always were women who never accepted the patriarchal gender definitions which defined them as inherently inferior and incapable of reasoning. Long before organized groups of women challenged male authority, the feminist Bible critics did just that" (Lerner, *The Creation of Feminist Consciousness*, 138–39).

2. Moltmann-Wendel and Moltmann, *Humanity in God*, 110. Louise Tappa, a theologian from Africa, denounces arguments such as: "The women's liberation movement is not a response to a genuinely African need," or "the African woman has always been one to give of herself." Tappa argues, on the contrary, that "women's liberation can be viewed only in the context of the liberation of all the oppressed of the earth" (Tappa, "The Christ-Event from the Viewpoint of African Women," 33).

3. Moltmann-Wendel and Moltmann, *God—His & Hers*, 53–54. See also Fabella, "Christology from an Asian Woman's Perspective," 3.

4. http://www.who.int/gender/violence/who_multicountry_study/en/.

5. Tertullian, *de Cult Fem* 1.1. Quoted by Ruether, *Sexism and God-Talk: Toward a Feminist Theology*, 167.

6. Rich, *Of Woman Born: Motherhood as Experience and Institution*, 33–35.

7. Douglass, *Women, Freedom, and Calvin*, 72–78; and Ruether, *Sexism and God-Talk*, 94–99.

8. On the question of women and the image of God, Augustine writes:

According to Genesis, human nature as such has been made to the image of God, a nature which exists in both sexes and which does not allow of our setting woman aside when it comes to understanding what the image of God is . . . The wife with her husband is the image of God, so that the totality of his human substance forms a single image; but when woman is considered as man's helpmate, a state which belongs to her alone, she is not the image of God. By contrast, man is the image of God by being solely what he is, an image so perfect, so whole, that when woman is joined with him it makes only one image. (From *De Trinitate XII*, 7:C.C.50, 363–64, quoted by Douglass in *Women, Freedom, and Calvin*, 74)

And this is what Aquinas has to say about the same question:

The image of God exists in man (*vir*) in a way that is not found in woman; as a matter of fact, man is the beginning and end of woman as God is the beginning and end of all creation. Once when the Apostle has said: "man is the image and glory of God whilst woman is the glory of man," he showed why he said that by adding: "It was not man who was taken from woman, but woman from man, and man was not created for woman, but woman was created for man" (From *Summa Theologica, I*, 93,4, ad 1, quoted by Douglass in *Women, Freedom, and Calvin*, 76)

9. Plaskow, *Sex, Sin, and Grace: Women's Experience and the Theologies of Reinhold Niebuhr and Paul Tillich*, 149.

10. Ibid., 156.

11. Ibid., 157. It is within the context of having identified the gender-specific character of sin that Plaskow questions whether one does not have to be "a bit Pelagian to be faithful to women's experience" (ibid., 157).

12. Daly, *Beyond God the Father: Toward a Philosophy of Women's Liberation*, 8. Daly argues that, "[under] patriarchy, Method has wiped out women's questions so totally that even women have not been able to hear and formulate our own questioning to meet our own experiences. Women have been unable even to experience our own experiences" (ibid., 12).

13. Ibid., 12.

14. Daly writes: "The distortion in Christian ideology resulting from and confirming sexual hierarchy is manifested not only in the doctrines of God and the Fall but also in doctrines concerning Jesus" (ibid., 69).

15. Young, *Feminist Theology/Christian Theology: In Search of Method*, 62–63.

16. Johnson, *She Who Is: The Mystery of God in Feminist Theological Discourse*, 62. In her book, Johnson discusses the critical consciousness arising among women as they turn away from "trivialization and defamation of oneself as a female person" and awake "to their own human worth" (ibid., 62–65).

17. Ruether argues that since "this lower part of the self is seen as the source of sin—the falling away of the body from its original unity with the mind and hence into sin and death—femaleness also becomes linked with the sin-prone part of the self" (Ruether, *Sexism and God-Talk*, 93).

18. Johnson, *She Who Is*, 75.

19. Grant, *White Women's Christ and Black Women's Jesus: Feminist Christology and Womanist Response*, 195.

20. Ibid., 199–200.

21. Ibid., 200.

22. See, for example, Ruether, *Sexism and God-Talk*, 20.

23. Carr, *Transforming Grace: Christian Tradition and Women's Experience*, 118.

24. Ibid., 65.

25. Ibid., 66.

26. Ibid., 67.

27. Ibid.

28. Johnson, *She Who Is*, 61. Ruether writes on this issue in her book *Sexism and God-Talk*: "The uniqueness of feminist theology lies not in its use of the criterion of experience but rather in its use of *women's* experience, which has been almost entirely shut out of theological reflection in the past. The use of women's experience in feminist theology, therefore, explodes as a critical force, exposing classical theology, including its codified traditions, as based on *male* experience rather than on universal human experience. Feminist theology makes the sociology of theological knowledge visible, no longer hidden behind mystifications of objectified divine and universal authority" (Ruether, *Sexism and God-Talk*, 13).

29. Young, *Feminist Theology/Christian Theology*, 67.

30. Johnson, *She Who Is*, 61.

31. Ruether, *Sexism and God-Talk*, 18.

32. Ibid., 19.

33. Fiorenza, *In Memory of Her: A Feminist Theological Reconstruction of Christian Origins*, 32.

34. For an important and critical discussion about the role of experience in feminist theology, see Eriksson, *The Meaning of Gender in Theology: Problems and Possibilites*, 127–44.

35. Hellwig, *Whose Experience Counts in Theological Reflection?* 45.

36. See Moltmann-Wendel and Moltmann, *God—His & Hers*, 78; Young, *Feminist Theology/Christian Theology*, 65–67.

37. Copeland, "'Wading through Many Sorrows': Toward a Theology of Suffering in Womanist Perspective," 109.

38. See Hall, *God & Human Suffering: An Exercise in the Theology of the Cross*, 57. Hall makes a helpful distinction between suffering "as *becoming*" or "integrative suffering", and suffering "which detracts from life" or "disintegrative suffering" (ibid., 67–68).

39. While "patriarchy" means the "rule of the father" and implies the rule of men over women, "androcentrism" signifies the assumption that the male is the normative human being.

40. Fiorenza, *Bread Not Stone: The Challenge of Feminist Biblical Interpretation*, xiii.

41. Cannon, "The Emergence of Black Feminist Consciousness," 40.

42. Fiorenza, *Bread Not Stone*, xvii.

43. Ibid., xi.

44. Ibid., 10–11.

45. Ibid., 13–15.

46. Fiorenza, "The Will to Choose or to Reject: Continuing Our Critical Work," 126.

47. Fiorenza, *Bread Not Stone*, 16–22. Phyllis Trible is another feminist who, like Fiorenza, looks for texts about women in the Bible that make a "universal solidarity among women of the past, present, and future possible" (ibid., 19). See, for example, Trible's book, *Texts of Terror*.

48. See Fiorenza's criticism of Ruether's method in *Bread Not Stone*, 12–15; and Fiorenza, "The Will to Choose or to Reject," 131–32.

49. Ruether, "Feminist Interpretation: A Method of Correlation," 115.

50. Ibid., 112. Ruether explains that in this context she is not talking about women's experience primarily in terms of "experiences created by biological differences in themselves but, rather, women's experiences created by the social and cultural appropriation of biological differences in a male-dominated society . . ." (ibid., 113).

51. Ibid., 117.

52. Fiorenza has criticized Ruether's method of "choosing one tradition, text, or biblical dynamics" for being in "danger of advocating a reductionist method of theological critique and of relinquishing the historical richness of biblical experience" (Fiorenza, *Bread Not Stone*, 13). Responding to Fiorenza, Ruether states that "continuity with the prophetic tradition . . . is not simply restatement of past texts but the constant renewal of the meaning of the prophetic critique itself" (Ruether, "Feminist Interpretation," 118).

53. Russell, "Authority and the Challenge of Feminist Interpretation," 138.

54. Ibid.

55. Ibid., 139–40.

56. Ibid., 144.

57. Ibid., 146.

58. It is important to recognize liturgies, hymns, and art as a part of the tradition, together with the written sources. An example of how art can be used as a valuable source is found in Moltmann-Wendel and Moltmann's book *Humanity in God*.

59. See Thistlethwaite, "Every Two Minutes: Battered Women and Feminist Interpretation," 96.

60. Stanton, *Women's Bible*, 5.

61. McLaughlin, "Feminist Christologies: Re-Dressing the Tradition," 137–38. Eleanor McLaughlin points out the problems with the appropriation of patristic or medieval constructions of devotion to the motherhood of God, Jesus, and Mary, because of the "anti-sexual and body-destroying asceticism which too often accompanied this piety." "These texts are therefore useful only to a point," argues McLaughlin, "the point of deconstructing the 'simply male' abstract and disembodied imagery and argument of the tradition." And McLaughlin continues:

What may be useful for us is not the historically intended meanings of late medieval images of the suffering mother/God—pieta or crucified one, but the way in which gender, and its symbolic freight, whether divine or human, was fluid, unfixed, and flowing in and out of the social constructions of sex and gender roles of the culture. Whatever was the symbolized sex of God suffering on the cross, he/she did not simply valorize the patriarchal order. There is a saving freedom for us in these gender-bending images, constructed out of the experience of celibate men in same-sex communities and celibate women amid communities of women (ibid.)

See also Bynum, *Jesus as Mother: Studies in the Spirituality of the High Middle Ages*, 170–262; Bynum, *Fragmentation and Redemption: Essays on Gender and the Human Body in Medieval Religion*, 151–71; Allen, "Christ our Mother in Julian of Norwich," 421–28.

62. See Florence, *Preaching as Testimony* (2007), in which the interesting story of three female preachers in the United States in the sixteenth and seventeenth centuries is told.

63. Russell, *Household of Freedom: Authority in Feminist Theology*, 45.

64. Daly, *Beyond God the Father*, 19.

65. Ruether, *Sexism and God-Talk*, 52.

66. Ibid., 66.

67. McFague, *Models of God: Theology for an Ecological, Nuclear Age*, 66.

68. Ruether, *Sexism and God-Talk*, 53.

69. Ibid., 54.

70. Ibid., 61.

71. Ibid., 69.

72. Daly, *Beyond God the Father*, 19.

73. Ruether, *To Change the World: Christology and Cultural Criticism*, 45.

74. See McLaughlin on Jesus as a transvestite: "Feminist Christologies," 138–39; and Fabella, "Christology from an Asian Woman's Perspective," 4.

75. For other attempts to give an overview of the early development in feminist Christology, see Young, "Diversity in Feminist Christology," 81–90; and Hampson, *Theology and Feminism*, 59–66.

2

Feminist Reconstruction of Christology—Typology

As we have seen from the previous chapter's introduction to feminist methodology, there is a broad spectrum of views among feminists on the possibilities for retrieving and reconstructing nonpatriarchal Christian faith. The full scale of such views is evidenced in the feminist discussion on Christology. In an effort to clarify the range of feminist christological proposals, this chapter presents a typology that distinguishes among three christological positions: first, the position which, on explicitly christological grounds, holds that Christianity and feminism are incompatible; second, that which reconstructs a feminist Christology that limits Jesus' significance to his humanity and his salvific role to that of an example or paradigm; and finally, the position which argues for a feminist retrieval of the ancient idea of incarnation, implying the understanding of Jesus as being truly human and at the same time truly divine. Before outlining these three groups, let us first turn to an important precursor to the modern feminist reflection of Christology: the so-called Jesus-the-feminist writings of the 1970s and early 1980s.

Jesus-the-Feminist Writings

The Jesus-the-feminist writings adopted an apologetic strategy to the feminist christological question, namely, to use scriptural arguments in order to prove that Jesus indeed was, according to a twentieth-century understanding, a feminist. Jesus' so-called feminism is seen in his advocacy of the equality of women and men in both his actions and his words.[1] Leonard Swidler's article, "Jesus Was a Feminist" (1971), is an early example of these writings. Swidler concludes his article in the following way:

> it should be clear that Jesus vigorously promoted the dignity and
> equality of women in the midst of a very male dominated society;
> Jesus was a feminist, and a very radical one. Can his followers
> attempt to be anything less—De Imitatione Christi?

By emphasizing the importance of scriptural stories about women, Jesus-the-feminist writings drew attention to the liberating effect of Jesus' relationship with women, as well as the prominent roles women played in the early Christian community.[2] These writings uncovered how the Christian tradition had previously overlooked the significance of stories about the interaction between Jesus and women. Given the radical difference between Jesus' treatment of women and the traditional role and status assigned to women at that particular time in history, such stories play a crucial part in the feminist critique of both traditional Christology and the patriarchal oppression of women through the centuries. As understood by the authors of the Jesus-the-feminist writings, Jesus' interaction with women in the Gospels is also significant for us today, not only in order to grasp how his contemporaries understood him, but also to unearth a previously overlooked aspect of his self-understanding.

In her books, *Jesus According to a Woman* and *Jesus and the Freed Woman*, Rachel Conrad Wahlberg presents a typical example of Jesus-the-feminist perspective.[3] Her goal is to reveal the liberating attitude Jesus had toward women by looking at stories about Jesus and his interaction with women. Wahlberg describes her task in the following way in her second book:

> In this sequel, I am continuing the process of looking afresh at
> neglected and/or distorted incidents in scripture—not only for their
> implications for women but for the Christian life. Thus we uncover a
> lost canon within the canon-stories not seen, stories not preached
> about, stories not used to affirm women.[4]

Wahlberg aims to correct the long-lasting tradition within the church of both neglecting stories that reveal Jesus' positive attitude toward women and lifting up "negative examples and passages from the Bible concerning women."[5] Looking back, Wahlberg admits that at "some level" her work was an attempt to "integrate the secular women's movement" with what she knew to be "the reality, the core, the kernel of Christianity."[6] This reality, for Wahlberg, is that women are indeed made in God's image (Genesis 1:27) and that in Christ the distinction between a Jew or a Greek, slave or free, male or female has been eliminated (Galatians 3:28).[7]

It was the secular women's movement in the sixties and the seventies that opened Wahlberg's eyes to insights in Scripture that were neither perceived nor mentioned in the average Sunday morning sermon or Bible study. "It occurred to me," she writes, "that Jesus in his relationships with women always treated women with intimacy, high regard and naturalness."[8] From Jesus' interaction with women and the "women imagery" he used in his preaching, as well as the fact that he chose women to "go and tell," Wahlberg concludes that Jesus was intentional in affirming women "in ways his contemporaries and later followers did not recognize."[9] For Wahlberg, the church regressed from what she considers "the freedom of the Gospel."[10] For example, the church has not acknowledged the significance of the biblical testimony that "not only did a woman proclaim *Jesus as Messiah*, but women were the first to preach *Jesus as risen*."[11] Thus, the church has not recognized the centrality of women to Jesus' mission, while excluding them from an active participation in the mission of the church today.

A second important aspect of Wahlberg's work—besides uncovering the important role women played in Jesus' ministry and the early Christian community—is her focus on the true humanity of Jesus and the way he himself was influenced by his interaction with women. Wahlberg argues that, despite being confessed as "truly human," Jesus' human qualities have frequently been downplayed within the Christian tradition.[12] Wahlberg uses the story of Jesus and the Canaanite woman to prove her point (Mark 7:24–30; Matthew 15:21–28). The way this story has been interpreted in the past reflects, according to Wahlberg, the tendency to play down the humanity of Jesus. While Wahlberg believes that traditionally Jesus has been excused from "the human necessity to make choices, to define himself, to mature in his own self-understanding, to interact with another person,"[13] the Canaanite woman was somebody who influenced Jesus, who made him reflect on his self-understanding and even change his mind. Wahlberg writes:

> [I]t seems that *this woman influenced Jesus*. Was he a limited
> Jew-healer, as he said, or one for all who needed healing? She prodded
> him to make a choice. Scripture says "Jesus grew in wisdom." How?
> Perhaps he grew in his self-understanding because of people like this
> woman. He matured in his concept of messiahship as she challenged
> him to recognize her need.[14]

Wahlberg encounters examples of how Jesus' humanness was repressed within the Christian tradition in the common disallowance of grief, anger, or love in

Jesus. She maintains that Jesus' divinity has been enhanced, while his human qualities have been either ignored or explained away, as well as his friends' "quite human treatment of him."[15]

Significant to Wahlberg's view of Jesus-as-a-feminist is her focus on the "horizontal," rather than "vertical," way in which Jesus related to his friends and coworkers as being characteristic of his "antihierarchical" ministry. According to Wahlberg, Jesus not only met people—women and men— "where they were" but also took them seriously "in the fullness of personhood."[16] Wahlberg perceives this to be a crucial yet neglected aspect of the stories about Jesus and women in the New Testament. Furthermore, Wahlberg relates this "antihierarchical praxis" as significant to Jesus' self-understanding as the "Servant of God." She points out that Jesus' ministry was focused on the needs of others, whether those needs were emotional, physical, or spiritual, and that he usually directed his ministry toward the downtrodden of his society. Still, not only did Jesus see himself as a servant, but also he offered himself as a model of service to his disciples. Wahlberg sees the reality of Christian congregations, in which women most frequently carry out the service activities while men continue to fill most of the authority positions, as characteristic of a church that still practices the hierarchy that Jesus himself sought to dismantle.

A Post-Christian Perspective: Daphne Hampson

I turn now to the first group of my typology, namely, those who have concluded—some on christological grounds—that feminism and Christianity are incompatible. The pioneer among these women was Mary Daly, a former Roman Catholic, who reached this negative conclusion in her book, *Beyond God the Father: Toward a Philosophy of Women's Liberation*, after trying in vain to reconcile feminism and Christianity in her earlier work.[17] According to Daly, the distortion in Christian ideology, which both results from and confirms sexual hierarchy, is manifested not only in the doctrines of God and of the Fall but most acutely in Christology. Daly highlights the problem with the image of the God-man (or the "God-male"), resulting from its one-sidedness "as far as sexual identity is concerned." Daly thinks this one-sidedness is "precisely on the wrong side, since it fails to counter sexism and functions to glorify maleness."[18] Given a patriarchal society, Daly is convinced that women need a one-sided God-female in order to counter sexism and to glorify women.[19]

I have chosen to focus more closely on another representative of the so-called post-Christian position, namely, Daphne Hampson, a British theologian, whose background is within the Anglican Church in Britain. Daphne

Hampson is Professor Emerita of Divinity, University of St. Andrews, Scotland. She is also a life member at Clare Hall, University of Cambridge.[20] Hampson started out as a historian and has a doctoral degree in comtemporary history from Oxford University. She later changed fields and finished her second doctorate in systematic theology at Harvard University in 1983. Hampson has been a productive writer and has published a large number of articles, together with the following books: *Theology and Feminism*; *After Christianity*; and *Christian Contradictions: The Structures of Lutheran and Catholic Thought*. She is also the editor of *Swallowing a Fishbone: Feminist Theologians Debate Christianity*, a collection of articles written by six British feminist theologians on questions regarding the compatibility of feminism and Christianity.

Before Hampson decided to leave Christianity behind, she was a member of the Anglican Church in Britain. In the late 1970s, she became active in the campaign for women's ordination within that church. Hampson wrote, for example, the theological statement arguing in favor of the ordination of women into the priesthood that was circulated to the members of the General Synod of the Church of England before the vote on women's ordination in 1978. Hampson's experience of fighting for women's ordination within her own church became a significant factor in her conclusion about the incompatibility of feminism and Christianity. For Hampson, like Daly earlier on, the church's failure to ordain women plays a significant, if unvoiced, role in her post-Christian position. Hence, they both reject Christ's ability to save women, as women have been rejected as "representatives" of Christ. Hampson herself gives the following definition of her post-Christian stance:

> Post-*Christian* because Christianity (and not Islam) is the historical context within which my religious sensibilities were formed. But definitely *post*-Christian because I do not believe that there could be this uniqueness: that God could be related in a particular way to a particular age or to one particular person Jesus Christ.[21]

In this sense, the term "post-Christian" is intended both to recognize her Christian background and to indicate her break away from it.[22]

Hampson contends that the question about the compatibility of feminism and Christianity really is "that of whether the equality of women is compatible with a religion which has come from a past patriarchal age."[23] In her book *Theology and Feminism*, Hampson presents an important christological case for the incompatibility of Christianity and feminism. What is distinctive about Hampson's argument compared with the work of other post-Christian feminist theologians is how she focuses the issue of compatibility christologically. She explains:

The nub of the question as to whether feminism is compatible with Christianity is that of whether a Christology can be found of which it may be said that at least it is not incompatible with feminism. By Christology is meant the portrayal of Jesus as the Christ. I have suggested that a meaningful way to set the limits as to what may rightly be called a Christian position, is that Christians are those who proclaim Christ to have been unique.[24]

Given her focus on Christology, more precisely on the unique claim of "Jesus as the Christ" as the litmus test for Christianity, Hampson concludes that "there can be no Christology which is compatible with feminism."[25]

For Hampson, the question of the compatibility of Christology and feminism needs to be viewed as two major questions. First is the question about the credibility of Christianity, which, she states, "has increasingly come to be raised during the last two hundred years."[26] The second question, which Hampson categorizes as the "feminist question," relates to the ethical nature of Christianity. Hampson maintains that her "post-Christian" stance has everything to do with the first question and "nothing to do with any feminist stance which I may espouse."[27] Hence, it is her worldview, and not her feminist conviction, that hinders her from believing in the uniqueness of Jesus Christ as the incarnation of God. Because Hampson believes God to be equally available to people everywhere and in all times, she denies that there could be a unique and normative revelation of God in any particular time and location.[28] This, she argues, is the basic problem with Christianity. The fact that Christianity is a historical religion, based on a belief in particularity and uniqueness, puts it into contradiction with modern scientific truth and makes it noncredible. The following description of Christianity constitutes the premise for Hampson's conclusion:

Christians believe in particularity. That is to say they believe that God was in some sense differently related to particular events, or may be said in particular to have revealed God's self through those events, in a way in which this is not true of all other events or periods in history. Above all they believe that that must be said of Christ which is to be said of no other human being. However they may express his uniqueness, they must say of Jesus of Nazareth that there was a revelation of God through him in a way in which this is not true of you or me. God is bound up with peculiar events, a particular people, above all with the person of Jesus of Nazareth. Therefore reference must needs always be made to this history and to this person.[29]

Based on her rejection of the uniqueness and particularity of Christ, and given her earlier definition of Christology and its necessity for a Christian position, Hampson admits she does not have a Christology and is therefore no longer a Christian.[30] She still argues that this does not exclude the possibility that she "may believe Jesus' teaching to have been exemplary, or that he was a man singularly in tune with God."[31]

The ethical question that feminism poses to Christianity has, according to Hampson, to do with the historical nature of Christianity and the fact that the history "to which it relates is a patriarchal history."[32] Hampson argues that because Christianity is rooted in a patriarchal past, it is difficult to think of God as anything other than "Father" and "Son," since most of the biblical metaphors for God are male, and Jesus was a male human being. Hence, despite the possibility of finding supplementary imagery, "the core imagery remains male."[33] As a historical religion, Christianity is therefore intrinsically bound to its past and is unable to overcome its patriarchal bias.

By asking the ethical question, Hampson maintains, feminists are raising a question to the Christian tradition that has not been raised before, at least not to the same degree. The uniqueness of this question comes from feminists taking seriously the effects symbols have on a "subconscious and pre-rational level."[34] Hampson finds the feminist approach significant precisely because it points explicitly to the fact that the Christian story has indeed harmed women at the "level of symbolism." She sees it as one thing to believe the Christian story, as "long as people find it good." However, when people start to have doubts about harmful effects outweighing the goodness of this story, Hampson is convinced that the truth question will inevitably follow. She believes this to be true for a lot of women because, as feminists, they realize

> the extent to which this Christian story has hurt women, indeed how far the fact that God has been seen as "male" in the west has served to undermine a sense of women as also made in the image of God. Questions will then inevitably be raised as to whether the Christian myth is true in any case. I would suggest that many women are coming to doubt that it is. In so far as our religion is our vision of the world, if that vision comes no longer to seem ethical, then it will be discarded. One's religion, at the end of the day, one might suppose, has to conform to one's ethical beliefs.[35]

To believe that one's religion has to comply with one's ethical beliefs signifies for Hampson her own "ethical a priori position," by which she means to hold certain principles a priori and consequently as not subject to qualification.

Hampson explains how her own decision to leave Christianity behind was reinforced by the ethical question. She refers to her experience when, in fighting for the cause of women's ordination, she found herself being forced to argue for the full humanity and equal dignity of women. This particular experience later made Hampson realize she could not, because of her ethical belief, stay within a religion that constantly refers to its "sexist history" as authoritative. Even to entertain the idea that questions of human dignity and equality are open to discussion, Hampson finds, is "deeply offensive." She believes these are not matters for which one should have to argue, as she had to do in advocating the ordination of women. The need, however, to continue such a discussion is strictly "owing to the fact that Christianity is a historical religion, having a necessary reference to a past period of human history."[36] However, any attempt to "close the gap between the past and present" by rereading texts in a more favorable light is not credible to Hampson and could, she says, make sense only to Christians who do consider the past to be normative.[37] She consequently advocates discontinuity with the past as a necessary step toward the goal of a "religious situation in which women and men are accounted equals."[38] This discontinuity with the past—for her, the necessary outcome of an "ethical a priori" position—makes all attempts to rework Christology useless and makes the step outside of Christianity unavoidable.

When it comes to the christological question, the focus is not simply on the mere fact that Jesus was a man but that this particular man has been considered unique and symbolic of God. Therefore "[t]he God-head, or at least Christology, appears to be biased against women."[39] In her work, Hampson highlights the attention that feminists are paying to the power of symbolism and ideology, and their claim that western religious thought has been "ideologically loaded against women."[40] She thinks that feminists are raising a question that strikes at the very core of Christology when they ask "whether a symbol which would appear to be necessarily male can be said to be inclusive of all humanity."[41]

In her own quest for a Christology that would be inclusive of women, Hampson found promise in the patristic era more than in any other period. Nevertheless, she concluded that "the philosophical framework which allowed the fathers to have a Christology which could be in some way inclusive of women" had disappeared.[42] Hampson considers the search of feminists of recent years for a Christology that is compatible with feminism to have been no more successful than her own. She insists that the problem in reconciling Christology with feminism has to do with the very fact that, "by definition, Christology speaks of Jesus as the Christ."[43] This is why, no matter how "high" a Christology one may have, Christ's divine nature is still tied to the human nature of a male human being. Thus, the dilemma with which feminists are faced goes back to the Chalcedonian agreement, which insists that one cannot speak simply of one nature without the other. Or, in Hampson's words: "Inescapably, if one is to have a Christology, one must bring the two natures together, and herein lies the problem."[44]

Looking for an example of high Christology, Hampson refers to Patricia Wilson-Kastner's book, *Faith, Feminism and the Christ*, in which she sees the focus being on a "non-gendered cosmic Christ."[45] This, Hampson argues, does not solve the problem. If, however, a solution is sought by going to the other extreme, she believes it does not matter how "low" a Christology becomes, "this human person, who is a man, is not simply human but his human nature is bonded to a divine nature."[46] Hampson finds this problem in Carter Heyward's Christology, which she maintains is "Christocentric," despite all attempts to present Jesus as "fully and only human."[47] The third attempt Hampson denounces as unsuccessful she identifies as "message" Christology. She chooses Ruether's Christology as an example. Hampson contends that, for Ruether, the interest is in Jesus' message, "a message in her case held to concern the coming of the kingdom, the vindication of the poor and the creation of a just social order."[48] Hampson does not believe that a Christology can exclusively focus on a message that exists independently of the person who preached it. "If it is to be a Christology, it must also concern Christ's person—whereupon all the problems which Christology entails are again present."[49] Furthermore, Hampson rejects the Jesus-the-feminist position, since, for her, there is nothing particularly exceptional about Jesus' behavior and attitudes toward women, as presented in the New Testament.[50] All that can be said is that he was not a misogynist, which does not make him special in any way, as there were others also in his society of whom that was also true. According to Hampson, there is "no positive evidence that Jesus saw anything wrong with the sexism of his day."[51] To look to Jesus in search of feminist models for human relationship is a vain enterprise, since Jesus was simply not concerned with those issues that contemporary women can no longer ignore.

Hampson's main critique of those feminists who want to remain within the Christian tradition is that they "often fail to recognize the crucial nature of symbolism."[52] In terms of the christological symbol, she criticizes them for downplaying the significance of Jesus' maleness.[53] Since Christology gives a male human being a status that is given to no woman (i.e., the incarnate divine), she believes there cannot be any Christology that is compatible with the feminist perspective.[54]

Daphne Hampson sees those who share her conclusion about the non-credible and unethical nature of Christianity as faced with two alternatives: one is atheism, which she herself does not find credible, the second, a reinterpretation of "what one understands by being a religious person who loves

God."[55] Hampson claims the second alternative for herself as she insists that despite the incompatibility of feminism and Christianity, a feminist can still be a religious person.[56] Looking for a way to conceptualize God independently of the Christian "myth," a myth Hampson believes is both untenable and immoral, her aim is to find new ways to "capture our experience of God in the language of our day."[57] She looks for a way beyond the anthropomorphically conceived God, while she does not want to give up the "theistic sensibility" that is reflected in what she perceives as "the possibility of prayer,"[58] or the "openness to that which we name God."[59] Hampson recognizes a need for a spirituality "which speaks. . .to the fact that human beings are a part of nature, and yet does not deny their peculiar transcendence."[60] She expresses a concern about contemporary feminist theology, a trend in which she also sees in much modern theology, toward a secularized position. What has happened with feminist theology is, according to Hampson, that women's experience has replaced "talk of God." Thus, Hampson's own feminist theological task is to find "new ways to conceive the presence of God in our world," from a position outside of Christianity.[61]

While I do not find Hampson's conclusion about the absolute incompatibility of feminism and Christology convincing, I think she is right about the important contribution that feminism has made in drawing attention to the effects that the exclusive male symbol of Christology have on "a subconscious and pre-rational level." Hampson also rightly points out that women should not have to argue for their equality, as for example has been the case in the debate about women's ordination. The fact that women have had to argue that they indeed are also made in the image of God, and are therefore equal to men, is a sad testimony to the patriarchal bias and potential abuse of power in the Christian tradition. Examples of such an abuse of power are unfortunately numerous, only one being the long history of men's monopoly on the administration of the sacraments and the preaching of the gospel. Instead of arguing for "women's rights" to join the ordained ministry, this should rather be addressed as a theological question, or rather a christological one, if a woman can represent Jesus Christ or if Jesus can represent women.[62] This leads us back to the christological question of the role and identity of Jesus Christ.

Jesus As Only Human: A Liberating Paradigm: Carter Heyward

A second group of feminist theologians resolves the feminist question about the male savior by focusing on the historical Jesus and his message and praxis, rather than on Christ and his divine identity. Even if women belonging to this group are not willing to take the step out of Christianity with Daly and Hampson, they still find the idea of Jesus as the sole savior and the unique revelation of God highly problematic. A feasible alternative for many is to describe Jesus' difference from other human beings as one of degree rather than of kind, and his salvific importance, a matter of his liberating influence on other human beings—his contemporaries as well as people today. Rosemary Radford Ruether's Christology belongs to this second category. For Ruether, Jesus' importance is based on his prophetic message and behavior counteracting the patriarchal bias of the tradition, which makes him an appropriate "example" for both women and men today.[63] Still, the claim that he is a fitting exemplar does not make Jesus truly unique or make him the only Christ, Christ meaning "the liberated humanity." On the contrary, Ruether sees Jesus as a representative of Christ, one among many paradigmatic women and men who continue the liberating work of Christ.[64]

Carter Heyward's Christology is another example of an "only human" approach to the person and work of Jesus Christ. Heyward's influence within feminist christological discourse has been significant since the publication of her dissertation in 1982. I will turn my attention to her writings on Jesus, after a short overview of Heyward's biological background.

Carter Heyward spent her teaching carrier at the Episcopal Divinity School in Cambridge, Massachusetts. She started teaching in 1975 and later served as Howard Chandler Robbins Professor of Theology, until her retirement in 2006. Heyward has written a number of books, amongst them: *The Redemption of God: A Theology of Mutual Relation*; *Our Passion For Justice: Images of Power, Sexuality and Liberation*; *Speaking of Christ: A Lesbian Feminist Voice*; and *Saving Jesus from Those Who Are Right: Rethinking What It Means to Be Christian*. In addition she is the author of a large number of articles.

Heyward was one of eleven women who in 1974 were "irregularly" ordained Episcopal priests and then banned immediately from functioning in the Episcopal Church. This ban was lifted two years later when women's ordination was authorized within the Episcopal Church. Her experience of fighting for women's rights within the church, as well as her resistance against any kind of injustice toward minority groups—be it women, blacks, the poor, or gay men and lesbians—has significantly influenced Heyward's theology. It is indeed her conviction that "the more theology reflects the specific and particular experience of those who shape it the more credible their theology is to others."[65] Hence, Heyward's personal identity has become like a "trademark" for her theology, as reflected, for example, in the title of one of her books, namely, *Speaking of Christ: A Lesbian Feminist Voice*. Heyward writes in the preface to her book:

> Nor is this book about lesbianism or feminism. The subtitle, "A Lesbian Feminist Voice," is a means of signaling for the reader my sense of primary accountability: Who are my people? For whom, primarily, am I speaking and writing? It is also a way of lifting up and making visible particular dimensions of who I am which the dominant powers in the world and church would prefer be kept invisible. It is important to me that the reader knows that this person who is speaking of Christ is a lesbian and a feminist who wants her readers to have this information.[66]

Heyward approaches the doctrines concerning the person and the work of Jesus Christ with a soteriological focus, by asking to what extent we are responsible for our own redemption. An important key to her work is her "operative theo-logical assumption," namely, that "God and humanity need to be understood as relational and co-operative, rather than as monistic (synonymous) or dualistic (antithetical),"[67] hence, her naming of God as "the power in relation."[68] Heyward insists that a "relational theology," such as her own, is "incarnational,"[69] and she perceives in Jesus—more precisely, "in what he did,"—"the human capacity to make God incarnate in the world," a capacity she believes to be "no less ours than his."[70] By focusing on what Jesus did instead of who he was, in her words, "to lay emphasis on Jesus of Nazareth rather than on the eternal Christ," Heyward develops *a functional Christology*, which limits the importance of Jesus to being "fully and only human."[71]

In her book (originally her doctoral work) *The Redemption of God: A Theology of Mutual Relation*, Heyward gives two reasons why she is interested in the christological question. The first reason has to do with her personal background:

> First, I am hooked on Jesus. I could no more pretend that the Jesus-figure, indeed the Jesus Christ of the kerygma, is unimportant to me than I could deny the significance of my parents and my past in the shaping of my future. As a "cradle-Christian"—a person who came to know the storybook Jesus long before I sat down and thought about God—I have no sane or creative choice but to take very seriously this Jesus Christ who is written indelibly in my own history.[72]

Beside this personal attachment to the person of Jesus Christ, Heyward claims that the person of Jesus is the most fundamental and problematic issue for feminists. Heyward maintains that the centrality, or the "Lordship," of Jesus ("the male god") has been employed—doctrinally, politically, psychologically, structurally—in the service of a fellowship of brothers and fathers—the Church—whose female members have been auxiliary or, in special cases, perceived to be enough "like men" ("the exceptional woman", "one of the boys") to be <u>relatively</u> welcome in the fellowship of men.[73]

Hence, Heyward is driven to the subject of Christology both by a personal fascination and by the patriarchal abuse of this particular doctrine.

Given her fascination with the "Jesus-figure," as well as her feminist concern about the traditional understanding of the person and work of Jesus, Heyward explains it is Christianity that has "compelled" her to be feminist, that is, "to search incessantly for ways to effect justice."[74] She has come to view the person of Jesus Christ as distorted within the Christian tradition, and this, "<u>despite</u> the most vocal articulations of dogma, worship, and discipline within our traditions." Through this experience, she has discovered Jesus as "more remarkable" than she had realized before: "More remarkable, more helpful, because he is more truly human than he has been made out to be in orthodox—both catholic and reformed—Christology."[75]

Heyward undertakes the task of "reimaging" Jesus in order to find this "more remarkable, more helpful," and "more human" Jesus. By reimaging Jesus "from our own experiences in the world," Heyward maintains, we are imaging Jesus' "most creative place in our consciousness."[76] To reimage Jesus involves "play[ing] freely" with Scripture and the Christian tradition, for the purpose of comprehending our own existence. To reimage Jesus may involve letting go of old images and finding new images of Jesus that will benefit our communities. These images, Heyward contends, will never fully coincide with any individual image of Jesus in Scripture or in the history of Christian thought. She believes that, for Jesus to become anything meaningful for humanity today and not just "an idol which lures us away from the world," he must be reimaged "on the basis of what we know already about ourselves in relation to the Jesus-figure about whom we have heard, to each other, and to that which we believe to be God." Only then will Christology evolve into an image of "relational experience," in the same way as Heyward assumes incarnation was "an image of Jesus' relational experience."[77]

Fundamental to Heyward's "reimaging" of Jesus is her presupposition that Jesus matters "only if he was fully, and only human." Jesus was not ontologically different from other human beings, and his "ousia" was not divine. Consequently, Jesus reveals the same capacity that all humans have to make God incarnate in the world.[78] For Heyward, Jesus belongs with a group of people who in a unique way have made God incarnate in the world. Still, she insists, she is not calling feminist attention to Jesus simply because of her Christian heritage. Rather, she argues,

> I invite attention to Jesus at this point because I believe that what he did may be instructive in our understanding of the power in relational experience, a power discernable not only in Jesus' life, but also in the lives of Socrates, Sappho, Sojourner Truth, King, Torres, Mother Theresa, and countless other women and men in history, in whose relations a compelling and creative power has been operative and strong.[79]

Thus, Jesus' "ousia" should be considered the "essence" of the human capability "to choose to act with God." Consequently, if Jesus is to be understood as divine, divinity can only be understood in functional terms. Whoever chooses to act "with God in the world" has consequently chosen to act "divinely." The person is still human, and God is God—that is, a transpersonal power. However, "on the basis of co-operation, the person may carry the weight of God's authority on earth."[80]

By redefining divinity, Heyward wants to correct what she perceives is "a misconception" of the person of Jesus, namely, the idea that Jesus was a divine person rather than "a human being who knew and loved God."[81] Heyward charges the councils of Nicea and Chalcedon with the "Hellenization of Jesus," which, she argues, "evolved from, and resulted further in, a spiritualization of the human Jesus."[82] The root of this problem is to be found in the mistake of focusing on Jesus' identity instead of on his work. Nicea and Chalcedon are therefore responsible for producing "a Platonic image of a divine man whose humanity is incredible." Heyward insists that if we continue to follow Chalcedon today, we know that we are unable to perform the same kind of acts, because we are not divine as he was.[83] For Heyward the bottom line is that, if Jesus was God, unlike us, then his story is incapable of encouraging us. However, if Jesus were human, in need of relationships like other human beings, then he can be an example for us.[84]

While Carter Heyward perceives Jesus' life as a meaningful example for women, she sees no redeeming quality in the event of the cross. On the contrary, a Christology that assigns positive redemptive significance to the cross sends out a message of "human passivity, powerlessness, and willingness to endure suffering."[85] Still, Heyward is willing to give a positive meaning to the voluntary aspect of Jesus' suffering and death. To Heyward, Jesus' death is an unnecessary, violent death and, as such, no different from other unjust deaths. Moreover, as "fully, and only human," Jesus' death can only be a final one. Nothing can remove the injustice of his death, nor transform it into a blessing or "cause for great thanksgiving." Any theology that promotes the idea that Jesus' followers are to endure and even welcome pain and death "as a sign of faith is," according to Heyward, "constructed upon a faulty hermeneutic of what Jesus was doing and of why he died." By encouraging imitation of Jesus' suffering and death, such theological masochism is not only unhelpful, but contradicts "Jesus' own refusal to make concession to unjust relation."[86]

Through her *functional* Christology, Heyward finally finds an answer to her initial question about our responsibility for our own redemption in history. After having rejected the idea of a protological or an eschatological redemption[87] and the image of a divine savior, Heyward comes up with her own alternative, which she calls "immediate redemption." Immediate redemption suggests that we are our own saviors, besides being "the saviors of God."[88] We do not need somebody else to save us, nor should we wait for redemption to take place in the future. Redemption is possible, and we can make it happen, through "right relation between and among ourselves here and now."[89] This makes God's incarnations "as many and varied as the persons who are driven by the power in relation to touch and be touched by sisters and brothers."[90] The importance of Jesus, as one of the incarnations of God, is strictly measured in terms of his ability to encourage us to incarnate God here and now. Thus, Heyward argues, if we are not encouraged to do so by his image, we should look elsewhere. However, if we are encouraged by his image, there is no good reason not to explore it.[91]

From early on, Heyward has expressed her conviction that a feminist theological agenda does indeed push for discontinuity with orthodox Christology[92] and has gone so far as to argue that classical Christology "as an arena of constructive work, is dead."[93] Heyward outlines this conclusion in an essay in which she tackles the tension between the Jesus of history and the Christ of faith. The thesis of her essay is that the tension between Jesus of Nazareth and Jesus Christ—the human Jesus and his divine significance— "is no longer, if it ever was, a place of creative christological inquiry." Moreover, Heyward contends this tension is itself a "distraction from the daily praxis of liberation."[94] Instead, Heyward wants to move the foundations of Christology from the ontology of dualistic opposition toward the "ethics of justice making," with the focus on "a praxis of relational particularity and cooperation."[95]

Feminist theologians, who identify with an "only-human" approach to Jesus Christ, share Hampson's and Daly's conviction that the argument for the uniqueness of God's revelation in Jesus Christ is no longer a credible claim. By focusing on his message and praxis, rather than on his person, they seek to avoid this exclusive claim about Christ. This is based on the assumption that if

Jesus' importance is limited to his influence on other people, and his signifi-cance is measured in terms of encouraging people to follow his example, then his identity is no longer important. Further, for theologians such as Heyward who advocate an exclusively functional (or rather ethical) Christology, there is no soteriological significance of the cross, except as reflection on the human ability to suffer "for the sake of justice."

I think Carter Heyward is absolutely right about the tendency in the Chris-tian tradition to minimize the significance of Jesus' humanity and what that means for our understanding of our human (or rather bodily) existence. Yet, I find her strictly human interpretation of Jesus not convincing, as I am not con-vinced by her argument why Jesus would continue to be so important if he is "nothing more" than human, like us. Why should we then bother to pursue the meaning of his story? I also find Heyward's rejection of the eschatological per-spective problematic. I understand her concern that it may take the focus away from the present, but still I think she overlooks the important difference between an abuse and use of eschatology, as the tendency to ignore present problems because of a glorious life awaiting in heaven is a clear misinterpreta-tion of the eschatological perspective. The possibility for such a misinterpreta-tion should, however, not dissolve the Christian hope, which looks forward to the fulfillment of the promises of the coming Reign of God. Yet, as is clear from Jesus' message, God's Reign is already affecting our lives today, calling Chris-tians to active participation in the furthering of Christ's mission amongst the last and the least. I think that, by simply rejecting the eschatological perspec-tive, Heyward is ignoring the importance of the Christian hope. Not only does hope motivate us to act here and now against the seemingly endless injustice we are faced with, but also hope forsees an end to this ongoing struggle we are called to participate in on behalf of God's Reign.

God Incarnated, Truly Human, and Yet Unique: Elizabeth Johnson

Unlike those feminist theologians who have left Christianity behind or limited Jesus' significance to his message and praxis, there are those who see the clas-sical doctrine of Jesus as Christ as not being intrinsically male-centered or in-compatible with feminism. A key to their standpoint is their conviction that "the classical doctrine of the Incarnation speaks of the divinity and humanity of Christ, *not* his maleness."[96] They, too, find the feminist critique important in pointing out the use (or rather misuse) of this particular doctrine against women in the history of the church. Given "an egalitarian Jesus of the gospels who accepted women as human beings on a par with men," these feminist theologians identify the "vexing issue" as the question of how this Jesus became a justification for male superiority, used for exclusive and often oppressive purposes.[97]

An important representative of those theologians who wish to retrieve the inclusive intent of ancient Christology is Elizabeth A. Johnson C.S.J. Currently a Distinguished Professor of Theology at Fordham University, The Jesuit University of New York, Johnson taught previously at The Catholic University of America. Johnson finished her dissertation, "Analogy/Doxology and Their Connection with Christology in the Thought of Wolfhart Pannenberg," from The Catholic University of America in 1981. She has written a number of books, among them is *Consider Jesus: Waves of Renewal in Christology*, in which she explores the development of Catholic Christology since 1950. Other books by Johnson are: *She Who Is: The Mystery of God in Feminist Theological Discourse*; *Friends of God and Prophets: A Feminist Theological Reading of the Communion of Saints*; *Truly Our Sister: A Theology of Mary in the Communion of Saints*; and *Quest for the Living God: Mapping Frontiers in the Theology of God*. Johnson has also written numerous articles and book chapters, amongst them are a few on feminist Christology.

In the beginning of the book *She Who Is: The Mystery of God in Feminist Theological Discourse*, Johnson states her strong commitment both to the Christian tradition and to the feminist critique that has been launched against the tradition. An important prerequisite is her firm conviction that the Christian tradition is neither intrinsically patriarchal nor incompatible with feminism. Hence, while Johnson agrees with those who argue that the classical tradition has both "aided and abetted the exclusion and subordination of women," she maintains it has also "sustained generations of foremothers and foresisters in the faith."[98]Given this double functioning of the tradition, Johnson is convinced of the possibility of a feminist retrieval of Christian tradition, that is, that we can find a "discourse about divine mystery that would further the emancipation of women."[99] She maintains that "a Christian feminist liberation theology," such as her own, makes an "a priori option for the human flourishing of women."[100] For Johnson herself, the goal of feminist religious discourse indeed "pivots in its fullness around the flourishing of poor women of color in violent situations."[101]

Feminist theology as an academic discipline is causing an "intellectual paradigm shift," argues Johnson. This happens when women's experience is placed at the center of inquiry and the call is made for a "transformation of oppressive symbols and systems."[102] Based on her notable statement, "the symbol of God functions," Johnson insists that upon examination it becomes clear that an exclusive speech about God "serves in manifold ways to support an imaginative and structural world that excludes or subordinates women."

Furthermore, "wittingly or not," she argues, "it undermines women's human dignity as equally created in the image of God."[103] It should be noticed that it is the exclusive, literal, and patriarchal use of male metaphors that Johnson finds problematic—both oppressive and idolatrous—and not the use of male metaphors per se.[104]

The crucial function of feminist Christology is, according to Johnson, to "redeem the name of Christ" *from* the exclusive and oppressive use of christological doctrines, *for* the healing of all humankind.[105] She explains how the Chalcedonian definition has often been used to advocate male metaphors and denounce female-language about God, despite all warning against mixing or confusing the two natures in Christ. "As visible image of the invisible God," Johnson asserts, "the human man Jesus is used to tie the knot between maleness and divinity very tightly."[106] A Christology done in the light of the gospel depiction of Jesus of Nazareth still has the potential to critique "the patriarchy of the God symbol."[107] That women have, despite christological abuses, found "life-giving power" in Jesus the Christ indeed "warrants the feminist theological effort to redeem the christological tradition from patriarchy."[108]

Johnson divides the task feminist theology is undertaking within the field of Christology into three parts.[109] First is the critical task of uncovering sexist interpretations of the narratives, symbols, and doctrines of Jesus the Christ that so often have distorted what was meant to be good news. The second is to look for alternative interpretations in Scripture, tradition, and women's experience. Third is the constructive part, the attempt to speak "anew about Jesus the Christ according to the feminist model of inclusion and reciprocity, to practical and critical effect."[110]

In terms of the first task, Johnson insists that during the first few centuries of Christianity, an imperial and patriarchal model triumphed over the liberating one, resulting in a sexist interpretation of Jesus' maleness.[111] Still, Johnson does not see Jesus' maleness as being problematic in itself, but rather constitutive for his personal identity, while being a part of both the perfection and the limitation of his historical reality. Instead, the problem has to do with the way this one historical particularity, unlike all the others, has been and still is interpreted in sexist theology and practice. "Consciously or unconsciously," she argues, "Jesus' maleness is lifted up and made essential for his christic function and identity, thus blocking women precisely because of their female sex from participating in the fullness of their Christian identity as images of Christ."[112]

Johnson gives three examples of how this sexist interpretation of Jesus' maleness is realized in theory as well as in praxis. First is the use of Jesus' historical maleness to reinforce an exclusively male image of God. Second, his maleness has been used to legitimize men's superiority over women, "in the belief that a partic-ular honor, dignity, and normativity accrues to the male sex because it was chosen by the Son of God 'himself' in the incarnation."[113] This is, for example, encoun-tered in the argument concerning men's so-called natural resemblance to Christ, which has been and still is used to keep women from ordination within the Roman Catholic Church. The third issue has to do with the question of salvation. Johnson points out how sexist Christology jeopardizes women's salvation, "at least in theory." Therefore, if "et homo factus est" in the Nicene Creed really means "et vir factus est"—that is, if "maleness is essential for the christic role,"[114] and female sexuality is furthermore not "assumed" in the incarnation—then women are indeed excluded from salvation. Consequently, the answer to the question, "Can a male savior save women?" has to be no. In order to correct such a distortion of the christological doctrine, Johnson looks to the wisdom tradition for hopeful signs. In wisdom Christology she sees the possibility of a Christology "which is faithful to the hard-won insights of the tradition" but at the same time provides tools to redeem the christological tradition from patriarchal distortion.[115]

Johnson advocates a reappropriation of wisdom Christology in order to provide an "alternative to dominant patriarchal language about God."[116] What Johnson considers the main advantage of wisdom Christology is that it "points the way to an inclusive Christology in female symbols."[117] In Sophia-Christology Johnson finds a necessary resource for much-needed female imagery. More spe-cifically, wisdom Christology provides a rich resource of female metaphors to be used to interpret both the saving significance and the personal identity of Jesus the Christ. Convinced of the importance of the choice of metaphors, Johnson argues that the gender symbolism

> not only casts Jesus into an inclusive framework with regard to his
> relationships with human beings and with God, removing the male
> emphasis that so quickly turns to androcentrism. But, the symbol
> giving rise to thought, it also evokes Sophia's characteristic gracious
> goodness, life-giving creativity, and passion for justice as key
> hermeneutical elements in speaking about the mission and
> person of Jesus.[118]

Wisdom categories therefore have the potential to correct sexist interpretations both in terms of Jesus' person and work and regarding his relationship with God and humanity.[119]

Johnson maintains that the early Christians' use of wisdom categories to articulate the "saving goodness" they experienced in Jesus the Christ had rad-ical consequences for the development of their understanding of "the identity and significance" of Jesus.[120] The identification of the human being Jesus with the divine Sophia led the early Christians to think about Jesus not simply as a human being inspired by God but as one related to God in a more personally unique way. Furthermore, the use of wisdom categories made it possible for the fledgling Christian communities to ascribe "cosmic significance to the crucified Jesus, relating him to the creation and governance of the world." Johnson concludes that wisdom categories became essential in the development of incarnation Christology.[121] She explains how a trajectory of wisdom Christology reveals the close association between Jesus and Sophia, and already by the end of the first century, Jesus is no longer simply presented as a wisdom teacher, a child or representative of Sophia, but as the embodiment of Sophia herself.[122] Thus, Johnson contends, Jesus "came to be seen as God's only begotten Son only after he was identified with Wisdom."[123]

While the ministry of Jesus, the prophet and child of Sophia, is characterized by his announcement of God as "the God of all-inclusive love who wills the wholeness and humanity of everyone especially the poor and heavy burdened,"[124] his death signifies rejection of the "friendship and inclusive care of Sophia."[125] Johnson rejects the idea that Jesus' death was required by God in payment for sin and insists that Jesus' death was an "act of violence," a result of his message and behavior.[126] Thus, instead of signifying a payment called for by human sinfulness, the cross becomes a sign of God's identification with human beings in the midst of their suffering and pain. Johnson finds wisdom categories helpful for the reappropriation of the story of the cross as, what she calls, a "heartbreaking empowerment." Moreover, within the context of the wisdom tradition, she understands the cross as a part of "the larger mystery of pain-to-life, of that struggle for the new creation evocative of the rhythm of pregnancy, delivery, and birth so familiar to women of all times."[127] The belief in the risen Christ is consequently the expression of "the victory of love, both human and divine, that spins new life out of this disaster."[128] And while the resurrection cannot be humanly imagined, in faith it represents that "evil does not have the last word." In the resurrection Sophia-God collects her child and prophet into new transformed life, which constitutes a "promise of a future for all the dead and the whole cosmos itself." Here, Johnson encounters the feminist vision of wholeness, "of the preservation of the bodily integrity of each, even the most violated, and the interconnectedness of the whole,"at the very core of the Christian message.[129]

One of the reasons for Johnson's retelling of the story of Jesus from a feminist perspective is to bring out the antipatriarchal character of the gospel story of Jesus. Johnson points out how Jesus' message and his "inclusive lifestyle" created a challenge to the reigning patriarchy and eventually brought him to the cross. She, furthermore, identifies a social significance to Jesus' maleness, since a woman, doing the same thing as Jesus did, would not have been taken seriously within a patriarchal culture. As the crucified Jesus becomes the embodiment of the very antithesis of the patriarchal prototype of the powerful man, and at the same time reveals the high cost to be paid in the struggle for liberation, Johnson recognizes the cross as a symbol of the "kenosis of patriarchy." The self-emptying or kenosis of patriarchy signifies more concretely the self-emptying "of male dominating power in favor of the new humanity of compassionate service and mutual empowerment." Thus, Jesus' maleness is turned into a prophecy proclaiming the end of patriarchy, "at least as divinely ordained."[130]

The possibility of an inclusive interpretation of the symbol of Christ is for Johnson one of the most important advantages of wisdom Christology, as the metaphor of Jesus the Wisdom of God indicates that "even as a human man, Jesus can be thought to be revelatory of the graciousness of God imaged as female."[131] Consequently, gender cannot be considered constitutive of the symbol of the Christ, nor does gender restrict the identity of the Christ within the human community. Johnson finds it important that the biblical symbol of Christ, as the one anointed in the Spirit, should be restricted neither to the historical Jesus nor, for that matter, to certain selected members of the community. "After his death and resurrection," she argues, "the focus of the ongoing story of Jesus-Sophia shifts from his concrete historical life to the community of sisters and brothers imbued with the Spirit."[132] To collapse the totality of the Christ into the human man Jesus signifies to Johnson "a naive physicalism," which is already challenged by biblical metaphors such as the Pauline body of Christ and the Johannine branches abiding in the vine. In accordance with these metaphors, the story of Sophia incarnate, anointed as the Christ, "goes on in history as the story of the whole Christ, *christa* and *christus* alike, the wisdom community."[133] The "Biblical cosmic Christology" expands the notion of Christ still further, by recognizing the destiny of the universe itself to become christomorphic in a reconciled new heaven and new earth (Colossians 1:15–20).[134]

Looking for helpful resources to correct a sexist Christology, Johnson does not limit her resources to the gospel story of Jesus and biblical speech about Christ. She finds the classical language of christological doctrines useful as well. The fact that the christological conflicts in the first five centuries circled around the authentic character of Jesus' humanity and not his sex, race, class, or any other particularity is a fundamental point here. Johnson stresses the significance of this particular issue, since what indeed was at stake in the christological debate was the question of salvation. Given the early Christian axiom "what is not assumed is not redeemed," (only if Jesus' humanity was genuine and not only partial), did the saving significance of the incarnation apply to the human being as a whole. The christological conflict was eventually solved by the affirmation of the genuine humanity (*vere homo*) of Sophia incarnate, which, in light of contemporary anthropology, Johnson explains, signified "a body of real flesh that could feel passion, suffer, and die and a soul with its own spiritual and psychological powers."[135] For this reason, Johnson is convinced of the inclusive intent of the christological doctrines. What christological texts in their historical context make clear is that it is *not* Jesus' maleness that is doctrinally important but his *humanity* "in solidarity with the whole suffering human race."[136] Consequently, without in any sense compromising the historical particularity of the incarnation, Johnson asserts that the idea of incarnation emphasizes the inclusion of the humanity of all human beings.[137]

Drawing her conclusions about "the practical and critical effects" of her attempt to "redeem the name of the Christ," Johnson claims that it will indeed be a sign of a theology coming of age when the focus shifts from Jesus' historical sex to his liberating message. The key here is "the scandal of his option for the poor and marginalized, including women, in the Spirit of his compassionate, liberating Sophia-God." For Johnson, this is "the scandal of particularity" that really counts, which aims toward "the creation of a new order of wholeness in justice." She continues:

> Jesus in his human, historical specificity is confessed as Sophia
> incarnate, revelatory of the liberating graciousness of God imaged as
> female; women, as friends of Jesus-Sophia, share equally with men in
> his saving mission throughout time and can fully represent Christ,
> being themselves, in the Spirit, other Christs.[138]

Johnson has no doubt this understanding of Jesus as Sophia incarnate and women as representatives of Christ will have serious consequences for ecclesiology, both in theory and practice, and eventually will lead toward a community characterized by a discipleship and ministry of equals.

Some of the implications of wisdom Christology Johnson lists are seen in the promotion of values that are closely related to women's experience. A particular example is the reconsideration of the widely accepted dichotomy between matter and spirit, in light of the notion that Wisdom herself did become a human being. Because of the resurrection, Johnson maintains, matter will always be "a treasure related to God," as the "body of itself is glorified in the power of Wisdom's spirit, not discarded."[139] Furthermore, based on the fact that it is "the tortured and executed body of Jesus that is raised," the Christian hope for a future for "all the dead and explicitly for all those who are raped, tortured, and unjustly destroyed in the continuing torment of history" is then established.[140] When done "in the struggle for women's equal human dignity," wisdom Christology's contributions can also be seen in the promotion of justice for the poor, respectful encounter with other religious traditions, and ecological care for the earth. Eventually, Johnson hopes, the whole church will be called to conversion, "away from sexism and toward a community of the discipleship of equals, for the sake of its mission in the world."[141] This conversion, according to Johnson, is to be brought about by the *retelling* of the story of Jesus, the *transformation* of the symbol of Christ, and the *reclaiming* of the original inclusive intent of the christological dogma.

In her work, Johnson has convincingly shown how a feminist retrieval of the basic intentions of the classical tradition can free Christology from its patriarchal distortion and thereby contribute to women's emancipation. I fully agree with her regarding the significance of the feminist critique to replace exclusive and oppressive use of the christological doctrines with an inclusive interpretation of the story of Jesus, the symbol of Christ, and the ancient christological dogma. Concurring with those who argue that the source of our oppression is the source of our power, Johnson rightly criticizes the patriarchal bias of the tradition, but at the same time reclaims the inclusive intent of the doctrine. Here, Johnson shows an important alternative to Heyward's contention for discontinuity with the classical Christology and to Daphne Hampson's insistence on a discontinuity with our patriarchal past. While Johnson argues that Jesus' maleness has a definite social significance, she maintains that the inclusive intent of the christological doctrine involves the affirmation of Jesus' genuine humanity, which is key to his solidarity with the entire suffering human race.

By affirming the importance of the cross in God's self-revelation, Johnson's work serves as a reminder of the significance that a suffering God might have to facilitate a praxis of hope for women. As she herself admits, her discussion of the Sophia-God as "compassion poured out" should be regarded only as "clues, starting points, commencements" for further feminist christological debate.[142] Indeed, Johnson's theology of the cross explicitly invites other Christian feminist theologians to attempt further critical retrievals of the classical theological tradition. It is to the cross—its role within the Christian tradition and the feminist critique of its function and meaning—that we will turn our focus in the following chapters.

NOTES

1. Swidler, "Jesus Was a Feminist," 183. In her book, *Beyond God the Father: Toward a Philosophy of Women's Liberation*, Mary Daly responds to Swidler's article by asking, "Jesus was a feminist, but so what?" (Daly, *Beyond God the Father*, 73).

2. Fiorenza points out a development within feminist biblical studies from the "apologetic-thematic focus" on "women in the Bible" and the concentration on what men have said about women in the Bible, to a critical reading of Biblical texts in a

feminist theological perspective. She writes: "In this process we have moved from discussing statements of Paul or the 'Fathers' and Rabbis about women to the rediscovery of Biblical women's leadership and oppression as crucial for the revelatory process of God's liberation reflected in the Jewish and Christian Scriptures" (Fiorenza, "To Set the Record Straight: Biblical Women's Studies," 111).

3. Other writings belonging to this group are, for example: Leonard Swidler, *Biblical Affirmations of Women* (1977); Frank and Evelyn Stagg, *Women in the World of Jesus* (1978); and Elisabeth Moltmann-Wendel, *The Women Around Jesus: Reflections on Authentic Personhood*.

4. Wahlberg, *Jesus and the Freed Woman*, 11.

5. Wahlberg, *Jesus According to a Woman*, 3.

6. Ibid., 1.

7. Wahlberg points out that Galatians 3:28 reminds us of the "three givens, accepted divisions or barriers of the day" (ibid. 14–15). This resonates with black women's "tridimensional experience of racism/sexism/classism," which Jacquelyn Grant talks about in *White Women's Christ and Black Women's Jesus: Feminist Christology and Womanist Response* (p. 209).

8. Wahlberg, *Jesus According to a Woman*, 3.

9. Ibid., 97. Wahlberg writes:

Not only did he astonish his contemporaries by speaking with women when such recognition of them was socially and religiously taboo, he actually chose women to go forth and spread the word of his ministry. The woman at the well left immediately to convert people in the nearby city; the women at the tomb received the message for the brethren that Christ was risen. And to a woman went the first post-crucifixion interview with the risen Christ that must have been the envy of the male apostles (Wahlberg, *Jesus and the Freed Woman*, 11).

10. Ibid., 6.

11. Wahlberg, *Jesus According to a Woman*, 86.

12. Ibid., 15. Elisabeth Moltmann-Wendel is another feminist theologian who stresses the human nature of Jesus, especially as depicted in the Gospel of Mark. See, for example, *The Women Around Jesus*, 95, 102.

13. Wahlberg, *Jesus According to a Woman*, 18.

14. Ibid., 17.

15. Ibid., 74.

16. Wahlberg, *Jesus and the Freed Woman*, 10.

17. See footnote in Daly, *Beyond God the Father*, xiii.

18. Ibid., 72.

19. Without wanting to deny "the charismatic and revelatory power of the personality of Jesus," Daly accuses Christianity of being guilty of "Christolatry," of idolatry concerning the person of Jesus. She believes this idolatry will not be overcome except through the revolution that is going on in women's conscious-ness. She writes: "As a uniquely masculine image and language for divinity loses credibility, so also the idea of a single divine incarnation in a human being of the

male sex may give way in the religious consciousness to an increased awareness of the power of Being in all persons" (Daly, *Beyond God the Father*, 71).

20. For further information, see Hampson's home page: http://www.standrews.ac.uk/~dh1/hamp1.html.

21. Hampson, *Theology and Feminism*, 42.

22. Ibid., 4.

23. Ibid., 11.

24. Ibid., 50.

25. Ibid., 58.

26. Ibid., 45.

27. Ibid., 41

28. Ibid.

29. Ibid., 8.

30. See ibid., 8 and 53. While agreeing with Hampson's criticism of the patriarchal character of traditional Christian theology and Christology, Ruether disagrees with her conclusion about the fundamental incompatibility of Christianity and feminism. See Ruether, "Is Feminism the End of Christianity? A Critique of Daphne Hampson's *Theology and Feminism*," 390–400.

31. Hampson, *Theology and Feminism*, 53.

32. Ibid., 9.

33. Ibid., 84.

34. Ibid., 161.

35. Ibid., 45.

36. Ibid., 32.

37. Hampson discusses the work of Elisabeth Schüssler Fiorenza and Phyllis Trible; see ibid., 32–41.

38. Ibid., 36.

39. Ibid., 51.

40. Ibid.

41. Ibid.

42. Ibid., 52.

43. Ibid., 59.

44. Ibid.

45. Ibid., 61.

46. Ibid., 59.

47. Ibid., 63.

48. Ibid., 6 5.

49. Ibid., 59.

50. Ibid., 87.

51. Ibid., 88.

52. Ibid., 76.

53. Unlike the Christian feminists, Hampson argues, conservatives and "feminist radicals" do grasp the importance of symbolism, as they both "see that the fact that God, and Christ, have been seen as 'male' is crucial to the religion" (ibid., 77).

54. Ibid., 76.

55. Ibid., 1.

56. Ibid., 46.

57. Ibid., 171.

58. Ibid., 168.

59. Ibid., 169.

60. Ibid., 13.

61. Ibid., 173.

62. I agree with Eleanor McLaughlin when she writes: "I argued for the priesthood of women not in the liberal or Enlightenment language of 'rights' but rather as a matter of theology—can Jesus Christ be represented by a woman-priest, does Jesus represent women? Can I, woman, made in God's image, see myself in God incarnate, and speak with the authoritative subjectivity of the New Adam, naming the world and offering with Christ the sacrifice of praise and thanksgiving?" ("Feminist Christologies: Re-Dressing the Tradition," 132).

63. In her book, *To Change the World: Christology and Cultural Criticism* (1981), Ruether explores how christological claims of the past have related to issues of classism, sexism, and ecology. Her Christology was further developed in her book *Sexism and God-Talk: Toward a Feminist Theology* (1983), which was probably the first example of a feminist systematic theology.

64. Ruether, *Sexism and God-Talk*, 138. McFague's understanding of Jesus is much in line with Ruether's, in which she talks about Jesus of Nazareth as "paradigmatic of God as lover" (McFague, *Models of God: Theology for an Ecological, Nuclear Age*, 150). Rita Nakashima Brock, in her book *Journeys by Heart: A Christology of Erotic Power* (1991), agrees with Ruether and McFague in denying the "individualizing of Christ." Brock suggests that we understand Christ, which she defines as the "revelatory and redemptive witness of God/ess's work in history," as "Christa/Community." She explains: "The Christa/Community in the biblical texts, in the stories of Jesus and other figures, is the church's imaginative witness to its experiences of brokenness and sacredness of erotic power in human existence" (Brock, *Journeys by Heart*, 69).

65. Heyward, *Our Passion for Justice: Images of Power, Sexuality and Liberation*, 223.

66. Heyward, *Speaking of Christ: A Lesbian Feminist Voice*, 10–11.

67. Heyward, *The Redemption of God: A Theology of Mutual Relation*, 1.

68. Ibid., 2.

69. Ibid., 31.

70. Ibid., 33.

71. Ibid., 34.

72. Ibid., 196.

73. Ibid.

74. Ibid., 197.

75. Ibid.

76. Ibid., 31. On the "danger" of "subjectivism" in assuming the authority of our own experience in doing theology, see ibid., 30.

77. Ibid., 30. Heyward demonstrates how reimaging is done "in relation to an image" by choosing to reimage the image of Jesus from the Gospel of Mark. She

believes the "Markan Jesus," who is imaged in "the prophetic tradition of Israel," is closer to her own than any other biblical image of Jesus. Starting out with the image the Gospel of Mark portrays of Jesus and his followers, Heyward's attempt is to reimage the Marcan Jesus in the light of "the immediate, critical needs" of people who are trying to understand themselves "in a world in which relation is broken violently" (ibid., 35).

78. Ibid., 33.

79. Ibid.

80. Ibid., 40.

81. Ibid., 32.

82. Ibid.

83. Ibid., 32. See also Appendix B on Chalcedon's Ontology (ibid., 189–92).

84. Ibid., 167.

85. Carter Heyward, "Suffering, Redemption, and Christ: Shifting the Grounds of Feminist Christology," 381–86.

86. Heyward, *The Redemption of God*, 57–58. Like Heyward, Sallie McFague has a very functional understanding of Jesus and his work, seeing him as one of many "paradigmatic figures" who "manifest in word and deed the love of God for the world" (McFague, *Models of God*, 136).

87. Heyward argues that to understand redemption eschatologically "is to attribute penultimate value to ourselves and to what we experience as real in the present world. There is always something more, something better, than our life together on earth" (Heyward, *The Redemption of God*, 131).

88. Ibid., 166.

89. Ibid., 132.

90. Ibid., 164.

91. Ibid., 169.

92. Heyward, *Our Passion for Justice*, 212.

93. Heyward, *Speaking of Christ*, 14.

94. Ibid., 13.

95. Ibid., 21.

96. Anne Carr, *Transforming Grace: Christian Tradition and Women's Experience*, 161. See also Russell, *Human Liberation in a Feminist Perspective—A Theology*, 138; and Moltmann-Wendel and Moltmann, *God—His and Hers*, 54.

97. Wilson-Kastner, *Faith, Feminism and the Christ*, 71. Many feminist theologians belonging to this group find it crucial to start with the historical Jesus. See, for example, Carr, *Transforming Grace*, 158; Wilson-Kastner, *Faith, Feminism and the Christ*, 92; Russell, *Human Liberation in a Feminist Perspective—A Theology*, 34.

98. Johnson, *She Who Is: The Mystery of God in Feminist Theological Discourse*, 9.

99. Ibid.

100. Ibid., 17. Johnson insists that making a fundamental option as such is not unique to feminist theology, as every theological reflection has "a center of gravity that unifies, organizes and directs its attention."

101. Ibid., 11.

102. Ibid., 33.

103. Ibid., 5.

104. Ibid., 40.

105. Johnson, "Redeeming the Name of Christ—Christology," 134.

106. Johnson, *She Who Is*, 35.

107. Ibid., 35.

108. Ibid., 134.

109. Johnson sees feminist theology in general engaged in these "interrelated tasks as it critically analyzes inherited oppressions, searches for alternative wisdom and suppressed history, and risks new interpretations of the tradition in conversation with women's lives" (ibid., 29).

110. Johnson, "Redeeming the Name of Christ—Christology," 116.

111. Johnson, *She Who Is*, 151.

112. Johnson, "Redeeming the Name of Christ—Christology," 119.

113. Ibid.

114. Ibid., 120. Johnson claims this is not a problem in which dualistic anthropology is embraced but appears once an androcentric Christology and egalitarian anthropology meet. She writes: "If women are not a lower order of creature subsumed in male humanity but equal partners in essential humanity along with men, then, according to the logic of male-centered Christology, they are not connected to what is most vital for salvation" (ibid.).

115. Johnson, "Jesus the Wisdom of God: A Biblical Basis for Non-androcentric Christology," 293.

116. Johnson, *She Who Is*, 103. See also pp. 241–45.

117. Ibid., 99. Johnson believes that an inclusive christological reflection "which makes room for female imagery has the potential to contribute in theory and practice to the appreciation of the dignity of real women. This kind of theological reflection, insofar as it is more liberating for all human beings, is finally more truly expressive of the reality of God incarnate" (Johnson, "Jesus the Wisdom of God," 289).

118. Johnson, *She Who Is*, 158.

119. Ibid., 213. For further discussion on wisdom Christology, see Johnson: *She Who Is*, 86–100, especially 94–100; "Redeeming the Name of Christ—Christology," 120–23; "Jesus the Wisdom of God," 261–94; and "Wisdom Was Made Flesh and Pitched Her Tent Among Us," especially 102–6.

120. Johnson writes: "Contemporary biblical exegesis has lifted the tradition of personified Wisdom from oblivion and demonstrated convincingly that it played a vital role in early Christian reflection on the creative, revelatory and saving significance of Jesus of Nazareth" ("Jesus the Wisdom of God," 291). See pp. 276–89 on the development of wisdom Christology in the New Testament.

121. Johnson, "Jesus the Wisdom of God," 261.

122. Johnson, *She Who Is*, 95.

123. Johnson, "Redeeming the Name of Christ—Christology," 121.

124. Ibid., 123.

125. Ibid., 124.

126. Johnson claims that this in fact is true for feminist theology in general, as well as for other forms of political and liberation theology. She argues that the idea of

the death of Jesus' being required by God in repayment for sin is today "virtually inseparable from an underlying image of God as an angry, bloodthirsty, violent and sadistic father, reflecting the very worst kind of male behavior" (ibid., 124).

127. Johnson, *She Who Is*, 159.

128. Johnson, "Redeeming the Name of Christ—Christology," 124.

129. Ibid., 125.

130. Johnson, *She Who Is*, 160–61. Concerning the social significance of Jesus' maleness, see also Johnson, "The Maleness of Christ," 112.

131. Johnson, "Redeeming the Name of Christ—Christology," 127–28.

132. Ibid., 128.

133. Ibid., 129. Johnson considers the role of the baptism and martyrdom traditions very important regarding the claim of women's and men's equal capacity to become "christomorphic" and to be transformed into *imago Christi*. Furthermore, she sees "the fundamental egalitarianism" of the baptismal and martyrdom traditions as continued today in the baptismal and funeral liturgies (Johnson, *She Who Is*, 75). See also Johnson, "The Maleness of Christ," 113–15.

134. Johnson, "The Maleness of Christ,"113.

135. Johnson, "Redeeming the Name of Christ—Christology," 130.

136. Johnson, *She Who Is*, 165.

137. Johnson, "Redeeming the Name of Christ—Christology," 130.

138. Johnson, *She Who Is*, 167.

139. Johnson, "Redeeming the Name of Christ—Christology," 132.

140. Ibid., 132.

141. Ibid., 134.

142. Johnson, *She Who Is*, 273.

3

The Life and Death of Jesus Christ from the Perspective of the Cross

From the overview of feminist reconstructions of Christology in the previous chapter, it is clear that the tendency to avoid the cross or strip it of any kind of saving significance has been prevalent within feminist Christology. The typology, however, stressed the diversity within this field, providing an example of an important feminist retrieval of a theology of the cross in Elizabeth Johnson's proposal. Agreeing with Johnson's call for another alternative to either the "impassible, omnipotent God" or "a victimized, helpless one,"[1] in the following, I will explore the tradition as a hermeneutical tool that allows for God's participation in the suffering of the world without turning God into a helpless victim of the radical suffering we so often encounter in our midst. Furthermore, I propose that theology of the cross is an important hermeneutical tool for our understanding of the life and death of Jesus Christ. By focusing on the cross as the locus of our knowledge of God, a theology of the cross maintains that the true nature of God is revealed in the person and work of Jesus Christ. From the standpoint of a theology of the cross, it is not only the human being, Jesus of Nazareth, who suffers on the cross, but, in the person of the Son, it really is God who suffers and dies. A God capable of suffering brings hope into hopeless situations. By embracing the sufferings of all those who suffer, God gives hope for a transformation of all suffering and death through the resurrection.

This chapter provides a survey of christological doctrines, with special attention given to the question of God's participation in Christ's sufferings and death. It starts with Paul's understanding of the "message about the cross," which is generally taken to be the foundation for all future theology of the cross. Special attention will be given to several recent interpretations of Paul's theology of the cross. Ernst Käsemann deserves particular notice for his significant contribution to the modern recovery of the theology of the cross,[2] as does Sally B. Purvis's proposal for a feminist retrieval of the cross.[3] From Paul we turn to the development of the christological doctrines that led to the agreement reached at Chalcedon in 451. The questions raised during this time regarding the widely accepted understanding of God's impassibility and the true humanity of Jesus Christ were vital for the development of the "truly human, truly divine" formulation affirmed in the Chalcedonian definition.

Moving to a consideration of Luther, it will become clear how important his controversy with Zwingli was to the forming of his theological position. Attempting to be faithful to the agreements of the early Christian councils, Luther found himself forced to emphasize the unity of the two natures to the extent that after the incarnation we can know God only "in the flesh." Luther's christological position, argued in defense of the real presence in the Lord's Supper, was developed within the context of his retrieval of Paul's *theologia crucis*. Luther's theology of the cross offered an important alternative to the theological discourse in his time and, moreover, played an important role in future interpretations of the cross and God's real involvement in Christ's suffering and death.

The nineteenth century directed much attention to Jesus Christ, undertaking a significant reevaluation of the widely accepted christological doctrines. The doctrine of divine impassibility also became the target of criticism initiated by a significant number of theologians and biblical scholars. After an exploration of the nineteenth-century background to the twentieth-century revival of trinitarian theology and the theology of the cross, the rest of this chapter will be devoted to Jürgen Moltmann's christological proposal. Moltmann represents a group of contemporary theologians who have found an important hermeneutical tool in the theology of the cross for an examination of the life and death of Jesus Christ. Moltmann's emphasis on the necessary relationship between our understanding of God and our daily life makes an important background for a feminist retrieval of a theology of the cross.

Paul's Theology of the Cross

In their writings on the role of the crucifixion and death of Jesus within the Pauline corpus, New Testament scholars have drawn attention to the infrequent use of crucifixion terminology in Paul's letters. They have also pointed out that there proves to be "no univocal role assigned to Jesus' death" nor "one fixed language employed in its depiction."[4] Scholars have, furthermore, questioned whether it is justifiable to talk about theology of the cross, given the important role Paul assigns to Jesus' resurrection within his proclamation.[5] However, it has been convincingly argued that it is not the message of the cross as such that is disputed, but rather "whether it is right to make this the real, or even the sole, theme of Pauline theology."[6]

The German New Testament scholar Ernst Käsemann has been called "the most vigorous and articulate advocate of understanding Pauline thought as a 'theology of the cross.'"[7] Käsemann was convinced that the center of Pauline theology "cannot be anything but a theology of the cross,"[8] despite "the multiplicity of other themes" in Paul's letters[9] and the fact that Paul proclaims Jesus' resurrection "as exclusively as his cross."[10] Furthermore, Käsemann considered it as his task to recover the "Reformation's insight," which for him consisted of showing that Luther's discernment that all theology must be seen as a "theology of the cross" (Luther's main thesis in his Heidelberg Disputation) is indeed true to the center of Paul's theology. For Käsemann, Paul interpreted the Christian message based on this theological center.[11] I will argue that it is not necessary to agree with Käsemann's exclusive argument for the cross as the center of Paul's theology, even if one recognizes his significant contribution to the contemporary retrieval of the theology of the cross.

What the Reformation expressed by its *crux sola est nostra theologia*, is, according to Käsemann, the center of Paul's doctrine of justification. A key here is the human incapacity to achieve salvation. The illusion that human beings are able to bring about their own salvation (in other words, do that of which only God is capable), by using their strength, wisdom, and piety, recognizes the cross as scandal and foolishness. For the same reason, the reversal of human expectations through the cross (which is Paul's view of the saving significance of the cross) is both "shocking and paradoxical." By justifying the sinner, the ungodly, and the enemy, God, who chooses to humble Godself, brings an end to the "self-transcending" human being. The saving significance of the cross becomes the basis for Käsemann's thesis that the center of Paul's theology cannot be anything but a theology of the cross, "just as, and just because, it cannot be separated from the message of justification, and counters all enthusiasm with a critical and realistic anthropology."[12]

That Paul does not display "any precise knowledge about the concrete circumstances of the crucifixion"[13] corresponds, according to Käsemann, to Paul's understanding of the primary role of preaching. "For Paul," Käsemann argues, "the 'facts of the redemption' cannot be separated from the Word of Christian preaching; nor can they be played off against it. They are undoubtedly the basis of preaching, but without preaching we cannot have them at all."[14] This gives Käsemann reason to insist on the need to see the theology of the cross and the theology of the Word as belonging together.[15] Crucial to Käsemann's argument is Paul's talk about the "message about the cross" and the "proclamation of Christ crucified" in 1 Corinthians 1:8ff, which he believes underscores Paul's conviction that there is "no other approach to the cross than preaching."[16] To reduce the cross to a purely historical event and to make the cross, as a historical fact, the object of faith, Käsemann believes, is contradictory to Paul's emphasis on the importance of the "word of the cross" as a ground of faith. While on one hand, the cross cannot be detached from Golgotha, on the other hand, the cross remains for Paul "an eschatological event."

Käsemann is not alone in assigning a key role to the passages in the beginning of Paul's Letters to the Corinthians in his interpretation of Paul's theology. Thus, it is important to take a closer look at these passages, which have often been considered the *locus classicus* for Paul's theology of the cross.[17] In his first letter to the "church of God" in Corinth, Paul is addressing a community divided among themselves. Hoping to convince his readers to overcome the divisions that have arisen among them and to search for unity, Paul brings his readers' attention to the cross of Christ. Paul finds the great antithesis to the wisdom of the wise in the cross, which he thinks has been proven incapable of communicating the true knowledge of God. Paul writes: "For since, in the wisdom of God, the world did not know God through wisdom, God decided, through the foolishness of our proclamation, to save those who believe"(1:21). What this "foolishness of our proclamation" consists of, Paul explains, is "Christ crucified," a stumbling block to the Jewish people and foolishness to the Gentiles, "but to those who are the called, both Jews and Greeks, Christ the power of God and the wisdom of God" (1:24). In order to underscore the real difference between human standards and God's standards, Paul then reiterates that while God's weakness exceeds human strength, God's foolishness is also "wiser than human wisdom" (1:25). Given his denunciation of human wisdom and power, it is not surprising that Paul decided to know nothing "except Jesus Christ, and him crucified"(2:2) when he came to preach to the Corinthians, so that their faith "might rest not on human wisdom but on the power of God"(2:5).

Responding to the situation in Corinth, Paul is offering another way of knowing God, over against the "superior wisdom" that was causing division within the community as well as disrespect for the cross of Christ.[18] Again, against the way of "eloquent wisdom" (1:17), Paul argues that the cross of Christ has vital importance for our knowledge of God, which is, indeed, located exclusively in the message of the cross. This kind of epistemology also excludes use of "an inferential method," what Luther would later call "a theology of glory."[19] Such "worldly wisdom," Paul claims, God has proven to be false, truly "foolish," and in stark opposition to the knowledge of God available in the message of the cross of Christ. The function of the cross is therefore first of all to dispute the "worldly" way of knowing, but also to reveal God's intention to save through the "folly" of the cross (1:21–25). Finally, the cross "has demonstrated God's destruction of the old world (with its valued human assets of strength, wisdom, nobility) and creation of the new world (into which he calls the weak, the ignoble, the non-existent; 1:26–31)."[20]

The picture painted by Paul of the "new creation" in Christ is full of contradictions and "strange reversals." The "new world," the "world of the cross,"

> is a world in which wisdom is folly, the least become the greatest, strength resides in weakness, and fullness of being arises from emptiness. To say that the Word of the cross creates a new world is to call an end to the present world. This is creation out of nothing.[21]

Charles Cousar makes an interesting comparison between Paul's understanding of God's power, righteousness, wisdom, faithfulness, freedom, and love and "the understanding they have often had in the history of Christian theology."[22] Cousar argues that by seeing these attributes through the cross of Christ, Paul is offering an alternative way of thinking about God's characteristics. It is by preaching "Christ, and him crucified" (2:2), Alexandra Brown maintains, that Paul delivers "this world-ending and recreating Word."[23] Thus, the power of the cross is located not simply in the past but also in the present Word about the cross that continuously re-presents it to the reader.

Focusing on the significance of Paul's understanding of power as the "power of the cross," Sally B. Purvis has made an important contribution to a feminist retrieval of the cross. In her book *The Power of the Cross: Foundations for a Christian Feminist Ethic of Community*, Purvis talks about Paul's commitment to form Christian communities "in accordance with his understanding of the Christ event."[24] Key to Paul's understanding of the life, death, and resurrection of Jesus Christ is, Purvis insists, a new understanding of power, the power of the cross, "articulated most clearly in Paul's first letter to the community at Corinth."[25] Purvis names this new understanding of power "power as life,"[26] while she calls the old understanding, which she believes was the widely accepted understanding of power in the first-century Roman Empire, "power as control."[27] Purvis writes:

> God's power as shown forth in "Christ crucified" is the reversal of power as violent control. It is the power to bring life, even in the face of the worst, most destructive power that can be brought to bear.[28]

The "old standards," the "wisdom of the world," would call this power "weak," since according to the traditional understanding of power as control, the cross stands for "victimization, loss of power, defeat."[29] On the contrary, to the new standard in the cross of Christ, this power "is really the greatest power of all, the power of God."[30] This new understanding of power is a total reversal of the older one, "a reality altogether different from the old understanding, as different as the cross is from the soldier's sword,"[31] and therefore is not to be understood on the basis of our knowledge of power as control. The power of the cross is the power of life, as both *unexpected* ("we do not expect to look at death and discover life") and *ongoing* ("we know about the power of the cross only from the continuing presence of the risen Christ among us, and Christian communities manifest that life in the world"). In line with Paul, who equates the power of God to the love of God, Purvis maintains that the power of the cross *is* love.[32]

So far the focus has been on how Paul, in his first letter to the Corinthians, presents the cross as the place where we get to know God's true nature. In his second letter to the same community, Paul goes on to claim that "in Christ God was reconciling the world to himself" (2 Corinthians 5:19),[33] without ever explaining to what extent Christ's sufferings on the cross did affect God the Father. Paul certainly wrote his letters before the christological controversy actually started. Regarding the pre-Nicean dating of Paul's writings, Charles Cousar maintains that Paul understands the relations between Father and Son "strictly on a functional level," which is why Paul is not preoccupied with the ontological questions that came to the forefront at the church councils of the fourth and fifth centuries. At the same time, Cousar concludes, "Paul as a Jew offers no support for the doctrine of divine impassibility, which underlies the later patri-passianist controversy."[34] It is to this debate about the divine ability to suffer, which was closely tied to the christological controversy taking place up to the Council of Chalcedon in 451, that I now turn.

The Road to Chalcedon and the Question of the Suffering God

In his book *The Incarnation of God*, German theologian Hans Küng writes about "the road to Classical Christology":

> It was. . .a long and immensely varied history which led to the Chalcedonian definition. With it the ontological interpretation of biblical Christology through the medium of Greek metaphysics, which laid the emphasis not on happenings and events, but on being, was at any rate provisionally completed: not only had the conceptual framework changed, but the points of emphasis had been shifted and some perspectives altered.[35]

Significant to Küng's reading of the development of the christological dogmas during the first few centuries is his emphasis on the difference between the scriptural witness to Jesus Christ and the interpretation of this witness provided by the Council of Chalcedon. Küng is consequently skeptical regarding a conclusion made by Alois Grillmeier, a German historian of dogma, who, in the end of his extensive study, *Christ in Christian Tradition*, stresses the affiliation between the biblical sources and the Chalcedonian definition, maintaining that there is a clear scriptural basis for the formula of the one person in two natures.[36] Küng's criticism of Grillmeier's conception is rooted in what he sees as stark evidence of Greek philosophy making its influence on "orthodox christology."[37] Küng highlights the contrast between the classical Greek idea of God and the "biblical testimony with reference to all God's attributes. . .especially his incomprehensibility and ineffability, immutability and simplicity, eternity and freedom." The questions concerning these attributes of God, Küng argues, were "bound to come to a head in Christology," in which the main focus was on the unity in the person of Jesus Christ, between "the most clear-cut antithesis," like "fleshly/spiritual, visible/invisible, unoriginated/born, perishable/imperishable, finite/infinite." Still, Küng maintains, in light of the Gospel stories the most prevalent pair of opposites has to be the one of suffering and not suffering.[38]

The attempt to resolve the tension between these antitheses became a continuous source of conflict and debate, as the early Christians tried to make sense of the one whom they claimed brought together a divine and a human reality in one single person. In the following, an effort will be made to highlight the major threads in the complicated patterns that make up the history of the christological controversy, with a special focus on the question of suffering. Of particular interest is the tension between the ideas of God's (Christ's) *apatheia* and the outspoken realism of Christ's suffering, present in the Gospels.[39]

The basic dilemma of the first centuries was to figure out the relationship between Christ's humanity and his divinity without playing down the one or the other. Thus the question: How can Christ be both human and divine, without either one of the two becoming absorbed into the other or a third reality (*tertium quid*) made. From the time the Gospels were written and up to the Council of Chalcedon in 451, there are two noticeable sides in the development of doctrines about the person of Jesus Christ. While one emphasizes the humanity of Christ, the other focuses on Christ's divinity.[40]

Many factors affected the shaping of the christological doctrines, the following three being particularly important. First of all, *the political circumstances* became increasingly influential from the time Christianity became the official religion of the Roman Empire. It was, for example, the emperor who summoned the first ecumenical council at Nicea in 325. At that time, the Arian controversy was threatening the unity of the church, and so the peace within the empire was in danger. *The liturgical life within the church* was a second important factor. Since Jesus was worshiped as the Lord from early on (at least as early as the time Paul was writing his letters, around the middle of the first century), every development that went against that practice was threatening to the faith of the church. This is why it has been argued that the doctrines were made necessary to protect the faith of the church, in harmony with the liturgical practice, and not because of speculations or intellectual interests. Third, *the use of philosophical terms and ideas* that were available from different philosophical schools was a debatable part of the christological discussion from early on. Was it possible to borrow the terms without running the risk of being taken over by foreign philosophical ways of thinking? This was, for example, a part of the debate concerning the term *homoousios* that took place at Nicea in 325. Hans Küng maintains that a certain "de-Hellenization" was taking place at the same time that new philosophical terms were introduced into Christian theology. Thus, Küng believes, Harnack's thesis of the "Hellenization" of the gospel needs to be critically reevaluated without minimizing the immence influence Greek philosophy had on the christological discourse.[41]

The Human Path

Christology that focused on the true humanity of Christ was guided by the history of Jesus given in the synoptic Gospels. In the second century, this emphasis became important in the fight against influences from Marcion and the Gnostics and their docetic interpretations. Reactions against docetism, which radically denied Christ's sufferings, led to extreme positions. *Ebionitism*, which was of Jewish origin, was a second-century position that believed Jesus was a mere man, who was the Messiah, "the elect of God and a true prophet."[42] According to ebionitism, Jesus earned the name Christ by fulfilling the Law, and "the Law, not Jesus himself, remained the true way to salvation."[43] In the third century, *adoptionism* (dynamistic monarchianism), as represented by Paul of Samosata, bishop of Antioch, continued the "ebionitic" line with its emphasis on Christ's humanity. But instead of arguing that Jesus was a mere man, its followers believed that Jesus became divine *from below*, by the indwelling of the Spirit of God and by his growth in godlike holiness.[44]

Arius, an Alexandrian presbyter of the fourth century, agreed with ebionitism and adoptionism that Jesus Christ truly endured and suffered, which is why he could not be divine to the same extent as God the Father.[45] Arius, who was highly concerned about the absolute transcendence and unity of God, denied the idea that the logos could be God. The logos had to be created, although still ontologically different from other created beings. Arius maintained so-called subordinationism, which means that the role of the logos was a mediatorial one in the relation of God to the world. Thus, the logos belonged to the created order but at the same time was "a quite superior creature, ranking above all others because he was brought into being by God 'before the ages,' to act as the agent of God in creation."[46] The relationship between the logos and Jesus was for Arius characterized by the idea that Jesus became the Son by virtue of his merits, which is why his communion with God was by grace and not by essence (when the logos became the soul of Jesus). Athanasius, the main opponent to Arius, accused him not only of polytheism but also of supporting a doctrine against liturgical and baptismal use. Athanasius also maintained that Arius's understanding of Jesus Christ undermined the idea of redemption, given the fact that salvation is only possible as long as the mediator is divine.[47] The Arian controversy became the main reason for the Council of Nicea, in which the term *homoousios* (which means "of the same nature") was introduced in order to secure the true divinity of Christ.[48]

During the fourth and fifth centuries, the two rival schools were the Antiochian and the Alexandrian. The Antiochian school was characterized by the so-called *logos-anthropos* Christology, with its emphasis on moral earnestness and the indwelling of the logos in the human being of Jesus of Nazareth. Hans Küng insists that it was the general assumption of God's impassibility within the Antiochian school that was the reason behind the emphasis on the radical distinction between the divinity and humanity in Christ, to make sure that suffering was only affecting the human nature without in any way touching upon his divinity.[49]

The most significant representative of the Antiochian school was Theodore of Mopsuestia, who stressed the two subjects, or two *hypostases* of Jesus Christ in the one *prosopon*. Theodore understood the relationship between the logos and Jesus, between God and humanity in the incarnation, in terms of will rather than substance (known as *conjunction Christology*). Thus, Christ is the result of the union of Jesus' will with the logos.[50] Theodore was particularly concerned about the full humanity of Christ, including his moral development. He wanted to take seriously the earthly life of Jesus, including his sufferings and death, which he thought affected him only as a human being. Thus, for Theodore, the incarnation represented "a very special kind of indwelling," making it possible to speak of Jesus "as a human being who truly shares the divine sonship of the Logos in a way that no prophet, apostle, or saint can."[51]

It was Nestorius, bishop of Constantinople, who took the Christology of Theodore of Mopsuestia one step further by talking about a relationship of two natures instead of an incarnation. Nestorius believed Jesus was a human being who was "intimately and completely indwelt by the logos."[52] Before the incarnation, Nestorius argued, there was a logos and a man, as two persons, so the only option was conjunction, not incarnation. A controversy arose around the question whether or not *theotokos* (literally: a god-bearer) was an appropriate name for Mary. Since Nestorius believed Mary gave birth only to a human being, he denied that Mary was properly called the mother of God.[53] Consequently, Jesus suffered only as a human being and not as God incarnated, while it was God the incarnated who raised Jesus the human being from the dead.[54] Nestorius's doctrine of the "two sons" was condemned at the Council of Ephesus in 431, and Nestorius himself was sent into exile.

Pope Leo I became a representative of the Antiochian school in the making of the Chalcedonian definition. Despite his emphasis on the two natures, it is clear from his letter to patriarch Flavian of Constantinople, written in June 449, that he believed the inner, ontological identity of Christ was the logos himself.[55]

The God-Side

While those who emphasized the human nature focused on a historical and exegetical approach, relying primarily on sources from the synoptic Gospels, the path in the opposite direction was first and foremost guided by the Christian liturgy and favored the divinity of Christ, depending heavily on the Gospel of John. The second-century Apologists made use of the concept logos (already known to Judaism and Stoicism) in order to explain the relation between God and Christ.[56] The identification of Christ with logos allowed the Apologists to insist that Christianity believed in the one to whom the Old Testament witnessed and to whom the pagan philosophers indistinctly pointed. For the Apologists, Christ was the logos, preexistent before the incarnation as the Father's mind or thought. As revealed in creation and redemption, Christ was the Father's expression and extrapolation. To emphasize the essential identity of the logos with the Father, the Apologists used the biblical image of son or child for the logos. Hence, the logos was not a creature but an offspring by generation. The danger of logos-theology consisted first and foremost of the logos being too restricted to the role of a subordinated mediator, in which procession of logos and creation was closely linked, both generated by will. Notably subordinationism, as in Arianism, followed.[57]

It was Origen who brought logos Christology into the third century. Origen asserted that logos was eternally begotten, so that there never was a time when the logos did not exist. For Origen, logos was not God but God's image, a "second God" who fulfilled a meditorial role.[58] Origen's Christology consists of two

stages. The first stage in the process of mediation "is fulfilled through the uni-
fication of the logos with the one rational spirit which did not fall away from
God—the soul which is Jesus." The second stage is realized "when this soul
which is united to the logos becomes embodied through a human birth."[59] It is
important to notice that for Origen, "the logos can never cease to be also outside of Jesus."[60] Because Origen's universe is hierarchical, "the divine does not
mix too directly with matter."[61] Consequently, through Origen's theory, the
gnostic opposition to the body found entrance into Christology.

Monarchianism is to be seen as a reaction against logos theology, motivated by
the fear that logos-theology endangered the unity of God. While *dynamic monarchianism* (adoptionism) emphasized Christ's humanity, *modalistic monarchianism*
(modalism) stressed his divine nature. Modalism (also called Sabellianism, after
Sabellius, one of its leading representatives) taught that there is one Godhead,
which expresses itself in relation to the world in three operations (or modes) at
different times in history. Trinitarian distinctions within God were therefore out of
the picture. A logical outcome was the idea of *patripassianism*, which suggests that
the Father (*pater*) suffered (*passio*) in the crucifixion and death of the Son.[62] During
the *patripassianist* controversy of the third century, Tertullian became an important
spokesperson for those who rejected the idea of the Father suffering in the Son, by
emphasising strict trinitarian distinctions. Furthermore, Tertullian became "the
first to argue for the impassibility of the divine nature in Christ."[63]

The Alexandrian school of the fourth and fifth century was characterized
by metaphysical profundity, allegorical interpretation of Scripture, and emphasis on the full divinity of Christ. Its Christology, which has been identified as
logos-flesh Christology, called attention to the *hypostatic union* within the person
of Jesus Christ. The premise of God's impassibility produced an inclination to
tone down the suffering of Christ's body and soul in order to safeguard the
divinity, as well as the impassibility of the logos.[64]

Athanasius, bishop in Alexandria from 328 to 373, became a leading figure
of the Alexandrian school. For soteriological reasons, Athanasius argued, in
opposition to logos theology, for a full divinity of the incarnated one, insisting
that there must be "a real and direct union of God with humanity in Christ."[65]
In the incarnation, the logos assumed human nature (or "human condition")
and should be seen as "the sole real subject" in the person of Jesus.[66] The likeness and unity of the Father and the Son therefore cannot consist just in harmony and concord of mind and will as the Antiochians argued, but must be in
respect of essence. The danger in Athanasius's position is that even though he
did not question the reality of the flesh the logos assumed, his position nevertheless suggests that Jesus was less than a complete human being, rather a
logos with a body.[67] This is why Athanasius makes a clear distinction between

what Jesus experienced "in flesh" and what affected his divine logos. He explains:

> It was appropriate for the Lord, when he was clothed in human flesh, to put it on in its totality, together with all the passions proper to it, so that just as we say that body was properly his, so also the passions of the body might be said to belong to him alone, even though they did not touch him in his deity.[68]

Regarding the question of suffering, it is important to note that despite widespread disagreement on important christological issues, the idea of divine impassibility was very often simply assumed, as was the case in the Arian controversy, where "both Arius and Athanasius assumed that God was incapable of suffering."[69]

It was Athanasius's friend and follower Apollinaris of Laodicea who openly denied what Athanasius had only hinted at, namely, that Jesus had a rational soul or "a human center of consciousness."[70] Contradicting the idea of a divine indwelling, Apollinaris believed that logos became an enfleshed intellect, in which the intellect was logos itself. Therefore, Jesus was one, "one composite nature, in which flesh and divine intellect share the same life."[71] Hence, Apollinaris evolved an understanding of Christ that emphasized the unity of his person as "one incarnate nature of the divine Word."[72] Consequently, Christ has bodily properties but not human nature. Apollinaris's Christology was rejected at Constantinople in 381, where Gregory of Nazianzus's principle that "what is not assumed by the Redeemer is not redeemed" became the key to the affirmation of Christ's full humanity.[73]

A prominent figure on the Alexandrian side in the preparation for the Chalcedonian agreement was Cyril, bishop of Alexandria from 413 to 444.[74] Cyril played an important role in the Nestorian controversy that was brought to an end at the Council of Ephesus in 431. Significant for Cyril's position was his emphasis on the union in hypostasis, or *the hypostatic union*, in which the "one hypostasis and the one nature are the logos himself, making a full human existence its own."[75] Against Apollinaris, Cyril affirmed "the fullness of Jesus' human nature, its possession of soul as well as of body."[76] For Cyril the union of the logos with the flesh "excludes division, but does not eliminate differences."[77] With reference to suffering and death, this means that it is

> not that the Logos of God suffered in his own nature, being overcome by stripes or nail-piercing or any of the other injuries; for the divine, since it is incorporeal, is impassible. Since, however, the body that had become his own underwent suffering, he is—once again—said

to have suffered these things for our sakes, for the impassible One
was within the suffering body. Moreover we reason in exactly the
same way in the case of his dying. . . . It is not that he actually
experienced death as far as anything which touches his [divine]
nature is concerned; to think that would be insanity. Rather it is that,
as I said earlier, his flesh tasted death.[78]

The emphasis on the union of the logos and flesh, manifested in this writing of
Cyril, became the key to his argument against Nestorius and, later, his contribution to the definition of the Council of Chalcedon.

Following the Council of Ephesus and the Formula of Reunion (433), which
had raised hopes for the possibility of peace, controversy would still arise concerning the relationship between the logos and Jesus' humanity. A major contributor to
this controversy was Eutyches, "a confirmed Cyrillian with wide connection in the
monastic world,"[79] who maintained that Christ had only "one nature after the
union."[80] Eutyches' Monophysitism was considered threatening to Christ's genuine
humanity as well as to his historical reality. In his letter to Flavian of Constantinople,
Pope Leo I attacked Eutyches' position, arguing for the truth of Tertullian's teaching
of "two natures in one person." For Pope Leo, it was important to hold on to the
unity of person, "which must be understood to subsist in a twofold nature." Pope
Leo maintained that, because of the unity, it could be argued that "the Son of
man came down from heaven (since the Son of God took on flesh from the Virgin of whom he was born)." He also thought it could be said that it was the Son
of God who "was crucified and buried (even though he endured these things not
in that divine nature in virtue of which, as Only Begotten, he is coeternal and
consubstantial with the Father, but in the weakness of his human nature)."[81]

Pope Leo insisted upon another council in order to set matters right. Meeting
Leo's demand, the emperor summoned a council to meet at Chalcedon and
called for a fresh pronouncement, "which would settle the christological debates
that were dividing his subjects."[82] Contrary to the pope's opinion, the eastern
bishops thought that Nicea was enough. Thus, the Council of Chalcedon in 451
accepted the councils of Constantinople and Ephesus as ecumenical councils
and the creed of Constantinople as an authentic interpretation of the faith of
Nicea. Despite the intention to please both parties with its emphasis on unity in
person as well as separation in natures, the agreement reached at Chalcedon
eventually satisfied the West much more than the East. What particularly trig-
gered the dissatisfaction in the East was the emphasis on the clear division
between the two natures, the human and the divine, which in the agreement is
described as being "without confusion, without change, without division, without separation."[83]

No Final Solution

During the christological controversy within the early church, the question of God's involvement in Christ's suffering and death was big on the agenda. For many theologians, it was crucial for the saving significance of Christ's life, suffering, and death that, not only the human side, but also "the *Son of God himself* lived, suffered and died."[84] Nevertheless, Christ's suffering continued to present a problem, while the principle of impassibility was by many regarded as nonnegotiable, despite the strong emphasis on the unity of the Christ's person. More often the question of Christ's suffering was not addressed directly, as was the case in the Chalcedonian agreement. Still, the statement about the Son's birth by a human mother has to imply that he was not exempted from human suffering. Thus, it can be argued, as Küng does, that "the question of suffering was decided in principle with the acceptance of the Theotokos formula into the Chalcedonian decree."[85]

The insufficiency of the Chalcedonian way of dealing with the question of sufferings—namely, by excluding it—became clear in the sixth century's debate about *theopaschitism* (meaning: one of the Trinity suffered). It was also apparent in the seventh century's *monothelite* (literally: one will) controversy, in which it was debated if it was possible that the person of Jesus Christ had two natures but only one will. From these post-Chalcedonian discussions and definitions it can be concluded that the question of Christ's ability to suffer was closely knitted to the question about the unity of the person of Christ. By many the idea of only the human side of Christ's suffering was rightly regarded as a real threat to the unity of the human and the divine nature of Christ in one person.[86]

The idea of God's immutability (implying God's impassibility) continued to be very influential, as well as problematic, in the theological discourse. During the middle ages, God's immutability became an important factor in different christological theories.[87] Luther's assertion of God's ability to suffer in Christ on the cross constituted a serious break with the tradition, which heretofore had fallen short of acknowledging God's ability to suffer.

Luther's Understanding of the Life and Work of Jesus Christ

A key to Luther's theological development was his retrieval of Paul's theology of the cross. Luther introduced his cross-centered theology in his Heidelberg Disputation in the spring of 1518. He considered his theology of the cross an alternative to the theology of glory, which he claimed was the prevailing theological tradition of the church. The focus on the cross was to become a key to Luther's entire theology, including his Christology, which was developing during Luther's debate with Zwingli regarding a plausible interpretation of the Holy Communion. The following survey of Luther's understanding of the life and work of Christ from the perspective of the cross will be based primarily on the Heidelberg Disputation and Luther's writings during the eucharistic controversy.[88]

Luther's Background and Breakthrough

In the preface to the 1545 complete edition of his Latin writings, Luther reflects back on his discovery of a new understanding of the righteousness of God. He recalls how he hated the term "righteousness of God," which he was taught to understand philosophically "regarding the formal or active righteousness," implying that God is a righteous God who punishes the unrighteous sinner.[89] It was through his meditation of Paul's words in his letter to the Romans that Luther came to a different understanding of God's righteousness. Coming close to the end of his life, Luther comments on his discovery in this frequently cited quotation:

> At last, by the mercy of God, meditating day and night, I gave heed to the context of the words, namely, "In it the righteousness of God is revealed, as it is written, 'He who through faith is righteous shall live.'" There I began to understand that the righteousness of God is that by which the righteous lives by a gift of God, namely by faith. And this is the meaning: the righteousness of God is revealed by the gospel, namely, the passive righteousness with which merciful God justifies us by faith, as it is written, "He who through faith is righteous shall live."[90]

In his preface, Luther indicates that it was not until after he had started lecturing on the Psalter the second time in 1518 that his understanding of God's righteousness changed so drastically. Scholars have contested the meaning and accuracy of Luther's autobiographical statement. While some have considered it a "mistaken recollection,"[91] others believe Luther's statement can be read as simply implying that his new theological insights *were complete by that date* and that they are incorporated into the substance of his second series of lectures on the Psalms.[92]

Regarding the development of Luther's theological position, Alister McGrath maintains that "Luther's thought over the period 1513–1519 demonstrates every evidence of continuous development, rather than cataclysmic alteration." Contrary to those who argue for a particular moment in which Luther discovered a fresh understanding of the gospel, McGrath suggests that there is no "single point at which a dramatic alteration in his theological outlook may be detected." Furthermore, McGrath believes Luther's theological breakthrough to be closely related to "the realization that the righteousness which God requires of man is faith," which he maintains happened "at some point in 1515, possibly having taken place during the final stages of the *Dictata*."[93] McGrath continues:

> . . . [T]his breakthrough represents the beginning, rather than the end, of Luther's early theological development, in that it is on the basis of his new understanding of *iustitia Dei* that Luther was obliged to begin the long and painful process of revising his understanding of the manner in which God deals with sinful man in a sinful world.[94]

An important result of Luther's newly discovered understanding of the righteousness of God is a new understanding of God and God's way of dealing with human beings. McGrath sums up Luther's answer to the question about God in the following way:

> Luther's insight into the true nature of the "righteousness of God" represents far more than a mere terminological clarification: latent within it is a new concept of God. Who is this God who deals thus with man? Luther's answer to this question, as it developed over the years 1513–19, can be summarized in one of his most daring phrases: the God who deals with sinful man in this astonishing way is none other than the "crucified and hidden God" (*Deus crucifixus et absconditus*)—the God of the *theologia crucis*.[95]

McGrath sees Luther's discovery of a new meaning of the righteousness of God as an important step in his reevaluation of the theological tradition. It was eventually to lead to his presentation of a new way of thinking and doing theology within the framework of a *theologia crucis*.

In order to appreciate the "genuinely creative and innovative aspects of Luther's *theologia crucis*," McGrath insists, Luther has to be seen as having begun his theological teaching career at Wittenberg in 1512 "*as a typical theologian of the late Middle Ages*,"who gradually distanced himself from his theological background.[96] As a theologian of the late middle ages, Luther was influenced by three main currents of thought, namely, humanism, nominalism of the *via moderna*, and the theology of his own Augustinian Order.[97] The humanist movement contributed significantly to the origin of the Reformation by providing Luther with "the tools" he needed for his biblical studies.[98] Luther identified strongly with the interest of the humanist movement in returning to Holy Scriptures and the early church fathers, as well as the rejection of scholasticism.[99] Despite these affinities, McGrath considers it questionable to see the humanist movement as a cause of the Reformation, even if it could be considered an "essential catalyst."[100]

Luther was trained in Erfurt, within the nominalist tradition (also known as the *via moderna*), but the implications of his academic background are still contested.[101] Even though the new university in Wittenberg was from the beginning committed to the *via antiqua*, there are strong evidences that the *via moderna* had already been introduced in Wittenberg before Luther arrived there in 1508.[102] From his study of Luther's first course of lectures on the Psalter (the *Dictata super Psalterium*, 1513–1515), McGrath reaches the conclusion that "the Luther of the early *Dictata* is unquestionably a medieval theologian, and displays considerable affinity at points with the theology of the *via moderna*."[103] But even if Luther started out holding on to a doctrine of justification that was typical for the "well-established medieval theological tradition," Luther's break with this tradition took place when he discovered the "new" meaning of the "righteousness of God," which is likely to have taken place at some point during the year 1515, possibly while Luther was still lecturing on the Psalms.[104] If McGrath is right, then the period between 1515 and 1518 was crucial for the development of Luther's theology, when the importance of his new understanding of *iustitia Dei* became evident.[105]

Characteristic of the soteriology of the *via moderna* is its presupposition of the conditional nature of God's promise of grace, namely, that God has promised to bestow grace upon human beings upon the condition that they do what is within their ability (*quod in se est*). If, however, human beings fail to meet this condition, God is not obliged to grant them grace.[106] McGrath insists that this understanding is present in Luther's earlier lectures on the Psalms, in which Luther maintains that the condition that human beings have to meet consists, on one hand, of a recognition of one's need for God's grace and, on the other hand, on an appeal to God to grant grace.[107] There is, nevertheless, a notable difference between Luther's interpretation of the *iustitia Dei*, with its christological emphasis, and that of the *via moderna*.[108]

Already toward the end of Luther's lectures on the Psalms there are indications that Luther was no longer agreeing with the presupposition of the soteriology of the *via moderna*. During his lectures on Romans, by the end of 1516, Luther's break with the soteriology of the *via moderna* seems complete.[109] McGrath insists that in this break, Luther developed a theology of justification that can be described only as his own creation. McGrath gives two reasons for his assertion of the uniqueness of Luther's position. First is Luther's insistence on the bondage of the will (*servum arbitrium*), which goes beyond Augustine's understanding of the debilitating effect of sin on the free will. The second relates to the development of the concept of the alien righteousness of Christ (*iustitia Christi aliena*), which McGrath considers "one of the most original and creative aspects of Luther's mature doctrine of justification."[110]

The concept of *iustitia Christi aliena*, which is first used by Luther in his lectures on Romans in 1515–16, is based on Luther's idea of the radical difference between human and divine understanding of rigtheousness (*iustitia*).[111] The human being who remains a sinner (*homo incurvatus in se*) is totally unable to contribute anything to her own justification (i.e., not able to do, *quod in se est*). God's righteousness is something that is alien and extrinsic to the human being (*iustitia extra nos*) and does not change the fact that the human being is a sinner inwardly and yet righteous in the sight of God (i.e., sinner and righteous at the same time, *iustus et peccator simul*).[112] By recognizing her unrighteousness, the human being becomes conscious of her need for another strange righteousness (*iustitia Christi aliena*) and thus turns to God, searching for a righteousness that is valid before God (*coram Deo*).[113] As God justifies *sinners*, Luther draws the conclusion that justification is contrary to reason, hence, his calling into question the role of reason in matters of theology. The origins of Luther's theology of the cross are to be found in his "initial difficulty in seeing how the idea of a righteous God could conceivably be good news for sinful man."[114] Hence, his criticism of human wisdom, which is based upon his reflections on the meaning of the "righteousness of God," foreshadows Luther's *theologia crucis*,[115] presented in his Heidelberg Disputation in the spring of 1518.

The Heidelberg Disputation

Luther prepared his theses for a meeting of the general chapter of the Augustinians of Germany at Heidelberg, at the invitation of Johann von Staupitz, the vicar-general of the German congregation of Augustinians. By request of Pope Leo X, Staupitz had been ordered to compel Luther to recant his position, but there are no indications of Staupitz calling for Luther's recantation. On the contrary, Staupitz gave Luther a chance to introduce his point of view to his fellow Augustinians. However, to "avoid arousing animosity against Luther," Staupitz had asked him "not to debate controversial subjects but to prepare theses concerning sin, free will and grace," topics that Luther had dealt with in his *Disputation Against Scholastic Theology* in the fall of 1517.[116] Responding to Staupitz's request, Luther prepared twenty-eight theological and twelve philosophical theses for the debate at Heidelberg. In addition, he wrote short proofs of the theological theses and a special explanation to the sixth thesis.[117]

In his Heidelberg thesis, Luther mentions neither indulgences nor the sacrament of penance, the main issues in his famous *Ninety-Five Theses* (or *Disputation
on the Power and Efficacy of Indulgences*), which he is believed to have nailed on the
Castle Church door in Wittenberg on October 31, 1517.[118] The focus in the Heidelberg Disputation is, in line with Staupitz's request, the same as in his *Disputation
Against Scholastic Theology*, presented in September the previous year. Luther starts
out by stating that the recognition of the inability of God's law and human works to
make a human being righteous (theses 1 and 2) directs one's attention to the grace
of God. As the idea of a "free will" turns out to be an illusion after the fall ("exists in
name only" [thesis 13]), the only proper response by human beings to their situation is an utter despair of their own ability to earn God's grace (thesis 18). In order
to bring about this humility and despair, God often makes use of "unattractive
works"—what Luther calls "the alien work of God." By this, Luther maintains, God
humbles us by leading us into despair, so that we may be given hope by God's
mercy (thesis 4). Instrumental here is the law of God, which makes human beings
aware of their sin by bringing about humility and despair, the necessary preparation for God's grace (theses 16–18 and 23–28).

In his Heidelberg Disputation (especially in theses 19–22), Luther introduces
a very different way of doing theology from the scholastic type of theology he had
denounced in his *Disputation Against Scholastic Theology*.[119] Luther believes his
theological standpoint to be faithful to Apostle Paul, as well as to Augustine, whom
he thought was Paul's "most trustworthy interpreter."[120] Theses 19–22 are particularly important for understanding the essence of Luther's theology of the cross:

19. That person does not deserve to be called a theologian who looks
upon the invisible things of God as though they were clearly perceptible
in those things which have actually happened.

20. He deserves to be called a theologian, however, who comprehends
the visible and manifest things of God seen through suffering and the
cross.

21. A theologian of glory calls evil good and good evil. A theologian of
the cross calls the thing what it actually is.

22. That wisdom which sees the invisible things of God in works as
perceived by man is completely puffed up, blinded, and hardened.[121]

Fundamental to Luther's theology of the cross is the distinction between a theology that relies on our *a posteriori* knowledge of God[122] "through suffering and
the cross" (a theology of revelation), and a theology that starts out with *a priori*

knowledge of God, available to human beings through the order of creation and moral works (a theology of speculation). Apart from the cross of Christ, a theologian of glory focuses on "the invisible things of God"—such as virtue, godliness, wisdom, justice, goodness—which are going to make him neither worthy nor wise, as the Apostle makes clear in his writing to the Romans.[123] A theologian of glory, moreover, "calls evil good and good evil." Luther explains:

> He who does not know Christ does not know God hidden in suffering. Therefore he prefers works to suffering, glory to the cross, strength to weakness, wisdom to folly, and, in general, good to evil. These are the people whom the apostle calls "enemies of the cross of Christ" [Philippians 3:18], for they hate the cross and suffering and love works and the glory of works. Thus they call the good of the cross evil and the evil of a deed good.[124]

Instead of loving the cross of Christ and looking there for a knowledge of God, a theology of glory seeks in vain for knowledge of God through creation and good works, putting trust in God's majesty and glory instead of "the humility and shame of the cross" (cf. 1 Corinthians 1:18ff). This does not mean that Luther denies that human beings do possess natural knowledge of God, but he believes such knowledge is limited to the cognitive level and thus does not give any assurance that it matters at all on the personal level or for the sake of *my* salvation (*pro me*).[125]

Unlike a theologian of glory, a theologian of the cross "comprehends the visible and manifest things of God seen through suffering and the cross" (thesis 20). To know God through the cross is to know God in God's human nature, weakness, and foolishness (1 Corinthians 1.25). A "true theology and recognition of God are in the crucified Christ," as God is to be found only in suffering and the cross.[126] Hence, a theologian of the cross "calls the thing what it actually is" (thesis 21).

Still, the revelation of God, according to a theology of the cross, is concealed and hidden under the contrary (*subcontrario specie*) and is not understood as a revelation of God, except with the help of faith. For Luther, this faith is a gift of God through the Spirit, which makes it possible to see God's strength as hidden under apparent weakness and God's wisdom hidden under apparent foolishness (thesis 22).

Luther's emphasis on the suffering of the true Christian was a continuous theme in Luther's theology all the way to the end. In his treatise *On the Councils and Churches* from 1539, Luther names suffering and persecution as the seventh characteristic of the church, together with sermon, baptism, Holy Communion, absolution, ordination, and divine worship. Luther writes:

Seventh, the holy Christian people are externally recognized by the holy possession of the sacred cross. They must endure every misfortune and persecution, all kinds of trials and evil from the devil, the world, and the flesh. . . by inward sadness, timidity, fear, outward poverty, contempt, illness, and weakness, in order to become like their head, Christ. And the only reason they must suffer is that they steadfastly adhere to Christ and God's word, enduring this for the sake of Christ.[127]

Luther's writings on suffering have caused people to question if he has become guilty of turning theology of the cross into a glorification of suffering, by encouraging people to enjoy their suffering and to accept it passively. In her book *Compelling Knowledge*, Mary Solberg writes about Luther's understanding of suffering, in which she stresses the importance that Luther's "emphasis on suffering as the form of true Christian discipleship is descriptive, *not* prescriptive, legalistic, or moralistic."[128] While Luther warned against self-chosen sufferings, usually related to suffering understood as good works, Luther saw suffering in terms of "conformation" to Christ. According to Luther, suffering is an unavoidable part of life and as such a part of the reality theologians have to speak to. Therefore, Solberg maintains, "Luther was no more interested in glorifying suffering than liberation theologians are in promoting grinding poverty when they insist that God is to be found particularly among the poor."[129] And Solberg continues:

To spiritualize suffering or treat it as an abstraction is to deny its meaning and its weight. To learn to see it, and risk experiencing it, we must pay attention to the real world in which it occurs, to those who suffer, and to those, including ourselves, who are complicit. To sharpen this focus on suffering is not to glorify it, but rather to notice it and name it. Noticing and naming are essential parts of a larger and ongoing program: the determination to overcome suffering.[130]

This is a helpful contribution to our discussion of the feminist critique of any glorification of suffering, coming up in chapter 4. To notice and name suffering, wherever it occurs, is in this sense a part of what a theologian of the cross is called to do, namely, to call the thing "what it actually is" instead of looking away and to call it what it is not, or to glorify it.[131]

Luther scholars have held different opinions about the role played by theology of the cross in the context of Luther's theological work as a whole. In his groundbreaking work, *Luthers Theologia Crucis* (1929), Walter von Loewenich maintains that the common assumption of Luther research from the second half of the nineteenth century up to the publication of his own book in 1929 was to understand Luther's theology of the cross as his "pre-Reformation theology."[132] Von Loewenich disagrees, as he believes the theology of the cross to be fundamental to Luther's entire theology and should therefore not be confined to any particular period in his theological development. Just as with Paul, von Loewenich maintains that the theology of the cross "offers a characteristic of Luther's entire theological thinking."[133] Elaborating on what he means by arguing for such a central role of the theology of the cross within Luther's theology, von Loewenich writes:

> For Luther the cross is not only the subject of theology; it is the distinctive mark of all theology. It has its place not only in the doctrine of the vicarious atonement, but it constitutes an integrating element for all Christian knowledge. The theology of the cross is not a chapter in theology but a specific kind of theology. The cross of Christ is significant here not only for the question concerning redemption and the certainty of salvation, but it is the center that provides perspective for all theological statements. Hence it belongs to the doctrine of God in the same way as it belongs to the doctrine of the work of Christ.[134]

Opposing the kind of theology that relies on speculation and theological conjecture, a theology of the cross is first and foremost a "theology of revelation." This implies a theological knowledge that is *a posteriori*, a reflection "after the fact about that which God has done." Hence, the theology of the cross "[does not] live out of ideas but out of experiences."[135]

In Luther's cross-centered theology, the cross is the key not only to his understanding of God but also to his interpretation about the person and work of Jesus Christ. To know God *a posteriori* is to know God wrapped in human flesh (*deus incarnatus*), thus, the close connection between an incarnational theology and a theology of the cross. By acknowledging the cross of Christ as "the sole authentic *locus*" of human knowledge of God, Luther exposes his understanding of Christ as "the perfect and visible manifestation of the nature of the invisible God."[136]

Luther was forced to develop his Christology during his debate with Zwingli about the meaning of the sacraments. A careful reading of the eucharistic controversy will help us understand better the relationship between Luther's theology of the cross and his understanding of the person and work of Jesus Christ.

Luther's Christology in the Making

Luther participated in two different controversies regarding the Lord's Supper. The first, with Rome, had to do with the use of the sacrament and Luther's

understanding of the sacrament as a gift of God in opposition to Rome's sacrificial interpretation of the mass.[137] The second controversy, with the Enthusi-
asts and the Swiss, concerned the sacramental presence of Christ. Against the
fanatics (as Luther called his radical opponents), Luther underscored the *real
presence* of the body and blood of Christ in the bread and wine, over against a
symbolic interpretation.[138] Paul Althaus distinguishes between two stages in
the development of Luther's doctrine of the Lord's Supper based on these two
controversies. The dividing point between the two stages is, acccording to
Althaus, the beginning of the dispute about the real presence around 1524.[139]
In his controversy with Zwingli, Luther felt pushed to clarify his understanding
of the person and work of Christ in connection with the development of his
doctrine of the sacrament of the altar.[140]

The breaking point in the sacramental controversy between Luther and
Zwingli had to do with the bodily presence of Christ in the eucharistic elements
of bread and wine. For Zwingli, Christ is present in the sacrament spiritually, and
therefore the words of institution are to be understood figuratively. Against
Zwingli's symbolic interpretation, Luther maintained a literal understanding of
the text. If Christ said, "this is my body," then, argued Luther, Christ's body is
really present in the bread, even if this is incomprehensible to human reason.[141]

Luther explained what he meant by a bodily presence in the following way: "In
plain language, we do not say that Christ's body is present in the supper in the
same form in which he was given for us. . . but that it is the same body which was
given for us, not in the same form or mode but in the same essence and nature. . . ."[142]
Althaus points out that the words of institution come to have a new and expanded
meaning for Luther in his controversy with Zwingli and his followers. No longer
are they conceived "only as the vehicle for the promise of the forgiveness of sin but
[they] are understood also as the promise of the real presence."[143]

Fundamental to Luther's position is his conviction that the finite is
capable of sharing in the nature of the infinite (*finitum capax infiniti*).[144]
Luther makes use of the idea of "truly divine, truly human" (*vere deus vere
homo*), from the christological controversies within the early church, in order
to defend his idea of the unity of the two natures within the person of Jesus
Christ. As the human body did not have to be transformed in the incarnation, so Christ can be physically present in the bread and wine.[145] For Luther
this means "that Christ's flesh either must avail in the Supper or must be of
no avail whatsoever whether in heaven or in the spirit."[146] The importance of
Christ's body as a dwelling place for the Spirit and its medium is beyond
question for Luther. He writes: ". . .Now Christ's body and flesh certainly are
quite compatible with the Spirit, indeed, he is the Spirit's dwelling place
bodily, and through him the Spirit comes into all others. . . ."[147] Luther's

radical understanding of the incarnation did indeed allow him to argue that after the incarnation, Christ is always present in both natures, in his divinity as well as in his humanity. Consequently, wherever Christ is, "it is the single, indivisible person, and if you can say, 'Here is God,' then you must also say, 'Christ the man is present too.'"[148]

The old patristic theory of the communication of the attributes (*communicatio idiomatum*) is significant in this context. The idea is already present with Apollinaris in the fourth century, even though he does not use the term. Still the difference between Apollinaris and Luther is significant. Apollinaris denied the true human nature of Christ and argued for "one composite nature," with the divine logos becoming an enfleshed soul. For Luther, unlike Apollinaris, it was very important to affirm the genuine humanity of Jesus, in which he becomes a truly human being ("like us") who eats, sleeps, suffers, and dies. While affirming the true human nature of Jesus, Luther still wanted to emphasize the unity of the divine and human in the one person of Jesus Christ. The radicality of this unity is expressed for Luther in the idea of the communication of the attributes (*communicatio idiomatum*), in which the attributes of both natures are shared in the person of Jesus Christ. This happens, without the mingling or the changing of the natures, in line with the Chalcedonian agreement. Luther defended himself against the charge of Monophysitism, while he accused the Zwinglians of Nestorianism. For Luther, the error of Nestorius consisted of his denial of communication of attributes.[149] Luther explains:

> They [i.e., the Zwinglians] raise a hue and cry against us, saying that we mingle the two natures into one essence. This is not true. We do not say that divinity is humanity, or that the divine nature is the human nature, which would be confusing the natures into one essence. Rather, we merge the two distinct natures into one single person, and say: God is man and man is God. We in turn raise a hue and cry against them for separating the person of Christ as though there were two persons.[150]

Crucial for the sacramental context of Luther's Christology is his understanding of God as being known to us "in the flesh."[151] This claim could not be made without the idea of the communication of attributes, which allows Luther to argue that Christ is present in the sacrament, not only in his divinity, but also in his humanity.[152] It also allows Luther to maintain that Christ suffers not only as a human being on the cross but also as God. This is essential for a theology that argues for the centrality of Christ and his cross as being the sole authentic locus of our knowledge of God. In the person of the Son it is God who suffers, dies, and rises again. This indeed makes Christ's life and passion unique. For Luther, it was certainly not satisfying to believe that Christ only suffered in his human nature," then Christ would be a poor Savior *for me*, in fact, he himself would need a Savior." Luther continues:

> Now if the old witch, Lady Reason, alloeosis'[153] grandmother, should say that the Deity surely cannot suffer and die, then you must answer and say: That is true, but since the divinity and humanity are one person in Christ, the Scriptures ascribe to the divinity, because of this personal union, all that happens to humanity, and vice versa. And in reality it is so. Indeed, you must say that the person (pointing to Christ) suffers, and dies. But this person is truly God, and therefore it is correct to say: the Son of God suffers. Although, so to speak, the one part (namely, the divinity) does not suffer, nevertheless the person, who is God, suffers in the other part (namely, in the humanity).[154]

Hence, because of the incarnation and the personal union between the divinity and humanity, Luther maintains that the deity or, rather, God suffers in Christ. To speak about one nature by using the expressions that belong to the other (what he refers to as *alleosis*), Luther insists, leads to the conclusion that only the human part of Christ suffered on the cross. For Luther, this makes redemption impossible. To exclude God from the suffering on the cross and to say that only humanity has suffered is to Luther the same as making redemption rest only on humanity: "For he who is redeemed only by humanity is surely not redeemed, and will never be redeemed."[155]

Luther's position always boils down to his key point: after the incarnation, God is found only in humanity. Thus, he accuses Zwingli of being guilty of the Nestorian fallacy, of attributing not only two natures to Christ but two persons as well. Siding strongly with the Alexandrian side of the ancient christological controversy, Luther thinks the idea of *theotokos* (originally directed against Nestorius, in Ephesus in 431) is crucial in affirming the unity of the two natures.[156] So, while Luther wants to hold on to the unity between the human and the divine in the one person, Zwingli's concern is to protect the true humanity of Christ.

At this point it is important to recall the core of Luther's theology of the cross and its significance for his understanding of the person and work of Jesus Christ, as well as the Lord's Supper. First of all, it has to be kept in mind that the presence of the divine in the person of Jesus Christ is always a *hidden* presence, not available to human reason. Thus, the significance of faith, as faith alone (*sola fide*), is that it is able to claim "that God has thus bound himself to the suffering and humiliated humanity of the man Jesus in order to reveal himself to human beings."[157]Seen from the perspective of *theologia crucis*, Christ is the prototype of God's actions hidden under the contrary. The outcome is the union in Christ of "the most astonishing opposites" such as life and death, suffering and joy, activity and passivity.[158]

Luther's insistence on the suffering of God certainly brings up the question of Luther falling prey to the *patripassionism* of the ancient modalists. In order to distinguish Luther's position from modalism, Marc Lienhard suggests the term *deipassianism* to indicate that, in Luther's case, instead of the Father's suffering in Christ, it is God who suffers.[159] A trinitarian understanding of God is a key here. As with the divinity of Christ, Luther bases his acceptance of the ancient doctrine of the Trinity on the scriptural witness, while reiterating that both Christ's divinity and the trinitarian nature of God are incomprehensible to human reason and will be known only through faith.[160]

When it comes to the trinitarian nature of God, it is crucial for Luther to hold on to the notion that the immanent Trinity is the same as the economic Trinity, or, he believes, the assurance of salvation is put in question. This notion underscores the difference between Luther's position and that of the modalists. While Luther's starting point is always with the economic Trinity, namely, God at work in history, he also finds it important to talk about the eternal relationships among the Father, the Son, and the Holy Spirit in order to prevent a separation between who God is and what God does. In his representation of a trinitarian understanding of God, Luther attempts to adhere to the trinitarian formula, which maintains that within the framework of intratrinitarian relationships the three persons must be distinguished, and not in their action, with regard to the creature.[161] Thus, Luther can argue that the humanity of Jesus is the work of the Trinity as a whole, while it is the Son alone who assumes humanity.

The controversy regarding the real presence, as already has been pointed out, became significant for the formation of Luther's Christology. This is true, for example, regarding the question of a suffering God. By arguing for the real presence of Christ in the eucharistic elements, grounded in the unity of the two natures in the person of Christ, Luther is able to maintain that *God* is suffering in Christ on the cross, contradicting the widely accepted notion that God cannot suffer. But it is also crucial for Luther to emphasize the reality of the suffering of the man Jesus.[162] For Luther, it is important to hold on to the reality of Christ's suffering, not only the physical part of it, but also the moral aspect. Luther denounces all interpretations that try to downplay the reality of Christ's abandonment by God, including some of the church fathers, among them his favorite, St. Augustine.[163] While the fathers of the church and the medieval theologians were willing to talk about Christ's physical suffering, they insisted that "the soul" remained untouched. This is where Marc Lienhard sees the real difference between Luther and his predecessors. Lienhard writes:

> Luther, on the contrary, envisages in a radical fashion the feeling of abandonment and damnation in the consciousness of Jesus Christ. Luther set out in this direction by understanding the humanity of Jesus Christ, no longer only in the categories of nature, but also in the perspective of his consciousness. And he has comprehended the humanity of Jesus Christ, thus characterized, beginning with his own struggles of conscience, as one confronted by the anger of God.[164]

For Luther, Christ's sufferings are both similar and different from our suffering.[165] While experiencing the depth of all human suffering, Christ's suffering gives hope for the eventual elimination of human suffering and sin. This indeed is the paradoxical interpretation of the mystery of the crucified Christ. The key here is the relationship between the cross and resurrection. If what happens on Good Friday is taken out of the context of Easter, then Christ's suffering and death do not leave humanity with much hope, as Christ becomes just one more victim of evil. Easter, on the contrary, confirms the hope that the cross is not the end. In light of the resurrection, the promise is given that suffering and death do not have the last word. It is indeed in Christ's death and his resurrection that the union and the distinction of the two natures are manifest in a critical way. In Lienhard's words: "Christ can die as a man, but he is invincible as God. The union of the two natures assures that the humanity will not remain in death."[166]

Since the whole person of Christ is present in the sacrament, and not only the divine part of him, the whole humanity has been taken up into the being of God through Christ. Hence, by participating in the Holy Communion, we are made participants in the life and being of Christ. Luther talks about the "happy exchange" that takes place when Christ so identifies with us that he becomes the sinner by taking our place, while we in turn take the place of the righteous one. Luther explains how this happens in his treatise *The Freedom of a Christian* (1520):

> The third incomparable benefit of faith is that it unites the soul with Christ as a bride is united with her bridegroom. By this mystery, as the Apostle teaches, Christ and the soul become one flesh . . . And if they are one flesh and there is between them a true marriage . . . it follows that everything they have they hold in common, the good as well as the evil. Accordingly the believing soul can boast of and glory

in whatever Christ has as though it were its own, and whatever the
soul has Christ claims as his own. . . .[167]

While faith precedes work, Luther's strong practical orientation is no less
important for his theology. Convinced that "good works do not make a good
man," Luther is equally sure that "a good man does good works."[168] Hence, for
Luther, a "faith active in love" is inevitable.[169]

Further Development of Luther's Theology after His Death

It became the task and the challenge for Luther's followers to further the theological development Luther initiated. The publication of *Formula of Concord*
(*Formula concordiae*) in 1577 was meant to settle controversies that had arisen
within the churches of the Augsburg Confession after Luther's death.[170] There
are important similarities to and differences from Luther's theology in the
Formula. The focus here will be on the articles that deal with the sacraments
and the person of Christ.

First of all, the *Formula* recognizes the relationship between the eucharistic
controversy and the doctrine of the person of Christ, crystallized in the main
question in article eight, regarding the person of Christ and the communion
between the two natures. While affirming the Chalcedonian argument of no
mingling and no changing of the two natures, the *Formula* opposes those who
argue that the divine and human natures in Christ "have in common nothing
more than the name alone" (*communia nomina*). By reiterating the ancient
illustrations of iron glowing with fire and of the union of body and soul in a
human being, the *Formula* maintains "that God is man and man is God, which
could not be if the divine and human natures had in deed and truth absolutely
no communion with one another."[171]

With the focus turned toward the personal union of two natures, and after
affirming the anicient teaching about Mary being the true mother of God
(*theotokos*), the question becomes the one of suffering and death:

> 8. Hence we also believe, teach, and confess that it was not a mere
> man who suffered, died, was buried, descended to hell, arose from
> the dead, ascended into heaven, and was raised to the majesty and
> almighty power of God for us, but a man whose human nature has
> such a profound [close], ineffable union and communion with the
> Son of God that it is [has become] one person with Him.
>
> 9. Therefore the Son of God truly suffered for us, however, according
> to the property of the human nature which He assumed into the

unity of His divine person and made His own, so that He might be able to suffer and be our High Priest for our reconciliation with God, as it is written 1 Cor 2.8: *They have crucified the Lord of glory.* And Acts 20.28: *We are purchased with God's blood.*[172]

The *Formula* goes on to address Luther's argument against Zwingli regarding the divine properties being shared with the human nature after the incarnation. Then the problem becomes Christ's true humanity. How could Christ be truly human and still participate in the divine properties of the Son of God? By abstaining from them "in the state of His humiliation." The articles reads on:

> . . . [T]herefore He exercised this majesty, not always, but when [as often as] it pleased Him, until after His resurrection He entirely laid aside the form of a servant, but not the [human] nature, and was established in the full use, manifestation, and declaration of the divine majesty, and thus entered into His glory, Phil. 2.6 ff., so that now not only as God, but also as man He knows all things, can do all things, is present with all creatures, and has under His feet and in His hands everything that is in heaven and on earth and under the earth. . . .[173]

The key issue is that the perfections that truly are divine are communicated to the human nature of Christ "in the abstract."[174] Instead of presenting the *kenosis* of Philippians 2 as a kenosis according to the deity, the *Formula* insists that the human nature, "during the state of humiliation," freely "abdicated from the full use of it."[175] Jaroslav Pelikan comments on the originality of Lutheran Christology in this regard:

> It was above all in its elaboration of the communication of the properties that Lutheran christology broke new ground, going far beyond the original eucharistic context of Luther's christological speculations but endeavoring to keep the soteriological emphasis on the continuing presence of Jesus Christ "also according to that nature by which he is our brother and we are flesh of his flesh."[176]

Pelikan distinguishes between three different "genera" of communication within the *Formula*. Beside the one, which deals with the communication of the divine properties to the human nature (*genus majestaticum*), the second maintains that qualities of either nature may be ascribed to the entire person, who is simultaneously God and human (*genus idiomaticum*). Pelikan warns that a carelessness of language here, not unknown among orthodox church fathers and more recent theologians, could lead to the accusation of a revival of the heresy of "Patripassianism" and Sabellianism. But fear of that accusation should not lead to a denial of the proposition that "the Son of God truly, really, and properly suffered, was crucified, and died"; for the statements of Scripture attested that it was not only the human nature that suffered, but the very Son of God, "Jehovah himself."[177]

Despite the danger of patripassianism, the authors of the *Formula of Concord* insisted that they found sufficiently strong scriptural support for ascribing the qualities that belong to only one of the natures, not only to the respective nature, but also to the person as a whole (see the *Formula Concord*, article VIII, 9).[178]

The same is true of the third type (*genus*), which concerns the "official works" (*apostelesmata*) of Christ. According to *genus apostelesmaticum*, actions of the one person are common to both natures "inasmuch as each contributes to them that which is its own and thus each acts with the communication of the other."[179] It is still made clear that Christ indeed suffered and died "according to the property of the human nature."[180] It has been pointed out that Lutheran orthodoxy differs at this point from Luther himself, who went further than these three genera allow by "conceiving in the person of Christ the communication of attributes as a real communication of the properties of one nature to the other nature considered in itself."[181] It is, however, important to keep in mind that Luther is not always very clear in expressing what he means by this, and neither does he make use of above-mentioned expressions for the different kinds of communication of attributes.

While the *Formula of Concord* follows Luther on the question of *genus majestaticum*, it does not agree with him in attributing the human properties to the divine nature. This form of the communication of the attributes is called *genus tapeinoticum*, *tapeinos* meaning humble or lowly. As *genus majestaticum* signified to the opponents of the Lutheran doctrine a threat to the true humanity of Jesus Christ, the idea of *genus tapeinoticum* was rejected by the followers of Lutheran orthodoxy because they believed it constituted a limitation of the divine nature. Luther's idea of the human properties being shared with the divine nature was to reappear in the writings of the so-called *kenotic* theologians in the nineteenth century. They will be the focus of the next chapter as they make an essential background to the twentieth-century revival of theology of the cross. But before we leave Luther behind, it is important to reiterate that for Luther himself, *kenosis* refers to the "attitude" of the incarnate, the humiliation of the earthly Christ, and not a self-limitation of the deity, as for the kenotic theologians of the nineteenth century.[182] This again goes back to Luther's theology of the cross, in which God's revelation is always *sub contrario* and the focus on God's embracing of the opposite, which opens up a new possibility of approaching the christological questions.

Post-Enlightenment Christology

While Luther and Lutheran orthodoxy took pride in grounding their theological arguments in the ancient creeds, many Enlightenment thinkers saw the creedal texts as outdated. Not only was the language considered outmoded, but the whole philosophical system that gave birth to this kind of language was thought to have been proven wrong by the advances made by the thinkers of the eighteenth and nineteenth centuries. The Enlightenment brought radical changes to the christological discourse. The critique of supernaturalism, revelation, and external authorities eventually led to a radically humanized Christ. Christ now became the perfect human being, the archetype, and the great moral example. The development of the historical-critical method then opened up the question of the authenticity of the Scriptures and consequently the historicity of the person of Jesus Christ.

With Lutheran orthodoxy growing out of the search for an accurate interpretation of the Augsburg Confession, the emphasis on doctrines became much stronger than during the Reformation. This prominence of the doctrinal element became the focus of criticism in Pietism, which originated as the seventeenth century's reaction to Protestant orthodoxy, and the "objectivity of theological and ecclesiastical organization."[183] Contrary to orthodoxy, pietism maintained the prominence of praxis and subjectivism.

Pietism is one of the three movements that make up the background of nineteenth-century Protestant theology. The other two are rationalism and romanticism.[184] Together with the rationalists' call for "reasonableness" in religion came a claim for the "omnicompetence of criticism," allowing nothing to escape subjection to rational criticism.[185] Despite its criticism of "positive" religions, eighteenth-century rationalism had a strong religious interest, signified by its quest for "natural religion," which very often was seen as in no need of revelation, but resting solely on "sound natural reason."[186] Hence, romanticism can in many ways be seen as a reaction to the prominence of reason in rationalism, with its emphasis on "the immediacy of feeling."[187] The concern and feeling for history, significant for the romantic thinkers, was to become very influential in the development of historical theology during the nineteenth century. The most important contribution of romanticism to the christological discourse was the reintroduction of the principle of the relation between the finite and the infinite. This principle had been crucial for Luther's interpretation of the presence of the divine in the sacramental materials and became important, for example, for Hegel's theological system in the nineteenth century.[188]

In the nineteenth century, there are three dominant theological tracks, originating with three major thinkers, namely, Immanuel Kant (1724–1804), Georg Wilhelm Friedrich Hegel (1770–1831), and Friedrich Schleiermacher (1768–1834). A brief overview of their contributions to the christological discussion is helpful at this point, as they provide an important background for the development within the field of Christology during the twentieth century.[189]

Immanuel Kant brought the critical attitude of the Enlightenment to its peak by subjecting knowledge and reason itself to rational criticism. Furthermore, Kant presented the end of natural religion by denying the ability of human reason to reach God. Theoretical knowledge is limited to the *phenomena*, argued Kant, and cannot extend to the *noumena*, or the thing in itself. Therefore, since humans cannot break through to God, God must come to us. Through the "turn to the subject," Kant wanted to direct the focus to morality and action, in which God can be known *a priori* through practical reason. This is the idea behind Kant's understanding of "religion within the limits of reason alone." Consequently, Kant could talk about "a practical faith in this Son of God" by presenting Christ as "an archetype," "already present in our reason," who encourages human beings to strive for "moral perfection."[190] Humans know God *a priori*, through reason, maintained Kant, apart from any historical experience. While the moral ideal is universally valid, it is hard to see that Christ is necessary at all for Kant's system. On the one hand, Kant's ethical Christology can be seen as ebionitic, in which Jesus, as a mere human being, functions as a historical example of the Ideal (the archetype), which is present in our reason. But, insofar as this ideal has an aprioristic reality (in which the archetype is the eternal Christ), Kant's Christology has much more in commom with ancient docetic Christology.

While Kant focuses on morality and action in his ethical approach to Christology, Georg Wilhelm Friedrich Hegel concentrates on knowing and speculation. In his work, Hegel searches for a synthesis of theology and philosophy, convinced that both are dealing with the same subject, namely, truth itself, or God. For Hegel, God is the absolute Spirit whose life is revealed in the history of the world. Underlying Hegel's system is his *panentheistic* understanding of God and the world, in which the one cannot be understood without the other. Hegel conceived in panentheism an alternative to dualism, between the infinite and the finite, transcendence and immanence, God and humans, which was characteristic of the Enlightenment.

Fundamental to Hegel's theology is the trinitarian framework.[191] When, for example, Hegel talks about the incarnation, which is central to his system, he is talking about the incarnation of the second person of the Trinity. For Hegel, Christ is the self-actualization of God, since God, whose true nature is love, expresses Godself in the other person. In the incarnation, God reveals that God and human are not ultimately separated but intimately one.[192] The aim of this unity is then achieved in reconciliation, which takes place on the cross.[193] On the cross, death, which is the ultimate characteristic of human beings (as finite beings), becomes the death of God, so that the finite is ultimately taken into the infinite (the *Aufhebung* of the finite into the infinite).[194] The role of the resurrection is then to confirm that the infinite is the true nature of the finite. Here Hegel discloses himself as a theologian of the cross, highly influenced by Luther.[195] For Hegel, as for Luther, God is revealed under the opposite. Likewise not only is the death of Christ the death of the human being, Jesus from Nazareth, but also in Jesus, God identifies with the humans to such an extent that the death of the human being becomes a death of God.

Since Hegel's main interest is in Christ, the second person of the Trinity, questions about the role of the historical Jesus within his system become unavoidable. It is indeed necessary for Hegel that the incarnation takes place in a particular individual within history, but less important how, where, and through whom it happens.[196] This is why the so-called left-wing Hegelians—such as David Friedrich Strauss, who opted for a total separation between the Jesus of history and the Christ of faith—have been considered a logical outcome of Hegel's system.[197] Hegel's influence is no less significant for the renewal of incarnation theology in the middle of the nineteenth century, presented in the works of Gottfried Thomasius, Isaak August Dorner, and Alois Emanuel Biedermann.[198]

Instead of focusing on doing, as Kant, or knowing, as Hegel, Friedrich Schleiermacher stresses the role of experience and feelings as the locus of authority for religion, by defining religion as "sense and taste for the Infinite."[199] The feeling Schleiermacher is referring to is what he calls "the immediate God-consciousness." Schleiermacher bases his understanding of religion on the assumption that humans can know God only "in relation," through their God-consciousness, which remains obscure and powerless in all human beings before they encounter Christ, the Redeemer. What makes Christ the Redeemer is his perfect God-consciousness. Christ is the archetype, who has magnetic power to draw others into his likeness. Because of his understanding of Christ, Schleiermacher's theology is indeed very Christocentric, as it is only through Christ that human beings have their God-consciousness restored.

Schleiermacher's Christology (sometimes labelled as "Second-Adam Christology") presents Christ as the perfection of creation, the ideality, and the norm of humanity.[200] Consequently, Christ does not have to be divine, except in virtue of his difference from other human beings.[201] Furthermore, the uniqueness of Jesus from Nazareth is located in his sinlessness.[202] Given Schleiermacher's understanding of sin as a shortcoming, or an obscured God-consciousness, Jesus' sinlessness does not present a problem for his true humanity. Yet, Schleiermacher finds the idea of Jesus' temptations and suffering problematic, as for him the "climax" of Jesus' sufferings was not real suffering but rather "sympathy with misery."[203]

Schleiermacher's focus on Jesus' true humanity, and his emphasis on Jesus being only and fully human, locates his Christology within the Christian tradition among other ebionitic interpretations of the person and work of Jesus Christ.[204] However, his emphasis on Christ as an archetype, with redeeming power, caused theologians such as Strauss and Baur to accuse Schleiermacher of Docetism, hence criticizing him for not taking Jesus' humanity seriously.[205] Schleiermacher has, furthermore, been accused of Apollinarianism, namely, for presenting Jesus as a divine person who has "swallowed the human."[206] But, wherever Schleiermacher's Christology is to be located within the spectrum of christological doctrines, his influence on theological development is unquestionable, earning him the distinctive title "the father of modern Protestant theology."[207] With the death of Schleiermacher, and the publication of Strauss' *Life of Jesus* in 1835, a new segment in the history of Protestant thought in the nineteenth century emerges, characterized by the christological problem, "both as a historical problem" and "as a problem of developing a christology genuinely *von unten nach oben*."[208] It is to the main representatives of this particular period that we now turn.

Searching for the Historical Jesus

The quest for the historical Jesus[209] reached its peak with the publication of David Friedrich Strauss's *Life of Jesus* in 1835. In his book *The Quest of the Historical Jesus: A Critical Study of its Progress from Reimarus to Wrede*, originally published in German in 1906, Albert Schweitzer distinguished between the periods "before and after Strauss."[210] Schweitzer maintained that the time before Strauss, starting with Hermann Reimarus, was characterized by its occupation with miracles. He believed the problem with miracles was solved by Strauss, who saw miracles as belonging to the mythological part of the Gospels. Strauss developed an understanding of myth as the production of the community and an expression of the *idea* in the form of a historical account. Convinced that no one had paid enough attention to the mythical elements in the gospel stories, Strauss proposed a mythological interpretation of the Gospels, which should provide the true meaning of the myth or the *idea* behind it.[211]

In his *Life of Jesus*, Strauss used the historical-critical method to look for the historical Jesus in the Gospels. Strauss searched the Gospels for all the mythical elements, for all inconsistencies, and for everything that could be labeled as supernatural. The result of his search was a historical figure about whom we know very little, and who could for no reason be the foundation for our faith.[212] In the conclusion of his book, and in his later work, *The Christ of Faith and the Jesus of History*,[213] Strauss denied that there was an incarnation in a single historical individual. Instead he believed that the central truth of Christianity was the divine incarnation in humanity as a whole.[214] Consequently, Strauss called for a total separation between the historical Jesus and the Christ of faith.[215]

It was Strauss's mentor and the founder of the Tübingen School, Ferdinand Christian Baur, who reacted against Strauss's negative conclusion, by insisting on the importance of the relationship between the Jesus of history and the ideal Christ. Highly influenced by Hegel, Baur still differed from Hegel in his emphasis on "the significance of the particularity and positivity of Jesus for the history of redemption."[216] A key to Baur's "historical theology" is his focus on the historical foundation of Christianity, while a necessary starting point and center for this kind of theology is Christology.[217] Baur's Christology is a Christology *from* below, starting with a critical analysis of the Gospel writings in order to avoid *docetic* Christologies of such theologians as Schleiermacher and Hegel.[218] Consequently, for Baur, the relation between the ideal and the historical Christ is a necessary one, as it is "in the humanity of Jesus that his divinity is to be seen."[219] Baur, however, refused to identify exclusively the idea of God-manhood with the historical Jesus.[220]

In *The So-Called Historical Jesus and the Historic Biblical Christ* (first published in 1892), Martin Kähler criticized the quest for the historical Jesus, denouncing the Jesus of the "Life-of-Jesus movement" as a "modern example of human creativity."[221] Kähler denied the possibility of using the Gospels as "documents for a *scientifically reconstructed biography* of Jesus," maintaining they were intended not as historical documents, but to "awaken faith in Jesus through a clear proclamation of his saving activity."[222] In the New Testament, Kähler insisted, the Jesus of history is the Christ of faith.

As an alternative to the "Jesus like us" approach of the historical-Jesus movement, Kähler's focus was on the Christ who is different from us. Kähler maintained that the distinction between Jesus Christ and ourselves was not one of degree but of kind, and therefore we should "refrain from depicting his inner life by the principle of analogy."[223] Without denying the significance of our likeness with Jesus, Kähler insisted that the urgency of the "biblical Christ" was his saving activity. Hence, the importance of holding together Christ's person and work. "His work is his person in its historic-super historic effect," argued Kähler. In order to know his work, we do not need to be convinced by the methods of historical research. That work is accessible to each of us: in the church as it marches through the centuries, in the confessing word and confessing deed of our fellow Christians, and in the living faith which Christ himself has evoked from us. The passionately held dogma about the Savior vouches for the reliability of the picture transmitted to us by the biblical proclamation of Jesus as the Christ.[224]

Kähler's intention was therefore not only to make theology independent of historical conclusions but also to explain why faith can never be based on history. The "real Christ" was for Kähler the "Christ who is preached."[225] And the Christ who is preached "is the Christ of faith." Hence, "for Christians," Kähler maintained, "Christ must always be the object of faith."[226]

The criticism of the search for the historical Jesus, raised by Martin Kähler, Johannes Weiss and others,[227] was continued by Albert Schweitzer in his *Quest of the Historical Jesus*.[228] Albert Schweitzer believed a new epoch had begun with Johannes Weiss, whom he claimed was "the first to achieve a consistent and inclusive understanding of the eschatological character of the person and message of Jesus."[229] In his extensive work on the quest of the historical Jesus, Schweitzer portrayed its failure, arguing that not only did the search for the historical Jesus reflect the time in which this search took place, but also that "each individual created Him in accordance with his own character."[230] Schweitzer agreed wholeheartedly with Johannes Weiss about the thoroughly eschatological character of the person and message of Jesus. Consequently, he was convinced that the historical Jesus would remain "a stranger and an enigma."[231] Instead of focusing on Jesus, as he is historically known, Schweitzer believed it was Jesus "as spiritually arisen" who was significant: "Not the historical Jesus, but the spirit which goes forth from Him and in the spirits of men strives for new influence and rule, is that which overcomes the world."[232]

Christ and Kenosis

The christological focus of the works of Schleiermacher and Hegel, as well as Strauss's critical work on the historical Jesus, elicited new responses to the question of the incarnation in mid-nineteenth-century German theology. Important contributions to the theological discussion of this particular period were made by Gottfried Thomasius, Isaak August Dorner, and Alois Emanuel Biedermann. The key problem dealt with by these theologians was metaphysical, centering on the being of God in the historical person Jesus Christ, or "the union of God and man in the God-man." But even though they were primarily concerned with the person rather than with the work of Christ, both Thomasius and Dorner insisted on the "inseparability and even the unity of person and work" by arguing that the unity of God and human in Christ itself was his "redemptive activity."[233] Christological reconstructions provided by Thomasius, Dorner, and Biedermann materialized as radically different proposals, even if they can all be seen as attempts to respond to the critical reconsideration of the human and divine aspect of the person of Christ, following the rise of the Enlightenment.[234]

Thomasius's *kenotic* theology has been labeled as "neo-Lutheranism," as his idea of kenosis grows out of the Lutheran emphasis on the communication of the attributes.[235] Thomasius was primarily concerned with two things in his Christology. First of all, he wanted to do justice to the two nature/one person doctrine of the early church. At the same time, he wanted to recognize the genuine humanity of the person of Jesus of Nazareth, "a person with actual human limitations of knowledge and power, with a 'gradually dawning infant consciousness' and a real growth—a person for whom sleep and death were real."[236]

Thomasius perceived two possibilities, with regard to the relationship between the human and the divine in the person of Jesus Christ. The first was the idea of juxtaposition or conjunction, emphasizing the distinction rather than the unity. The alternative, and the one Thomasius chose, was Luther's idea of the communication of attributes. By insisting on a real communication of the attributes, in which the divine and human natures were "actually imparted to each other, in as complete a penetration as could take place without destroying the integrity of each,"[237] Thomasius believed he could show that Christ suffered not only as a human being but also as God. Consequently, Christ is received in the Lord's Supper not only according to his divine nature but also as a human being. In his interpretation of the idea of the communication of the attributes, Thomasius wanted to maintain a true communication that goes both ways. This was contrary to the tendency within the Lutheran tradition to interpret the communication only as a one-way impartation from divine to human. In order to hold on to a communication of the human properties to the divine (*genus tapeinoticum*), Thomasius made use of the concept of *kenosis*, representing "the idea of a self-limitation of the *divine* in the incarnation."[238] Thomasius's kenotic theology has later become an important theoretical background for those who have wanted to highlight the true participation of Jesus in the human condition, all the way to suffering and death.

In his explication of the kenotic theory, Thomasius makes a distinction between the *immanent* and the *relative* attributes of God. The *relative* attributes are the ones God needs while dealing with the world (i.e., omniscience, omnipresence, and omnipotence), but the *immanent* attributes are necessary for God's essential being (i.e., holiness, love, power, and justice).[239] *Kenosis* then consists of laying aside the relative attributes, as, during the earthly life of Jesus, the divine actually accepts human limitations, while the human receives the properties of the divine. Thus, the communication of attributes becomes genuine and mutual.[240]

It was Isaak August Dorner who became Thomasius's strongest contemporary critic. Dorner insisted that, while the idea of kenosis did justice to the true humanity of Christ, God's immutability made kenosis impossible.[241] Hence, in order to empty Godself, God had to cease to be God. Holding on to the centrality of God's immutability, Dorner maintained that there is in God not a fixed but a "living immutability," which is love.[242] The true nature of God as love is to become the other, first in the creation[243] and later in the incarnation and reconciliation in Christ.[244] Dorner clarified what this means in regard to the incarnation of Christ in the following way:

> The possibility and necessity in general of the incarnation has its
> ultimate foundation in God as holy love; the actuality of the incarnation,
> and its necessary form, brings the pre-Christian history of humanity
> and revelation into consideration as a presupposition. When the time
> was fulfilled, God sent his Son (Gal. 4:4).[245]

Without emptying Godself or ceasing to be God, and not implying an identity of the divine and human, God enters a "unity in difference" in the God-man. Hence, Christ's true humanity is preserved, since it "does not have to count the divine as eternally part of its original being, but only be receiving throughout." Contrary to a pantheistic conception, Christ's humanity is therefore not directly divine "but is only filled with God by the free love of the Logos." In other words, "the Logos makes it his own in participation, in order to give it a share in himself and thus to receive it into his trinitarian life."[246]

Distinctive for Dorner's Christology is his idea of *progressive incarnation*, which was meant to serve the same purpose as Thomasius's idea of kenosis (i.e., to secure the true humanity of Christ). As development is fundamental to humanity, it has to pertain also to Christ, as long as he represents a truly human being.[247] But development is not limited to Christ's humanity. Dorner explains:

> Since on the other hand God can be perfectly manifest in Christ
> only when the whole fullness of the divine Logos has become this
> man's own fullness in knowledge and will, and has thus become
> divine-human, a development of God-manhood is also necessarily
> given in him along with the development of the human side.[248]

In order to avoid, on one hand, Schleiermacher's rejection of a true moral process and, on the other hand, the idea of Christ's sinful flesh, Dorner wanted to present an ethical and yet sinless life, in which there still remains a place for "wrestling and struggle."[249] Therefore, he argued, during Jesus' earthly life, God is already in him, but he must also be in God; which means he "must grasp the divine with his will and make it his own."[250]

The renewed emphasis on the trinitarian understanding of God early on in the twentieth century was an important attempt to bridge the gap between the kerygmatic Christ and the historical Jesus. Trinitarian theology embraced the critique of the search for the historical Jesus, as well as the conclusion about the eschatological character of the preaching of Jesus Christ, reached by Johannes Weiss and Albert Schweitzer. From a trinitarian perspective, the focus shifted away from the historical Jesus to Jesus the Son of God as the object of Christology. Jürgen Moltmann, one of the leading trinitarian theologians of the second half of the twentieth century, explains what he means when he argues that

> the doctrine of the Trinity is not a speculation over mysteries in
> heaven, which nobody knows; it is rather the short formulation of the
> God story of Jesus, the son of the Abba-father in heaven and our
> brother on earth.[251]

Moltmann's trinitarian theology is characterized by the central role assigned to Christ and his cross. Another important feature of Moltmann's theology is his emphasis on a strong relationship between theory and praxis, fundamental to his practical and political interpretation of the cross.

Jürgen Moltmann's Retrieval of *Theologia Crucis*

While the resurrection plays the center role in Moltmann's *Theology of Hope: On the Ground and the Implications of a Christian Eschatology*, the focus shifts to the cross and the crucified Christ in his next book, *The Crucified God: The Cross of Christ as the Foundation and Criticism of Christian Theology*. In the latter, Moltmann intends to show that "the theology of the cross is none other than the reverse side of the Christian theology of hope." The order in *Theology of Hope*, namely, "the *resurrection* of the crucified Christ," is shifted to "the *cross* of the risen Christ" in Moltmann's *Crucified God*. Moltmann writes:

> I was concerned then with the remembrance of Christ in the form of
> the *hope* of his future, and now I am concerned with hope in the
> form of the *remembrance* of his death. The dominant theme then was

that of *anticipation* of the future of God in the form of promises and hopes; here it is the understanding of the *incarnation* of that future, by way of the sufferings of Christ, in the world's sufferings.[252]

But Moltmann is not only shifting the focus from Easter to Good Friday. He also wants to change the locus of the question of Christ's suffering and death. Instead of asking about the meaning of the cross for human beings, he asks about its meaning for God. Looking back, Moltmann observes:

> In my book *The Crucified God* I came upon a trinitarian theology of the cross by reversing the soteriological question "what do the suffering and death of Christ mean for us?" so that it became the theological question "what do the suffering and death of Christ mean for God?"[253]

Moltmann finds an answer to his question in his perception of God's suffering in Christ. Crucial for Moltmann's answer is Paul's statement in 2 Corinthians 5:19: "God was in Christ, reconciling the world to himself." "If God the Father was *in* Christ, the Son," Moltmann argues, "this means that Christ's sufferings are God's sufferings too, and then God too experienced death on the cross."[254]

For Moltmann, the event of the cross is understood only within a trinitarian framework, in which the cross is located at the center of the trinitarian being of God, functioning as the dividing point between the persons of the Trinity.[255] As the Son reveals God the Father through the life and message of Jesus of Nazareth, his death on the cross discloses the "essential passion of the eternal love of God."[256] A trinitarian understanding of the cross perceives what happens within God on the cross. As the Son suffers abandonment by the Father ("My God, my God, why hast thou forsaken me"), the Father suffers the death of the Son.[257] Hence, the cross "divides God from God to the utmost degree of enmity and destitution."[258]

Moltmann maintains that the idea of a "crucified God," as presented within the tradition of the theology of the cross, runs counter to the strong emphasis on God's immortality and impassibility within the Western theological tradition.[259] Moltmann traces this problem with a suffering God back to the theology of the early church, which, he argues, only acknowledged two possibilities, either a suffering God or a God who is incapable of suffering.[260] The ontological concept of God, gradually taking over the theological thinking of the ancient church, protected the being of God from becoming affected by the suffering and death of Jesus on the cross. Then the doctrine of the two natures, which became the framework for christological thinking, further ensured that the God-man could have suffered only as a human being.[261] Moltmann affirms the need of contemporary theology to confront what he considers "the unsolved problems of the past." He writes:

The Council of Nicea correctly opposed Arius with the assertion that God is not subject to change as creation is. He does not change as creation does. But this is not an absolute statement; rather it is a comparison. We must not turn the statement into a thesis of God's absolute unchangeability. This negative stipulation says only that God, unlike men, is not subject to what is not divine. Therefore, the denial that God can change, this distinction between God and world, is not to lead us to conclude that God is inwardly unmoved, but rather we can draw from it the conclusion that God has sovereign freedom.[262]

So, while God differs from human beings in their changeability, it does not mean God is not able to change Godself or freely to become subject to change by others. For Moltmann it means that, even if God "cannot be divisible as creation is," God can still choose to share Godself with humans. Therefore, despite "the relative assertion of God's unchangeableness," God is not "absolutely unchangeable inwardly."[263]

In addition to opening up the possiblity of change within God, Moltmann makes a critical distinction between "involuntary suffering" and what he calls "the suffering of love" in order to make God's participation in suffering and death possible. Thus, while Moltmann agrees with those who argue that God cannot suffer "because of some lack in his being," he still believes God is able to suffer "out of the fullness of his being, that is, his love."[264] With this distinction Moltmann rejects the idea of God's *apatheia*, insisting that

> a God who cannot suffer is poorer than any man. For a God who is incapable of suffering is a being who cannot be involved. Suffering and injustice do not affect him. And because he is so completely insensitive, he cannot be affected or shaken by anything. He cannot weep, for he has no tears. But the one who cannot suffer cannot love either. So he is also a loveless being.[265]

To understand fully the event on the cross, Moltmann calls for a shift from the doctrine of the two natures toward a trinitarian perception of the relationship between Jesus and his Father on the cross. Instead of starting with the differentiation between a human and a divine nature, Moltmann finds it more appropriate "to start from Jesus' special relationship to God. . .in order to elicit from this mutual relationship between the messianic child and the divine Father what is truly divine and what is truly human." Moltmann continues:

> By first of all developing christology and the doctrine of God in specifically Christian—which means trinitarian—terms, we are not denying the task of christology in the framework of metaphysics in

general. But the New Testament is not concerned about the relationship between Christ's human and his divine nature. It is concerned with Jesus' relationship as child to the Father, and with God's relationship as Father to Jesus. It is only the trinitarian concept of God which makes it possible to understand God for Jesus' sake in his relationship as Father, and Jesus for God's sake as the child and Son of the Father.[266]

Hence, Moltmann insists, if the assumption that the crucified Christ is the risen one holds, then we cannot start our Christology either from below (anthropological Christology) or from above (metaphysical Christology), but we have to keep the two in tension.[267] Instead of starting from below or above, Moltmann wants to start with a *pneumatological* Christology, since it is through the Spirit that Jesus knows that he is the Son of God.[268] The title of his volume on Christology, *The Way of Jesus Christ: Christology in Messianic Dimensions*, indicates Moltmann's understanding of the Sonship being something Jesus grows into on his way to the cross. The resurrection then "qualifies the one who has been crucified as the Christ, and his sufferings and death as a saving event for us and for many." This does not imply that the resurrection "relativizes" the cross. "The resurrection 'does not evacuate the cross,'" argues Moltmann, "but fills it with eschatology and saving significance."[269] Hence, the resurrection has to be the starting point for all further interpretations of the cross.

Not only does Moltmann argue for the importance of the trinitarian framework for our understanding of the cross, but also he stresses the significance for the event of the cross for the meaning of the Trinity. The uniqueness of the Christian faith, argues Moltmann, consists of the cross and the poor, rejected, suffering, and abandoned God crucified on it. This God is truly "different from the projection of man's desire."[270] The death of Jesus also has little in common with that of heroes such as Socrates, the Zealot martyrs, the wise men of the Stoics, and the Christian martyrs, who all faced death with confidence and joy.[271] Moltmann maintains, "the dialectical principle" of the theology of the cross claims that "the deity of God is revealed in the paradox of the cross."[272] Implied is the reversal of human expectations and contesting of the principle of likeness and similarity. The fact that Jesus was accused of blasphemy but was crucified as a political rebel[273] can be understood in the context of his life and message. It is all the more difficult to understand what it means that "Jesus died the death of God's Son in God-forsakenness."[274]

Making use of trinitarian terms, Moltmann explains the cross event in the following way:

> The Father is the one who abandons. He abandons Jesus to the abyss of being forsaken, and that is the real abyss of this world forsaken by

God. The Father's pain is the death of the Son in this absolute destruction. The Son is the one who is abandoned by the Father and the one who gives himself in self-surrender. He suffers the hell of this death. The Spirit is the Spirit of surrender of the Father and the Son. He is creative love proceeding out of the Father's pain and the Son's self-surrender and coming to forsaken human beings in order to open to them a future for life.[275]

Moltmann claims that through his trinitarian interpretation of the event of the cross, he is able to avoid the dangers of the two natures doctrine and, with it, "any concept of God—metaphysical, moral, or political—that is assumed to have general validity."[276] He, furthermore, maintains that the trinitarian approach eliminates the old dichotomy between the immanent and a functional Trinity, as well as the general nature of God and God's inner triune nature.[277] Here Moltmann complies with Karl Rahner's famous trinitarian formulas, namely, that "the Trinity *is* the nature of God and the nature of God *is* the Trinity" and, furthermore, that "the economic Trinity *is* the immanent Trinity, and the immanent Trinity *is* the economic Trinity."[278] Finally, Moltmann wants to correct earlier statements about "the death of God," or at least warn against a literal understanding of the term. In trinitarian terms, argues Moltmann, Jesus' death is to be understood as death *in* God, instead of as the death *of* God, so that the triune nature of the Godhead will not be overlooked.[279]

As a political theologian, Moltmann does not limit his questions to the ones about the being of God, but he is also interested in the relationship between our understanding of God and our daily life. A key to Moltmann's practical interpretation of the "crucified God" is the inclusive character of Christ's suffering, meaning that in his suffering, the suffering of the whole creation is embraced. The revelation of the "suffering God" "allows people to understand their suffering in God and to participate in the 'suffering of God in the world.'"[280] In trinitarian terms, this means that human history, everything included, becomes a part of God's history through the event of the cross. Moltmann explains:

> When the Christian faith is put in trinitarian terms it says that forsaken men have, by virtue of Christ's being forsaken, already entered his "divine history," and that we are living "in God" because through the death of Christ we share in the eschatological life of God. God is, and God is in us. God suffers in us when love suffers. We take part in God's trinitarian process in history. As we take part both actively and passively in God's suffering in the world, we also take part in God's joy in the world wherever we love and pray and hope.[281]

Moltmann assumes that only a God capable of suffering can bring hope into hopeless situations. By embracing the sufferings of all suffering people, God gives hope for a transformation of all suffering and death through the resurrection. But the theology of the cross is also a call to an active following of the crucified Christ. To join Christ on "his way to the cross" means "solidarity with the sufferings of the poor and the misery both of the oppressed and the oppressors."[282] Hence, Christology becomes Christopraxis, when the practical aspect of the theology of the cross becomes actualized.

Even if theology of the cross can bring hope and liberation to suffering people, it does not always do so. Moltmann recognizes the danger of an "abused" theology of the cross, which can, and has been, "perverted into a justification of suffering itself."[283] Moltmann finds examples of such a distortion in the church's interaction with peasants, Indians, and black slaves. An example is Luther's interaction with the peasants, as Moltmann believes Luther would have been better off giving a sermon on the cross to the princes and the masters of the peasants than encouraging the peasants to accept their suffering as their cross:

> In a world of domination and oppression one must pay close
> attention to the concrete function of any preaching and any devotion.
> As "opium for the people," produced by those who caused the
> suffering, this mysticism of suffering is a blasphemy, a kind of
> monstrous product of inhumanity.[284]

Despite the distortion, "the Christ of the poor has always been the crucified Christ,"[285] as the poor, the humiliated, and the oppressed have found in Jesus not a passive fellow sufferer but a "divine Brother" who has voluntarily taken on suffering and death "for the sake of the many."[286] This is the Jesus of the Gospel narratives, the one who sided with the outcast of his society and preached the coming of the kingdom of God to sinners and taxcollectors. The road to the cross was his own choice:

> Jesus did not suffer passively from the world in which he lived, but
> incited it against himself by his message and the life he lived. Nor did
> his crucifixion in Jerusalem come upon him as the act of an evil
> destiny, so that one could speak of a heroic failure, as heroes have
> often failed and yet remained heroes to posterity. According to the
> gospels, Jesus himself set out for Jerusalem and actively took the
> expected suffering upon himself.[287]

The key here is to recognize the voluntary aspect of the passion story. "The more the mysticism of the cross" recognizes this aspect, maintains Moltmann, "the less it can accept Jesus as an example of patience and submission to fate."

Hence, instead of encouraging mere *conformitas crucis*, the theology of the cross opens up the possibility for suffering people to join Jesus on his way by accepting his mission and actively following in his footsteps.[288]

Where Do We Go from Here?

In this survey of the Christian tradition, a theology of the cross presents an important alternative to a God who is above and beyond all human suffering but also to a God who is an impotent victim of evil. Faithful to the biblical witness to a God who is actively involved in the human predicament, theology of the cross sees in the story of the passion, death, and resurrection of Jesus Christ God's response to a suffering humanity in an act of deep solidarity. Through what has continued to be a "stumbling block" and "foolishness" to many, theology of the cross sees in the cross the power and wisdom of God revealed *sub contrario*. This is in stark contradiction to the prevailing understanding of God as being unable to suffer. By focusing on the cross as the place where we meet the suffering God, whose power and wisdom are revealed through that which is "low and despised in the world" (1 Corinthians 1:28), theology of the cross brings about a reversal of our expectations. Seen from the angle of the cross, the story of the life and death of Jesus Christ is bound to do just that.

While affirming the significance of that part of the Christian tradition that locates the cross at its center, it is nonetheless important to be aware of the potential danger of the twisting of theology of the cross into "a justification of suffering itself."[289] Thus Moltmann's warning and his emphasis on the significance of the identity and interests of the one who is speaking as well as the one who is listening are essential parts of all theological discussions, particularly those that focus on the cross as a central point of reference.

For a feminist retrieval of a theology of the cross, it is particularly important to be aware of the danger of making suffering into a virtue. This is because women, more than men, have frequently been encouraged to "carry their crosses" silently and patiently because of their likeness to Christ's cross. Thus, the feminist critique of an "abusive" theology of the cross is an essential part of a feminist retrieval of the cross. While affirming the feminist critique, the fourth chapter presents a proposal of a feminist theology of the cross that seeks to unveil patriarchal distortions of traditional Christology but also to reveal lost dimensions in the person and work of Jesus Christ.

NOTES

1. Johnson, *She Who Is: The Mystery of God in Feminist Theological Discourse*, 254.

2. Käsemann, "The Saving Significance of the Death of Jesus in Paul" (English translation).

3. Purvis, *The Power of the Cross: Foundations for a Christian Feminist Ethic of Community*.

4. Cousar, *A Theology of the Cross: The Death of Jesus in the Pauline Letters*, 2. Describing the variety of language used by Paul to depict the importance and role of the death of Jesus, Cousar writes: "Sometimes the death is spoken of as a self-giving on Jesus' part (Gal 2.20), at other times as a giving on God's part (Rom 8.32); sometimes the language of crucifixion is used (1 Cor 1.23), at other times not (2 Cor 5.14); sometimes believers as a community are made participants in Jesus' death (Rom 6.1–11), at other times the death imparts significance to the individual (1 Cor 8.11); sometimes the death is asserted exclusively (1 Cor 2.2), at other times it is linked to the resurrection (Rom 4.25); sometimes it is affirmed as the event by which God effects atonement for human sinfulness (Rom 3.24–26), at other times it is identified as the cause of persecution (Gal 5.11)" (ibid.).

5. See, for example, 1 Corinthians 15:14–15.

6. Käsemann, "The Saving Significance of the Death of Jesus in Paul," 47.

7. Cousar, *A Theology of the Cross*, 9.

8. Käsemann, "The Saving Significance of the Death of Jesus in Paul," 46.

9. Ibid., 47.

10. Ibid., 54.

11. Ibid., 58.

12. Ibid., 46.

13. Ibid., 49.

14. Ibid., 50.

15. Ibid., 50–51.

16. Ibid., 49–50.

17. Both Cousar (*A Theology of the Cross*) and Brown (*The Cross & Human Transformation: Paul's Apocalyptic Word in 1 Corinthians*) focus on 1 Corinthians 1:18–2.5.

18. Pannenberg, "A Theology of the Cross," 163.

19. Cousar, *A Theology of the Cross*, 42.

20. Brown, *The Cross & Human Transformation*, 96.

21. Ibid., 93–94.

22. Cousar, *A Theology of the Cross*, 45–48.

23. Brown, *The Cross & Human Transformation*, 94.

24. Purvis, *The Power of the Cross*, 49.

25. Ibid., 13.

26. Purvis has chosen Paul as an early messenger of the power of the cross as the power of life,

> first because his letters offer us the clearest picture of a group of people
> struggling to understand and embody a "new world," a world shaped by a
> power that seemed odd and surprising and that called forth new ways of

being together in community. Second, Paul's letters, especially 1 Corinthians 1, offer a sustained if not a systematic discussion of the cross and its implications for Christians' understanding and embodiment of power" (ibid., 39).

27. Ibid., 13. Explaining what she means by "power as control," Purvis writes:

"Power as control assumes the superiority and the greater entitlement of one or some over another or others. By its very nature, power as control undermines and abrogates the commitment to fundamental, if minimal, equality to which all Christians are obligated. Therefore, power as control cannot function as the basis for a Christian ethic of community without deep and violent self-contradiction. Yet such power has been and is the most prevalent understanding and practice of power within Christian community" (ibid., 21).

28. Ibid., 50.

29. Ibid., 74.

30. Ibid., 51.

31. Ibid.

32. Ibid., 77.

33. On different options of translating and interpreting this particular passage, see footnote 43 in Cousar, *A Theology of the Cross*, 50–51.

34. Cousar, *A Theology of the Cross*, 49.

35. Küng, *The Incarnation of God*, 518.

36. Ibid. See also Grillmeier, *Christ in Christian Tradition: Vol One. From the Apostolic Age to the Chalcedon*.

37. On Küng's discussion on "orthodoxy" and "heresy," see Küng, *The Incarnation of God*, 510.

38. Ibid., 519.

39. Ibid., 520.

40. Ibid., 512–15.

41. Ibid., 518–19.

42. Davis, *The First Seven Ecumenical Councils (325–787): Their History and Theology*, 34.

43. Ibid.

44. Davis, *The First Seven Ecumenical Councils*, 40–41. See also Tillich, *A History of Christian Thought: From Its Judaic and Hellenistic Origins to Existentialism*, 65.

45. Küng, *The Incarnation of God*, 521.

46. Norris, *The Christological Controversy*, 18.

47. See parts from Athanasius's *Orations against the Arians*, in Norris, *The Christological Controversy*, 83–101.

48. The Nicene Creed: ". . . eternally begotten of the Father. . . . true God from true God. . . . of one being (*homoousios*) with the Father. . . ." On the events and significance of the Council of Nicea, see Davis, *The First Seven Ecumenical Councils*, 56–75.

49. Küng, *The Incarnation of God*, 521.

50. Norris, *The Christological Controversy*, 115.

51. Ibid., 25.

52. Ibid., 26. See also Davis, *The First Seven Ecumenical Councils*, 145–48.

53. Norris, *The Christological Controversy*, 124–25.

54. Ibid., 139.

55. Ibid., 148.

56. Macquarrie, *Jesus Christ in Modern Thought*, 44.

57. Justin Martyr was one of the leading theologians among the Apologists. See Norris, *The Christological Controversy*, 6–9; and Tillich, *A History of Christian Thought*, 24–32.

58. Tillich, *A History of Christian Thought*, 60.

59. Norris, *The Christological Controversy*, 16.

60. Tillich, *A History of Christian Thought*, 62.

61. Norris, *The Christological Controversy*, 16.

62. Tillich, *A History of Christian Thought*, 42.

63. McWilliams, *The Passion of God: Divine Suffering in Contemporary Protestant Theology*, 12, footnote 25.

64. Küng, *The Incarnation of God*, 521.

65. Norris, *The Christological Controversy*, 19. Athanasius writes in his *Orations Against the Arians*: "If the works of the Logos' Godhead had not been done by means of the body, humanity would not have been divinized" (ibid., 91).

66. Ibid., 19–20.

67. Ibid., 20.

68. Ibid., 90.

69. McWilliams, *The Passion of God*, 13.

70. Norris, *The Christological Controversy*, 21.

71. Ibid., 22.

72. Davis, *The First Seven Ecumenical Councils*, 105.

73. Ibid., 106.

74. Ibid, 148–53.

75. Norris, *The Christological Controversy*, 28.

76. Ibid., 27.

77. Davis, *The First Seven Ecumenical Councils*, 151.

78. A quotation from Cyril's second letter to Nestorius, in Norris, *The Christological Controversy*, 133–34.

79. Davis, *The First Seven Ecumenical Councils*, 170.

80. Norris, *The Christological Controversy*, 28.

81. From Pope Leo I's letter to Flavian of Constantinople, in Norris, *The Christological Controversy*, 151.

82. Ibid., 30.

83. Grillmeier, *Christ in Christian Tradition*, 544.

84. Küng, *The Incarnation of God*, 522.

85. Ibid., 523–54. Regarding the subject of incarnation and the question of Jesus' ability to suffer, Hans Küng maintains that the "subject of the incarnation remains the

subject of all that is related of the incarnate One in life, suffering and death."
Therefore, he explains, if

> the subject of the incarnation (according to Nestorius) is the man Christ,
> then suffering and dying also must be predicated of the man Christ; if the
> subject of the incarnation (according to Ephesus and Chalcedon) is not the
> man Christ (whose humanity is in fact without a human subject and who has
> his own hypostasis in the divine subject of the Logos), but God the Logos,
> then suffering and dying also must be predicated of God the Logos (ibid.,
> 524–25).

86. Ibid., 524.

87. Ibid., 530–32.

88. Wolfhart Pannenberg writes on Luther's discovery of Paul's theology of the cross:

> It is a commonplace that Christian theology is concerned with that kind of
> knowledge about God that is obtained through Jesus Christ. But it is not a
> commonplace that the cross of Jesus is the criterion for the authenticity of
> such knowledge. It was Paul who first emphasized the cross in such a way.
> And later on it was Paul's argument against the supposedly superior wisdom
> claimed by the Corinthians that Luther called upon when, in his Heidelberg
> Disputation of 1518, he praised the theology of the cross in contrast to the
> theology of glory which speculates about the nature of God on the basis of
> his work in the creation of the world (Pannenberg, "A Theology of the
> Cross," 162).

89. Luther, *Martin Luther, Selections from His Writings*, 11.

90. Ibid., 11.

91. Dillenberger, "Introduction to Martin Luther," xvii.

92. McGrath, *Luther's Theology of the Cross*, 145. *Dictata* is an abbreviation of
Dictata super Psalterium, referring to Luther's first course of lectures of the Psalter in
1513–1315. On the debate about the nature and date of Luther's theological breakthrough, see ibid., 141–47; and Dillenberger, *Martin Luther: Selections from His Writings*,
xvii–xviii. See also Lohse, *Martin Luther: An Introduction to His Life and Work*, 145.

93. McGrath, *Luther's Theology of the Cross*, 146.

94. Ibid., 146–47.

95. Ibid., 147.

96. Ibid., 25.

97. See McGrath's chapter "Headwaters of the Reformation at Wittenberg:
Studia Humanitatis, Via Moderna, Schola Augustiniana Moderna" (ibid., 27–71). See also
Oberman, *Luther. Man Between God and the Devil*, 113-150.

98. McGrath, *Luther's Theology of the Cross*, 47.

99. Ibid., 50.

100. Ibid., 53.

101. Oberman, *Luther: Man Between God and the Devil*, 120. On the difference
between the *via antiqua* and *via moderna* McGrath writes:

The distinction between the *via antiqua* and *via moderna* dated from the second half of the fourteenth century. The former is usually taken to refer to the well-established Thomist and Scotist schools, characterized by their metaphysical realism, while the latter is usually held to refer to the new philosophy associated with men such as William Ockham, Marsilius of Inghen and Gregory of Rimini, characterized by their metaphysical nominalism (McGrath, *Luther's Theology of the Cross*, 30).

102. McGrath, *Luther's Theology of the Cross*, 30.

103. Ibid., 92.

104. Ibid., 98.

105. Ibid., 178.

106. Ibid., 107.

107. Ibid., 89.

108. Ibid., 76.

109. Ibid., 133.

110. Ibid.

111. Ibid., 135.

112. Ibid., 133. McGrath maintains that Luther's concept of the alien righteousness of Christ "must be considered to lie in his holistic understanding of man. In particular, Luther argues that 'flesh' (*caro*) and 'spirit' (spiritus) are not to be regarded as man's lower and higher faculties respectively, but rather as descriptions of the whole person considered under different aspects" (ibid.).

113. Ibid., 135.

114. Ibid., 92.

115. Ibid., 141.

116. LW 31:37. In his *Disputation Against Scholastic Theology*, Luther repudiated scholasticism as a whole, together with Aristotle and reason (LW 31:9–16).

117. WA1, 353–74. An English translation in LW 31:39–70. Regarding the significance of academic disputations in Luther's time, Lohse writes: "Particularly in thinking about the early period of the Reformation and Luther's early writings, we need to be aware of the role and function of a university during the late Middle Ages and its special right to raise critical questions about the most sacred dogmas in the course of academic disputations" (Lohse, *Martin Luther: An Introduction to His Life and Work*, 121).

118. LW 31:25.

119. Harold J. Grimm writes in an introduction to his translation of Luther's *Disputation Against Scholastic Theology*:

Luther's studies soon led him to the conclusion that there was an irreconcilable conflict between his evangelical theology and scholasticism. By means of Aristotelian logic the schoolmen sought a synthesis of all things, divine and human. By means of reason they would explain their faith. In search of principles for achieving this, they studied the philosophical writings of ancient philosophers from Plato to Boethius; for them the prince of them all was Aristotle (LW 31:5).

120. LW 31:39. Wolfhart Pannenberg writes on the commonalities and differences in Paul's and Luther's understanding of *theologia crucis*, where he highlights the distinct historical contexts of their writings. See: Pannenberg, "A Theology of the Cross."

121. LW 31:40–41.

122. "*Posteriora et visibilia Dei*" (WA1:362). Here Luther refers to the story of Moses' encounter with God in Exodus 33:21–23, in which God says to Moses: "See, there is a place by me where you shall stand on the rock; and while my glory passes by I will put you in a cleft of the rock, and I will cover you with my hand until I have passed by, then I will take away my hand, and you shall see my back; but my face shall not be seen."

123. Romans 1:22. See Luther's explanation of thesis 19, LW 31:52.

124. LW 31:53.

125. McGrath, *Luther's Theology of the Cross*, 162.

126. LW 31:53.

127. Ibid., 41:164–65.

128. Solberg, *Compelling Knowledge: A Feminist Proposal for an Epistemology of the Cross*, 154.

129. Ibid., 155.

130. Ibid., 156.

131. While recognizing the boldness of Luther's program, Heiko Oberman believes its "darker aspect" should not be ignored. Oberman writes: "Exhorting the persecuted to defenseless acceptance of the cross and passive suffering can reinforce the status quo and have so conservative an effect as to obstruct change and reform" (Oberman, *Luther, Man Between God and the Devil*, 255).

132. Loewenich, *Luther's Theology of the Cross*, 12. For a brief overview on the definitions of the concept "theology of the cross" in literature on Luther's theology, see Loewenich, 169–73 n. 2.

133. Ibid., 12–13.

134. Ibid., 17–18. See also: Althaus, *The Theology of Martin Luther*, 30; and Lienhard, *Luther: Witness to Jesus Christ*, 65–66.

135. Loewenich, *Martin Luther: The Man and His Work*, 124. On the role of experience in Luther's theology of the cross, see Solberg, *Compelling Knowledge*, 82–84.

136. Siggins, *Martin Luther's Doctrine of Christ*, 86.

137. Althaus, *The Theology of Martin Luther*, 375. Luther's basic writings in opposition to Rome's understanding of the sacraments are: *The Babylonian Captivity of the Church* (1520); *The Misuse of the Mass* (1521); *Receiving Both Kinds in the Sacrament* (1522); and *The Adoration of the Sacrament* (1523). They are all printed in LW 36.

138. Althaus, *The Theology of Martin Luther*, 376.

139. The first publication of Luther's writing on this issue was in the fall of 1526. Then three sermons Luther had preached in Wittenberg the previous spring were printed under the title *The Sacrament of the Body and Blood of Christ—Against the Fanatics* (LW 36:329). On the history of the eucharistic controversy, see Oberman, *Luther: Man Between God and the Devil*, 232–45.

140. Paul Althaus writes: "The conflict about the real presence gave his Christology its final form and has dominated Lutheran theology since then. Christology and the

doctrine of the Lord's Supper have mutually conditioned each other" (Althaus, *The Theology of Martin Luther*, 398).

141. LW 38:22.

142. LW 37:195.

143. Althaus, *The Theology of Martin Luther*, 380.

144. Zwingli, who stressed the diversity of the two natures rather than the unity within the person, disagreed with Luther on this point, arguing that the finite is not able to share in the nature of the infinite (*finitum non capax infiniti*).

145. This had also been a key to his renunciation of the doctrine of transformation of the bread and wine in his controversy with Rome.

146. LW 37:85.

147. LW 37:95.

148. LW 37:218.

149. Luther maintained that the most important council was the Council of Ephesus, where the controversy about *theotokos* was the main issue. See Luther's treatise, *On the Councils and the Church*, LW 41:95. See also Lienhard, *Luther: Witness to Jesus Christ*, 310.

150. LW 37:212. Lienhard thinks Luther comes dangerously near to Monophysitism in his use of the theory of the communication of attributes. He questions the use of this particular theory and wonders how helpful such a metaphysical concept can be for explaining the biblical image of an active God (Lienhard, *Luther: Witness to Jesus Christ*, 345).

151. This is known as Luther's emphasis on God "in the flesh and never outside of the flesh" (*infra carnem et numquam extra carnem*). Zwingli, on the contrary, would argue for the idea of *extra carnem*, in which the logos, despite the union of the two natures in the person of Christ, is still to be found outside of the human flesh (*asarkos*). To Luther, this meant giving way to a theology of glory, in which God is to be known *a priori*, away from the flesh and the cross. In this context it is important to pay attention to different understandings of *flesh* and *spirit* present in Luther's and Zwingli's writings. While Zwingli and his followers understood spirit "as the opposite of flesh in the sense of bodiliness," for Luther, "spirit is the opposite of flesh in the sense of sinfulness." Hence, Christ's flesh is "spiritual" "because it comes from the Spirit, and the bodily eating is spiritual because it is done in faith in God's word" (Althaus, *The Theology of Martin Luther*, 395–96). See LW 37:237, 250, on Luther's understanding of flesh and spirit.

152. For the history of the term *idiomata*, see Siggins, *Martin Luther's Doctrine of Christ*, 238–39. The idea of the communication of attributes became one of the key concepts of Luther's Christology after 1530. See Lienhard, *Luther: Witness to Jesus Christ*, 337.

153. By *alleoisis*, Luther refers to a way of speech; when speaking of one nature of Christ, one uses the expressions that belong to the other. Sasse, *This is My Body: Luther's Contention for the Real Presence in the Sacrament of the Altar*, 120).

154. LW 37:210.

155. WA 26:342, 19. Quoted by Lienhard, *Luther: Witness to Jesus Christ*, 214–15.

156. LW 41:93.

157. Lienhard, *Luther: Witness to Jesus Christ*, 65.

158. Ibid., 61.

159. Ibid., 171.

160. On Luther's understanding of the Trinity, see Althaus, *The Theology of Martin Luther*, 199–200.

161. Ibid., 200.

162. Lienhard, *Luther: Witness to Jesus Christ*, 116.

163. Ibid., 25.

164. Ibid., 117.

165. About Luther's understanding of the sharp limits of the analogical approach, see Solberg, "All that Matters: What an Epistemology of the Cross Is Good For," 140–41.

166. Lienhard, *Luther: Witness to Jesus Christ*, 67.

167. LW 31:351.

168. Ibid., 31:361.

169. Which is indeed the thesis of George Forell's book, *Faith Active in Love*. Mary Solberg writes about the practical implications of Luther's theology: "A Christian's job is not to work for salvation, nor is it to save other—unless from injustice, suffering, loneliness, and hunger. It is to live fully, "a perfectly free lord of all, subject to none [and] . . . a perfectly dutiful servant of all, subject to all" (Solberg, "All That Matters," 153).

170. Sasse, *This Is My Body*, 270.

171. *Concordia Triglotta*, 819.

172. Ibid., 821.

173. Ibid.

174. Pelikan, *Reformation of Church and Dogma (1300–1700)*, 357.

175. Ibid., 358.

176. Ibid., 356.

177. Ibid., 356–57.

178. Lienhard, *Luther: Witness to Jesus Christ*, 339.

179. Pelikan, *Reformation of Church and Dogma*, 358.

180. *Concordia Triglotta*, 821.

181. Lienhard, *Luther: Witness to Jesus Christ*, 339.

182. Althaus, *The Theology of Martin Luther*, 194.

183. Tillich, *A History of Christian Thought*, 284.

184. Welch, *Protestant Thought in the Nineteenth Century. Vol. 1. 1799–1870*, 22–55.

185. Ibid., 30–32.

186. Ibid., 35.

187. Ibid., 52.

188. Tillich, *A History of Christian Thought*, 372–78.

189. Yerkes, *The Christology of Hegel*, 312–14.

190. Kant, *Religion within the Limits of Reason Alone*, 56.

191. Hegel, *Lectures on the Philosophy of Religion*, 417–32.

192. Ibid., 418. According to Hegel's system, incarnation is the *Vorstellung* (representation or religion) that expresses the *Begriff* (concept or philosophy), the

universal truth, that God and humans are intimately one. Further, on the incarnation, see Yerkes, *The Christology of Hegel*, 161–73.

193. On reconciliation, see Hegel, *Lectures on the Philosophy of Religion*, 452–70.

194. "God is the movement toward the finite and thereby is, as it were, the elevation (*Aufhebung*) of the finite to himself" (Yerkes, *The Christology of Hegel*, 87).

195. On Hegel's indebtedness to Luther, see Lohse, *Martin Luther: An Introduction to His Life and Work*, 214–15.

196. Hegel, *Lectures on the Philosophy of Religion*, 455–56.

197. Thus, Strauss argues for a total separation between the *Vorstellung* and the *Begriff*. Contrary to both Lessing and Strauss, Hegel argues for an ontological significance of a historical event. Hegel also differs from the followers of the Enlightenment, including Kant, by stressing the significance of Jesus as the incarnation of the idea of the God-man, instead of Jesus as the teacher of virtue.

198. Welch, *Protestant Thought in the Nineteenth Century*, 1:104. For the works of Thomasius, Dorner, and Biedermann, see Welch, *God and Incarnation in Mid-Nineteenth Century German Theology*.

199. Schleiermacher, *On Religion: Speeches to Its Cultured Despisers*, 39.

200. In his chapter on the person of Christ, Schleiermacher concludes that "ideality is the only appropriate expression for the exclusive personal dignity of Christ" (Schleiermacher, *The Christian Faith*, 379).

201. Schleiermacher reinterpreted the two-natures doctrine through Christ's perfect God-consciousness (ibid., 391–417).

202. Ibid., 397.

203. Ibid., 436. On Schleiermacher's rejection of the theory of *communicatio idiomatum*, including the capacity for suffering, see ibid., 411–13.

204. Schleiermacher wanted to get rid of all the supernatural qualities of Jesus, except his perfect God-consciousness, including the resurrection and the ascension (see ibid., 417–24).

205. See, for example, Strauss, *The Christ of Faith and the Jesus of History: A Critique of Schleiermacher's Life of Jesus*, 148.

206. Karl Barth has presented one of the sharpest critiques of Schleiermacher's theology and his influence on Protestant theology into the twentieth century. On Barth's critique of Schleiermacher, see Karl Barth, *The Theology of Schleiermacher*. See also, Duke and Streetman, *Barth and Schleiermacher: Beyond the Impasse?*

207. Tillich, *A History of Christian Thought*, 387. On the importance of Hegel's and Schleiermacher's theological writings, Paul Tillich writes: "These two thinkers, Schleiermacher and Hegel, are the points toward which all elements go and from which they then diverge, later bringing about the demand for new synthesis" (ibid., 301).

208. Welch, *Protestant Thought*, 1:6.

209. According to Albert Schweitzer, the search for the historical Jesus started with Lessing's publication of Hermann Reimarus's book *The Aims of Jesus and His Disciples* in 1778 (Schweitzer, *The Quest of the Historical Jesus: A Critical Study of Its Progress from Reimarus to Wrede*, 13–26).

210. Ibid., 10.

211. That is, the *Begriff* in the *Vorstellung*. See Welch, *Protestant Thought*, 1:148–54.

212. Strauss writes: "Jesus is to be regarded as a person, as a great—and as far as I am concerned, the greatest—personality in the series of religious geniuses, but still only a man like others . . ." (Strauss, *The Christ of Faith and the Jesus of History*, 160).

213. *The Christ of Faith and the Jesus of History* was published in 1864/65, as a reaction to the publication of Schleiermacher's *Leben Jesu*, published posthumously in 1864.

214. Strauss, *The Christ of Faith and the Jesus of History*, lviii.

215. Ibid., 169.

216. Hodgson, *The Formation of Historical Theology: A Study of Ferdinand Christian Baur*, 3.

217. Ibid., 261.

218. Baur believed that "the basic heresy of the Christian church has always been docetism in one form or another, and it is against docetism that his entire historical-critical theological program is postured." Furthermore, Baur insisted that it was "the docetism in the Christologies of Schleiermacher and Hegel which marks the focal point of the failure of these two great theologians" (Hodgson, *The Formation of Historical Theology*, 70).

219. Welch, *Protestant Thought*, 1:157.

220. Hodgson, *The Formation of Historical Theology*, 269.

221. Kähler, *The So-Called Historical Jesus and the Historic Biblical Christ*, 43.

222. Ibid., 127. In order to explain his understanding of the nature of the New Testament writings, Kähler made the distinction between the historical (*historisch*) and the historic (*geschichtlich*). He insisted that the Gospels were written as a *Geschichte* and not a *Historie*.

223. Ibid., 53–54.

224. Ibid., 95.

225. Ibid., 66.

226. Ibid., 68.

227. See for example, Weiss, *Jesus' Proclamation of the Kingdom of God* (English translation).

228. This quest was reintroduced in the so-called new quest of the historical Jesus in the second half of the twentieth century. See for example, Robinson, *A New Quest of the Historical Jesus*; and Käsemann, *Essays on New Testament Themes*.

229. Welch, *Protestant Thought*, 2:162.

230. Schweitzer, *The Quest of the Historical Jesus*, 4. "There is no historical task which so reveals a man's true self as the writing of a Life of Jesus," writes Schweitzer. And he continues:

> No vital force comes into the figure unless a man breathes into it all the hate or all the love of which he is capable. The stronger the love, or the stronger the hate, the more life-like is the figure which is produced. For hate as well as love can write a Life of Jesus, and the greatest of them are written with hate, that of Reimarus, the Wolfenbüttel Fragmentist, and that of David Friedrich Strauss (ibid.).

231. Ibid., 397.

232. Ibid., 399.

233. Welch, *God and Incarnation in Mid-Nineteenth Century German Theology*, 7. By focusing on the question of the person of Jesus Christ, they are responding to an almost exclusive focus on the work of Christ in, for example, Albrect Ritschl.

234. Ibid., 8.

235. Regarding the indebtedness of the Kenotic theologians to Luther, Lienhard writes: "In the 19th century, the Kenotic theologians such as Thomasius and Franck will appeal to Luther's thought in order to go beyond Luther, in fact far beyond him, in admitting the limitations, freely accepted, of the hypostatic union at the moment of the incarnation" (Lienhard, *Luther: Witness to Jesus Christ*, 390–91).

236. Welch, *Protestant Thought*, 1:233.

237. Welch, *God and Incarnation in Mid-Nineteenth Century German Theology*, 27.

238. Ibid., 28.

239. Welch, *Protestant Thought*, 1:238; Welch, *God and Incarnation in Mid-Nineteenth Century German Theology*, 67–70.

240. Thomasius found a scriptural base for his theory in the following description of Jesus Christ in Philippians 2: "who, though he was in the form of God, did not regard equality with God as something to be exploited, but emptied himself, taking the form of a slave, being born in human likeness. And being found in human form, he humbled himself and became obedient to the point of death—even death on a cross" (ibid., 6–8). Thomasius maintained that the author of Philippians 2 is referring to an exchange of forms of existence: from God to servant. This is an act with two moments: "the renunciation of the divine condition of glory, due him as God, and the assumption of the humanly limited and conditioned pattern of life" (*God and Incarnation in Mid-Nineteenth Century German Theology*, 53).

241. Welch, *Protestant Thought*, 1:280.

242. Welch, *God and Incarnation in Mid-Nineteenth Century German Theology*, 159.

243. Ibid., 165.

244. Ibid., 170.

245. Ibid., 209. Dorner used the doctrine of the immanent Trinity to explain the possibility of the incarnation: "It was not God in his absolute totality who became incarnate. Rather, here again the doctrine of the immanent Trinity enters to elucidate and opens the possibility which monarchianism lacks. For because God is distinguished in himself, he can maintain himself in self-impartation without self-loss, remaining in himself and also being and acting outside himself" (ibid., 215).

246. Ibid., 229. Welch writes on Dorner's idea of the God-man: "The God-man is a new creation, a higher reality, but one toward which all God's activity moves; thus it is the factual resolution of all problems of the relation of God and world. The incarnation can be shown to be necessary from the ethical being of God. Thus 'the Christ of history, the Christ of faith, and the Christ of the Idea are one'" (Welch, *Protestant Thought*, 1:281–82).

247. Welch, *God and Incarnation in Mid-Nineteenth Century German Theology*, 247.

248. Ibid.

249. Ibid., 275.

250. Ibid., 277.

251. Moltmann-Wendel and Moltmann, *Humanity in God*, 70.

252. Moltmann, *The Crucified God: The Cross of Christ as the Foundation and Criticism of Christian Theology*, 5.

253. Moltmann, *History and the Triune God: Contributions to Trinitarian Theology*, xvi.

254. Moltmann, *Jesus Christ for Today's World*, 37.

255. Moltmann, *The Crucified God*, 207. On Moltmann's trinitarian theology of the cross, see McDougall, *Pilgrimage of Love: Moltmann on the Trinity and Christian Life*, 37–58.

256. Moltmann, *History and the Triune God*, xvi.

257. Moltmann writes: "The abandonment on the cross which separates the Son from the Father is something which takes place within God himself; it is *stasis* within God—'God against God'-particularly if we are to maintain that Jesus bore witness to and lived out the truth of God" (Moltmann, *The Crucified God*, 151).

258. Ibid., 152.

259. Moltmann, *History and the Triune God*, 172.

260. Moltmann, *The Crucified God*, 230. On "the apathetic theology of the ancient world," see Moltmann, *The Future of Creation*, 67–69.

261. Moltmann maintains that "Luther's Christology of the crucified God remains within the framework of the early Church's doctrine of the two natures" but still "represents an important further development of the doctrine of the *communicatio idiomatum* and radicalizes the doctrine of the incarnation on the cross." Luther, however, argues Moltmann, "never arrived at a developed doctrine of the Trinity" (Moltmann, *The Crucified God*, 235).

262. Moltmann, "The 'Crucified God': A Trinitarian Theology of the Cross," 287.

263. Ibid., 287–88.

264. Ibid., 288.

265. Moltmann, *The Crucified God*, 222.

266. Moltmann, *The Way of Jesus Christ: Christology in Messianic Dimensions*, 53.

267. Moltmann, *The Crucified God*, 112, 160.

268. Moltmann, *The Way of Jesus Christ*, 73-78.

269. By reclaiming the historical presupposition of Christology, that is, "the messianic promise of the Old Testament, and the Jewish hope which is founded on the Hebrew Bible," Moltmann wants to reunite Christology and eschatology, which Christian theology separated early on (ibid., 1). It is then through the eschatological direction of Christology (i.e., with a Christology that points forward) that Moltmann confronts "the metaphysical 'christology from above,' and the anthropological 'christology from below'" (ibid., 3). On the inability of a Christology "from below," as well as "from above," to solve the problem of Jesus' forsakenness on the cross, see also, Moltmann, "The 'Crucified God,'" 290.

270. Ibid., *The Crucified God*, 37.

271. Ibid., 145–46.

272. Ibid., 27.

273. Ibid., 144.

274. Moltmann, *The Way of Jesus Christ*, 167. While recognizing the religious and political significance of Jesus' death, Moltmann believes that "the soteriological inclusions and the political dimensions can only be substantiated and developed when what happened on the cross solely between Jesus and his Father becomes clear to us" (Moltmann, *The Future of Creation*, 72).

275. Moltmann, "The 'Crucified God,'" 294–95. Moltmann believes he escapes the ancient heresies of patripassianism and theopaschitism by emphasizing the different modes of suffering of God the Father and God the Son (ibid., 292).

276. Ibid., 288.

277. Ibid., 295.

278. Moltmann, *The Crucified God*, 240.

279. Ibid., 207.

280. Moltmann, *History and the Triune God*, 25.

281. Moltmann, "The 'Crucified God,'" 299.

282. Moltmann, *The Crucified God*, 25.

283. Ibid., 48.

284. Ibid., 49.

285. Ibid.

286. Moltmann, *History and the Triune God*, 48.

287. Moltmann, *The Crucified God*, 51.

288. Moltmann warns against an entirely political or moralistic understanding of the following of Christ through his idea of the Lord's Supper as a "practiced theology of the cross." He writes: "A practice which corresponds to the christology of the crucified One cannot be merely ethical and political. It must be sacramental too, for it is the practice of Christ before it determines our lives. In discipleship, men and women try to become like Christ. But in his Supper, Christ is wholly there for human beings, so that through his self-surrender he may take them with him on his way into his future" (Moltmann, *The Way of Jesus Christ*, 204).

289. Moltmann, *The Crucified God*, 48.

4

The Cross of Christ

Symbol of Hope or Sign of Oppression?

Toward the end of the twentieth century, the late Catherine LaCugna made the following remark about the critical role of Christology:

> The life of Jesus Christ is at odds with the sexist theology of complementarity, the racist theology of white superiority, the clerical theology of cultic privilege, the political theology of exploitation and economic injustice, and the patriarchal theology of male dominance and control.[1]

Regardless of a strong emphasis on the social significance of the life and work of Jesus Christ in the second half of the twentieth century, christological arguments continue to be used by those in power to secure their own territory. One example is how Jesus' maleness has been made into a universal principle, which has been and still is used to question women's ability to represent Christ and correlatively to depict women as inferior human beings. Furthermore, women's sufferings have been justified by appealing to the salvific significance of their suffering. A traditional example is found in the first letter to Timothy, which reads:

> Let a woman learn in silence with full submission. I permit no woman to teach or to have authority over a man; she is to keep silent. For Adam was formed first, then Eve; and Adam was not deceived, but the woman was deceived and became a transgressor. Yet she will be saved through childbearing,

provided they continue in faith and loves and holiness, with modesty.
(1 Tim 2:11–15)

For centuries, women's suffering has been justified, based on the idea of its salvific meaning. As was the case in the teaching of the medieval church regarding the use of painkillers during labor, when, in line with God's words of punishment to Eve in the third chapter of Genesis, church leaders maintained that to use painkillers in order to reduce women's pain in childbearing would be against God's will.[2]

Despite the abuse of theological arguments in order to justify women's suffering, women have been able to experience Jesus' solidarity with them not only in their suffering but also in their fight against unjust causes of their suffering. This is why the christological question, "Who do you say I am?" receives a response with yet another dimension, when answered from the perspective of women's experience of suffering. Hence, the Christ who sided with women as "the oppressed of the oppressed" reminds us that also today the knowledge of God is to be discerned in the midst of suffering. By identifying with the suffering woman, the foreigner, the deserted, the sick, and the social outcast of our time, we are identifying with Christ among us.[3] At the same time, we are participating in God's ongoing struggle against injustice, inequality, and oppression.

The persistent critical reaction to the cross in feminist theological literature prompted Elisabeth Moltmann-Wendel to pose the question in the beginning of the nineties: "Is there a feminist theology of the cross?"[4] While I agree with the overall criticism of the abuse of the cross, I disagree with those who have come to a negative conclusion regarding the possibility of a feminist theology of the cross. I will argue that the prerequisite for a tenable feminist theology of the cross is a sharp distinction between *use* and *abuse*. To me it is absolutely clear that even if theology of the cross has been used for abusive purposes, "abuse does not abolish the use."[5] Indeed, the cross itself launches the harshest criticism of any abuse of power represented in abusive theology of the cross.

In the first chapter I explored three major issues of feminist theology: the role of women's experience, the patriarchal bias of the Christian tradition, and the sexism of our God-language. Those issues serve an important role in the feminist reconstructions of Christology presented in chapter 2. The typology of feminist christologies in the second chapter included three different responses to Jesus' question: the post-Christian perspective (Daphne Hampson), the limitation of Jesus' significance to a moral example (Carter Heyward), and the attempt at feminist reconstruction of classical christological doctrines (Elizabeth

Johnson). Unlike Daphne Hampson and Carter Heyward, Elizabeth Johnson affirms the importance of the cross in revealing God's participation in the suffering
of the world, a standpoint that makes her work particularly important for the
basic argument of this chapter. While Johnson agrees with Heyward in understanding Jesus' death as an act of violence, and a logical result of his message and
behavior, she sees the cross also as an important symbol of the *kenosis* of patriarchy. Johnson explains:

> Above all, the cross is raised as a challenge to the natural rightness
> of male dominating rule. The crucified Jesus embodies the exact
> opposite of the patriarchal ideal of the powerful man, and shows
> the steep price to be paid in the struggle for liberation. The cross
> thus stands as a poignant symbol of the "kenosis of patriarchy,"
> the self-emptying of male dominating power in favor of the new
> humanity of compassionate service and mutual empowerment. On
> this reading Jesus' maleness is prophecy announcing the end of
> patriarchy, at least as divinely ordained.[6]

Thus, by reclaiming the cross, Johnson seeks to affirm the basic intention of
classical christological doctrines, as well as the importance of the feminist
critique for such a retrieval. Significant for Johnson's approach is her focus on
practical implications. By emphasizing the practical aspect of theology, Johnson
maintains that our understanding of the triune God affects the way we think
and act.[7] The suffering God, who is "in solidarity with violated women," encourages resistance, calling for an action on behalf of the Christian community. This
is indeed a call for participation in the ongoing work of God against the forces
that "dishonor women, and indeed all human beings and living creatures."[8]
Stressing the close connection between theology and ethics, Johnson's proposal
agrees with Luther's understanding of Christians being called to be "Christ to
each other."[9] Hence, Christian praxis is understood as a continuation of the incarnation, in which God becomes truly involved in the human condition.

    In order to establish a hermeneutical tool for our understanding of the life
and death of Jesus Christ, in the third chapter, I undertook an abridged survey of
the christological tradition, focusing on the question of the divine capacity to
suffer. In this survey of what has been labeled the "thin tradition,"[10] I started out
with Paul's theology of the cross, which then led into the christological controversy of the first five centuries. Since this survey was not meant to do justice to all
periods but to highlight significant contributions, I proceeded from Chalcedon to
Luther, who revitalized the *theologia crucis* and made it a key issue in his theology.
In the last part of the third chapter, I explored the influence of Luther's cross-
centered theology on the christological discussion of the nineteenth century and

its significant comeback in the theological discussion undertaken in the shadow of Auschwitz, particularly through the writings of Jürgen Moltmann.

In light of the preceding chapters, the aim of this chapter is to explore what it means for a feminist interpretation of the person and work of Christ to focus on the cross as the locus of our knowledge of God. Hence, the question: Is the cross of Christ a symbol of hope or a sign of oppression? Attempting a feminist reconstruction of a theology of the cross, I propose a twofold purpose for this reconstruction: (1) to show the patriarchal distortion of traditional Christology and (2) to retrieve concealed dimensions in the classical interpretation of the person and work of Christ. I maintain that a theology of the cross can become an important hermeneutical tool when appropriated to unveil the distortion of patriarchal Christology. It can also help demonstrate how the cross of Christ provides an inherent critique of all abuse of power. It is important to highlight *passive* and *active* aspects of the symbol of the cross: the passive aspect demonstrated in Jesus' solidarity with women in their suffering and the active aspect as it is found in his empowering of women in their struggle for liberation. Thus, a theology of the cross becomes a theology of hope as women find meaning and strength in their discernment of Jesus, not simply as a moral example, but as a God who becomes *truly* human, fully participating in their human predicament. By all means it has to be stressed that the symbol of the cross cannot be recovered without a recognition of its *abuse*, as it has often been used to justify oppressive behavior, resulting in suffering and abuse. Recognizing the significance of a feminist critique of the abuse of the cross, I start this chapter by reflecting on the critique women of various backgrounds have placed against what they consider either an *essentially abusive* or *abused* theology of the cross. As I propose that the significance of the cross depends upon the identity of the person who is hanging on the cross—implying that Christology and soteriology are fundamentally connected—I will in the second part of this chapter focus on different responses to Jesus' question, "Who do you say I am?" In the third and last part, I present a proposal of a feminist theology of the cross. This is a theology of the cross that takes seriously the feminist critique, while it sees the center of the gospel maintained in the "message about the cross."[11]

An Essentially "Abusive" or Explicitly "Abused" Theology of the Cross?

In 1973, a year before Moltmann's book *The Crucified God: The Cross of Christ as the Foundation and Criticism of Christian Theology* was first published in English, Mary Daly launched her harsh criticism against Christianity and its "scapegoat mentality." In *Beyond God the Father: Toward a Philosophy of Women's*

Liberation, Daly accuses Christianity of idealizing, particularly for women, the qualities of the victim. Daly names qualities such as sacrificial love, passive acceptance of suffering, humility, and meekness. Because these very same qualities have been idealized in Jesus, Daly maintains that Jesus' example "reinforces the scapegoat syndrome for women." She continues:

> Given the victimized situation of the female in sexist society, these "virtues" are hardly the qualities that women should be encouraged to have. Moreover, since women cannot be "good" enough to measure up to this ideal, and since all are by sexual definition alien from the male savior, this is an impossible model. Thus doomed to failure even in emulating the Victim, women are plunged more deeply into victimization.[12]

It probably goes without saying that Daly finds absolutely no redeeming elements in the story of Christ. Daly maintains that, in addition to reinforcing the scapegoat mentality for women, by presenting Jesus as a male son of a male God, Christianity suggests the divine nature of all men. Hence, in order for women to break free from their patriarchal oppression, they also have to leave Christ and Christianity behind.[13]

Daly's denunciation of the traditional understanding of the suffering and death of Jesus made a powerful impact within the theological discourse for decades to come. Agreeing with her reading of the cross, many feminist theologians writing after Daly have rejected any salvific significance of the cross-event. Hence, the radical criticism of the cross, initiated by Daly, was to become an important theme in the writings, not only of white Western feminist theologians, but also of womanist theologians as well as female theologians from other parts of the globe. Whatever significance theologians had previously attributed to the suffering and death of Jesus, after Daly, it became more difficult to ignore abusive interpretations of the cross, past and present.

The Cross and the Spiritualizing of Suffering

The "glorification of suffering," which Mary Daly accuses Christianity of, has by some feminist theologians been seen as a primary force behind the abuse of women and children within a patriarchal society. Such is the case with a number of authors from the essay collection, *Christianity, Patriarchy, and Abuse*, for example, Joanne Carlson Brown and Rebecca Parker. In their article, titled "For God So Loved the World?" Brown and Parker denounce any theology that ascribes redemptive significance to suffering, including Jesus' suffering and death on the cross. They point out that not only does the image of the crucified Christ as the savior of the world communicate the message that "suffering is redemptive," but also it encourages self-sacrifice and total obedience to the will of the Father.[14] Therefore, they argue, through its idea of the heavenly Father sacrificing his only Son (what they label as a "divine child abuse"), patriarchal Christianity has not only justified but actually prompted the abuse of women and children.

In order to find out whether it can rightfully be argued that it is indeed contradictory to the gospel to maintain that suffering is redemptive, Brown and Parker present a survey of atonement theories within the Christian tradition, as well as some twentieth-century criticism of those theories.[15] While Brown and Parker agree with recent critique in insisting on the negative quality of suffering, they maintain that this critique falls short "of pushing the challenge to its logical conclusion."[16] A closer look at Brown and Parker's analysis of the recent critical proposals will help us understand what they mean by that.

The first example is Moltmann's fundamental distinction between human suffering and Jesus' suffering and his positive interpretation of the latter. While Brown and Parker consider Moltmann's idea of the "suffering God" to be a sign of a "theological progress," they think it does not go far enough.[17] By making a distinction between what he calls "active suffering" (i.e., chosen suffering) and acquiescence to suffering viewed as fate, Brown and Parker argue that Moltmann continues "a theology that cloaks the perpetrator of violence and calls the choice *for life* a choice *to suffer*." Therefore, they think Moltmann "fails to present a theology capable of moving beyond suffering as fate to be endured."[18]

The second critical proposal Brown and Parker discuss is presented in the works of Martin Luther King, Jr. and Archbishop Oscar Romero. This proposal presupposes the necessity of suffering and, like, for example, Abelard's moral influence theory, assumes that innocent suffering can indeed transform perpetrators of violence and consequently bring an end to unjust suffering. Brown and Parker criticize this theology for expecting innocent people to suffer in order to help the guilty ones recognize their evil doings. They think such a theology is simply wrong because it "makes victims the servants of the evildoers' salvation."[19]

The third approach resembles Brown and Parker's own proposal as it rejects any positive or redemptive aspects of human suffering.[20] An example is the work of Jon Sobrino. But unlike Brown and Parker, Sobrino claims a positive meaning of the cross of Christ, which they consider a significant shortcoming in his approach. The same they think is true for so many other Latin American liberation theologians. Brown and Parker base their criticism of Sobrino on their presupposition that the "glorification of anyone's suffering allows the glorification of all suffering." Thus, they think, the danger of focusing on the cross as the key to salvation is equivalent to making God a divine sadist and a child abuser.[21]

Another important representative of the third approach is Carter Heyward. Brown and Parker maintain that, because of her understanding of Jesus' death as both unnecessary and final, Heyward is the theologian who has made the most radical move away from traditional understanding of the cross.[22] They still think Heyward does not go far enough as she fails to acknowledge the doctrine of the atonement as the main cause for Christianity's oppressive nature. They assume it is Heyward's attempt to stay within the Christian tradition, which finally prevents her from denouncing Christianity as essentially abusive.[23]

Brown and Parker go so far as to argue that any critique that stops short of rejecting Christianity as "an abusive theology that glorifies suffering" is simply not enough. They, furthermore, insist that the future of Christianity depends on our willingness to abandon the idea of atonement, which they understand as

> this idea of a blood sin upon the whole human race which can be washed away only by the blood of the lamb. This bloodthirsty God is the God of the patriarchy who at the moment controls the whole Judeo-Christian tradition.[24]

Instead of being saved from original sin, Brown and Parker insist, human beings need to be "liberated from the oppression of racism, classism, and sexism, that is, from patriarchy."[25] In other words, they assume that all humanly made suffering and evil are caused by patriarchal abuse of power. It is certainly true that much suffering is caused by abuse of power, which can be traced to patriarchal social structures and ways of thinking. However, I think it cannot be argued convincingly that all suffering is rooted in patriarchy. Instead, I think patriarchy is a manifestation of *hubris*, which makes the self the center of the universe and has therefore elevated the self in the place of God. As such, patriarchy has, by its abuse of power, caused a lot of suffering and evil in the world.

In a more recent book, *Proverbs of Ashes: Violence, Redemptive Suffering, and the Search for What Saves Us* (2001), Rita Nakashima Brock and Rebecca Ann Parker develop further the critical evaluation of the Christian tradition that they began in their respective articles in *Christianity, Patriarchy, and Abuse* from 1990. Coauthored and autobiographically styled, Brock and Parker's book is a collection of stories, their own mixed with those of people they have known, family and friends, and those that they have encountered in their work within the church and the academy. By using personal testimony to prove the correlation between violence and the Christian faith, Brock and Parker seek to provide firsthand evidence in support of their demand for a critical reevaluation of Christianity. Brock and Parker point their fingers at the cross-event as the source of the problem, more than any other theological theme, and the main reason why they search for a "new theology," free of violence and abuse.[26]

Women in violent situations who believe they are to suffer "like Jesus" is a recurrent theme in Brock and Parker's book. Brock and Parker maintain that the church expects women to be Christ-like, by encouraging women to remain passive and helpless in violent situations. Parker offers the testimony of a woman, named Anola Reed, whose priest told her to tolerate her husband's violence because it made her Christ-like. This woman came to Parker, hoping a woman priest would understand her problem and offer assistance:

> "I haven't talked to anyone about this for a while," she began, the smile fading, and sadness deepening in her eyes. "But I'm worried for my kids now. The problem is my husband. He beats me sometimes. Mostly he is a good man. But sometimes he becomes very angry and he hits me. He knocks me down. One time he broke my arm and I had to go to the hospital. But I didn't tell them how my arm got broken."
>
> I nodded. She took a deep breath and went on. "I went to my priest twenty years ago. I've been trying to follow his advice. The priest said I should rejoice in my sufferings because they bring me closer to Jesus. He said, 'Jesus suffered because he loved us.' He said, 'If you love Jesus, accept the beatings and bear them gladly, as Jesus bore the cross.' I've tried, but I'm not sure anymore. My husband is turning on the kids now. Tell me, is what the priest told me true?"[27]

Through encounters with women in violent situations who have been told, like Anola Reed, by representatives of the church to endure their sufferings, Brock and Parker have become alarmed by what they describe as a "spiritualizing of suffering" in Christianity. They point out how suffering is frequently given a spiritual significance as God's way to "edify or purify human beings,"[28] which not only prevents people from resisting suffering but even more renders them passive and acquiescent to it.[29]

Furthermore, Brock and Parker maintain that Christianity has promoted "self-sacrificial love" as the true and higher version of love, a love that focuses exclusively on the desire of the other (agape) instead of one's own (eros). Here, too, Brock and Parker claim a strong analogy between an abusive relationship of parent to a child and how Christian tradition has interpreted the cross-event. They believe moreover that the image of God as a benevolent and almighty Father, who does not spare his own son, has helped explain away the violence exercised by earthly parents, as a just expression of love.[30]

Based on their own and others' experiences of violence and abuse, Brock and Parker demand a radical reinterpretation of the Christian message. What they think is needed is a different understanding of the person and work of Jesus Christ, in addition to a radical revision of the Christian image of God. Instead of a theology that spiritualizes suffering and supports victimization and helplessness regarding abuse, they call for a theology that empowers people "to affirm their own agency, to resist abuse, to take responsibility for ethical discernment, and to work for justice."[31] For Brock and Parker, this kind of theology is supported by a model of Jesus as "a prophet who confronted injustices and risked opposition,"[32] whose death was "an unjust act of violence that needed resolution."[33] Such a theology, they insist, does not have to cover up Jesus' death with a belief in resurrection in order to avoid facing the horror and anguish of his death. Rather, it presents an image of God who "delights in revolutionary disobedience and spirited protest."[34] Parker wonders what a difference such an image of God might have made for the woman whose husband abused and finally killed her. She writes:

> . . . [I]f Anola Reed had believed in a God who supported protest, might she have protested and resisted her husband's violence, rather than accepted and endured it? If her husband didn't regard God as the divine enforcer of obedience, would he have enforced obedience from his wife with violence. Would they have had more of a chance at life?[35]

I agree with Parker, that a different image of God could have encouraged Anola Reed to react differently to her violent husband. At the same time, I find it hard to see her husband's understanding of God "as the divine enforcer of obedience," as the cause of his violent behavior, even if it might have supported it. It is important to keep in mind that abuse of women did not originate within the Jewish-Christian tradition, and neither did the patriarchal structure of society. However, that does not undermine the fact that Judaism and Christianity have at times been highly influenced by patriarchal idealogy and power structures, which have caused extensive harm and abuse of power.

While I find the radical criticism of abusive interpretations of the cross and severe consequences of such interpretations, particularly for women and children, helpful, I nevertheless think this critique suffers from serious misrepresentations, first of all, by not differentiating between use and abuse of the cross, between abused and essentially abusive theology of the cross.

While I agree with Brock and Parker about the abuse, I think it is radically different to talk about something being abused and to argue that something is abusive in itself. Like Leanne Van Dyk, I think "misuse in abusive fashion does not make Christianity an abusive theology per se."[36] On this issue I also strongly agree with those who maintain that to "abandon the symbol because it has been misused would be once again to turn over the power of interpretation to those who have misused it."[37] This is why I think the cross can still bring hope and life, even if it has been (ab-)used for abusive purposes.

Second, I find the criticism of twentieth-century theologians' reinterpretations of classical atonement theories, presented in the writings of Brown, and Parker and Brock, misleading. It is one thing to insist on the saving significance of self-sacrifice, suffering, and death in and of themselves, but something very different to recognize that they *can* lead to something good. When Martin Luther King, Jr. encouraged his people to risk suffering and death in their fight against the injustice of racism, he recognized that fighting for justice might cost suffering and death. What King thought could justify such a suffering and death was transformation of the social situations and eventually a just society. The same is true for Archbishop Oscar Romero and other liberation theologians who have encouraged nonviolent resistance against forces of oppression.[38] While the critique of any glorification of suffering is valid and necessary, it is important to acknowledge that suffering and death can be transformed into the opposite. This is why a theology of the cross maintains that the cross of Christ has the potential to become a source of hope and life. What makes a difference here is the perspective because only afterward (*posteriori*) are we able to see the horrific instrument of suffering and death being transformed into its opposite.[39]

Third, mujerista and non-Western women have been instrumental among those who have wanted to hold on to the cross as a symbol of hope and life. Not only to critique abusive interpretations of the cross, but also to reject the cross as an abusive theological symbol in itself, is to "trivialize" the theological reflection of all those women.[40]

Jesus, the Ultimate Surrogate Figure

In her book *Sisters in the Wilderness: The Challenge of Womanist God-Talk*, womanist theologian Delores S. Williams agrees with theologians such as Brown, Brock, and Parker, about the problematic understanding of a redemptive significance of Jesus' suffering and death. African American women's experience of surrogacy (coerced or voluntary) serves as a hermeneutical key to Williams's christological interpretations. Williams explains:

> Surrogacy has been a negative force in African-American women's
> lives. It has been used by both men and women of the ruling class, as
> well as by some black men, to keep black women in the service of
> other people's needs and goals.[41]

By comparing the Christian understanding of Jesus' cross to black women's
experience of surrogacy, Williams rejects the idea of human salvation taking
place through suffering and death. Jesus, "the ultimate surrogate figure," who
stands in the place of a sinful humankind, only supports the exploitation that
surrogacy brings. Hence, based on the social context and experience of African
American women, Williams is convinced that salvation of black women cannot
depend on surrogacy of any kind. In other words, if womanist theologians are
going to take seriously black women's experience of surrogacy and oppression,
Williams maintains, they

> must show that redemption of humans can have nothing to do with any
> kind of surrogate or substitute role Jesus was reputed to have played in
> a bloody act that supposedly gained victory over sin and/or evil.[42]

While Williams sees the image of the cross as an image of degradation, a clear
indication of collective human sin, the focus of hope shifts toward the wilderness
and Jesus' act of resistance.[43] Instead of being saved by Jesus' death, Williams
believes black women's salvation

> is assured by Jesus' life of resistance and by the survival strategies he
> used to help people survive the death of identity caused by their
> exchange of inherited cultural meanings for a new identity shaped by
> the gospel ethics and world view.[44]

By understanding Jesus' life of resistance in the sociopolitical context of African
American women, Williams maintains that redemption is freed from the cross at
the same time that the cross is freed from patriarchal interpretations of Jesus'
death.[45] As redemption comes through Jesus' ministry and not through his death,
black women are reminded that their surrogacy experience is not according to
God's will.[46] Hence, without developing a comprehensive womanist Christology,
Williams promotes a functional understanding of the person and work of Christ,
guided by black women's "voices, faith and experience" rather than by christological doctrines of the past.[47]

"Making Meaning Out of Suffering"

All over the world, women's oppression is frequently associated with abusive interpretations of the cross. A significant difference is still noticeable,

as white Western women tend to focus more on women's choices to serve and suffer for the sake of others, while African American and mujerista women, as well as women in other parts of the world, are mostly concerned about women's experience of involuntary suffering and servanthood.[48] Delores Williams, for example, maintains that, despite the fact that she makes the distinction between involuntary and voluntary surrogacy (referring to their experience of surrogacy before and after emancipation), African American women are still under enormous social pressure to accept surrogacy roles. Jacquelyn Grant, another womanist theologian, argues in her article "The Sin of Servanthood: And the Deliverance of Discipleship," that the history of black women in the United States shows that African American women have been the "servants of the servants." Because service has so often turned out to be "a life of suffering for those 'relegated' to that state," the questions have been raised: "Why do black women suffer so? Or even more pointedly, why does God permit the suffering of Black women? Does God condone the fact that Black women are systematically relegated to being 'servants of servants?'"[49] Grant's response to those questions is based on her assertion that "Christ is a black woman," as well as the image of Jesus as "the divine co-sufferer."[50] Writing about Grant's understanding of the role of Jesus Christ in the lives of African American women, JoAnne Marie Terrell maintains that significant for Grant's Christology is her starting point, namely, "the Johannine christological presupposition that Jesus is God-become-human." Terrell writes:

> Among womanists, Grant consistently lifts up the image of Jesus as the "divine co-sufferer." For Grant, that Jesus Christ was born, lived, struggled, and died among the poor was an affirmation that his ultimate victory is theirs to appropriate. That "Christ came and died, no less for the woman as for the man" was an affirmation of black femininity, indicating that Christ's significance lay not in Jesus' maleness but in his humanity. For Grant, the bold declaration that "Christ is a black woman" carries a step further black theologians' assertion that "Christ is black" by radicalizing black women's conceptual apparatus for imaging God. . . .[51]

In Grant's understanding of who Jesus Christ is for African American women who suffer from a "triple oppression" of racism, classism, and sexism, we encounter a very different interpretation of Jesus' person and work from what we have seen with Williams, as well as with Brown, Parker, and Brock. While Grant is willing to consider Jesus's death—not only his life and work—bringing an important message to suffering women, the others agree with Mary Daly's negative conclusion about the hopeless model of the crucified Son of God.

For women who suffer, not only because of their race and class status, but also because of their gender, "making meaning out of suffering" can for sure function both as "a seed of liberation and an opium for oppression."[52] Virginia Fabella, a Catholic theologian from the Philippines, maintains that theologians have to take into account in their work the meaningless suffering of women, caused by the injustice of their society. She uses examples of Indian women to explain what she means by that:

> In India, the theology of sacrifice thrust upon women is of no purpose. Indian women theologians tell us that their women silently bear taunts, abuse, and even battering; they sacrifice their self-esteem for the sake of family honor, subject themselves to sex determination tests, and endure the oppressive and even fatal effects of the dowry system. A woman who is raped will invariably commit suicide rather than allow her husband and family to suffer the ignominy of living with a raped woman. While we seek in Jesus' passion, death, and resurrection a meaning for our own suffering, we cannot passively submit ourselves as women to practices that are ultimately anti-life. Only that suffering endured for the sake of one's neighbor, for the sake of the kingdom, for the sake of greater life, can be redeeming and rooted in the Paschal mystery.[53]

Fabella claims that many women suffering from injustice and oppression, find hope in Jesus the suffering servant who is with them in their own suffering, while others are encouraged by Jesus the liberator, who accompanies them in their struggle for liberation. Unfortunately, she admits, too often the understanding of Jesus held by suffering women is limited to the suffering or crucified one who understands their suffering, while the liberator remains unknown to them.

In another article, Fabella makes an important distinction between the passive and the active moments of Jesus' suffering. Contrary to the experience of "undergoing" passive suffering,

> "doing" and "accompanying" are acts of solidarity which constitute the other moment of Jesus' passion. How Jesus was able to stand his ground during his arrest and trial brings us to a consideration of his passion as an act of being in solidarity.[54]

Fabella insists that Filipino women have been able to identify with this active side of Jesus' passion, as they have resisted the consequences of unjust and oppressive powers on behalf of their suffering sisters and brothers.

A Theology of (Self-)Sacrifice

While denouncing the church's oppression and sacrifice of women, African theologian Mercy Amba Oduyoye nevertheless promotes the self-sacrificial life of women as a model for the whole church. Key to her argument is the difference between voluntary and involuntary sacrifice. Oduyoye contends that "the 'expected kenosis' of women and their compliance have enabled men to be the chief architects of history."[55] Women's *involuntary* "kenosis" differs radically from that of Christ, who *voluntarily* took on the form of a servant (Philippians 2:6–7). Thus, only a *voluntary* self-sacrifice, by men *and* women, can bring hope to the church. Oduyoye writes:

> My thesis . . . is that if the church can begin to function more effectively as an instrument of Christ it must follow the sacrificial life of the woman. Not as the sacrificed, but as the one consciously and deliberately becoming a living sacrifice, taking up the cross voluntarily. In this way it will be following its Lord who dedicated his whole life to the announcement of the kingdom by word and deed.[56]

It is clear from Oduyoye's writings that, to her, Jesus, whom she calls "Lord," is more than a human being. The identity question is truly crucial to Oduyoye's argument, as I think is indeed true for everybody thinking or talking about Christ. One's understanding of the cross has everything to do with who she believes is hanging on the cross. If the person suffering and dying on the cross is just one more exceptionally good human being sacrificing his life for a good cause, then we should be worried about the precedent he gives to women, particularly to those who, to begin with, find it difficult to claim anything for themselves. The martyr image can easily become an excuse not to stand up for oneself and resist the evil forces that threaten the well-being of women all over the world. But it is radically different when women's oppression and their fight against its causes is understood as a participation in God's work against evil.[57] Then the cross of Christ represents God's concerned and active presence in our human condition instead of a passive presence. Becoming truly human by "emptying" himself and "taking the form of a servant," Jesus Christ gives hope by identifying with those who suffer, but also by giving them courage to stand up and resist. If God's loving nature is revealed in Jesus' work and words and God is truly involved in the suffering and death of Jesus on the cross, then, despite examples of abused interpretations of the cross, theology of the cross can truly become a theology of hope for all suffering people.[58]

I will come back to Oduyoye's thesis about self-sacrifice as a model for the church after taking a closer look at the question regarding the person of Jesus Christ.

Who Is Hanging on the Cross?

In the Gospel of Mark, there is the story of Jesus asking his disciples who people said he was. After listening to their responses, Jesus turns the question to his disciples: "But you, who do you say I am?" (8:29). The Christian tradition can be understood as a collection of different responses to that very same question. For two thousand years, Christians have tried to understand the story of Jesus of Nazareth, his life, death, and resurrection, in the light of their own traditions and experiences. Jesus' contemporaries engaged in this very process of interpretation when they called him a prophet, the Messiah, the Son of God, or even Satan's disciple. The development of the Christian tradition up until the Council of Chalcedon (451) is a good example of how contemporary philosophy and worldview help shape people's interpretation of the person of Jesus Christ.

Jesus' self-understanding has been and continues to be a subject of critical, scholarly debate, as well as reflections of the ordinary believers. How did Jesus understand himself—as a prophet, the Messiah, the Son of God, the Son of Man? It is not easy to decide from the sources in the New Testament. Whether or not Jesus used those titles himself, it is clear that by the time of the writing of the Gospels, his followers did. An example is the well-known confession of Peter in the eighth chapter of Mark, as well as the less-quoted response of Martha in the Gospel of John: "I now believe that you are the Messiah, the Son of God who was to come into the world" (11:27).[59]

As noted in my analysis of Luther's theology of the cross in the previous chapter, Luther's main criticism of his contemporaries was their optimism regarding the human capability to know God through creation as well as through good works. By presenting the theology of the cross as the core of all theological discussion, Luther radically shifted the focus of theological discussion of his time. To do theology from the standpoint of the cross, as Luther did, forces us to abandon our preconceptions about God. This abandoning involves a reversal of expectations as well as a "hiddenness" in the very act of revelation; the Jesus we see on the cross sways our understanding of the Christ-event; Jesus as suffering Messiah is different from the Messiah the Jewish nation expected; Jesus as serving king is different from the traditional understanding of an authoritative figure; Jesus the man is different from the stereotypical understanding of maleness nourished by patriarchy.

A theology of the cross presents the cross as the locus of our knowledge of God, in which God is found revealed and yet paradoxically hidden in that revelation. By presenting God known through suffering and dying, a cross-centered theology reveals how the crucified and hidden God is the God whose strength lies hidden behind apparent weakness and whose wisdom lies hidden behind apparent folly. For women who have suffered from physical and/or emotional oppression, the cross can therefore become a hopeful sign, representing God's solidarity as well as freedom from all suffering and pain.[60]

God Incarnated and Crucified

The cross has remained an enigma for Christians from the time Jesus' followers witnessed the cruel death of their master and friend. The Gospels as well as other contemporary sources provide limited information about the praxis of crucifixion. What we know for sure is that crucifixion was a common criminal, as well as political, punishment during antiquity. In the Roman Empire, it was most often used for dangerous criminals and members of the lower class. Martin Hengel maintains in his book *Crucifixion* that the main reason for its use was "its allegedly supreme efficacy as a deterrent," which is why it was exercised in public, "usually associated with other forms of torture, including at least flogging." Crucifixion was an especially harsh punishment, securing a maximum humiliation of the victim, who frequently was left on the cross, "served as food for wild beasts and birds of prey."[61] For Jews, God's curse was furthermore believed to be on those who were crucified, as Paul reminds his readers in his letter to the Galatians, in which he writes, citing the book of Deuteronomy (21:23): ". . . for it is written, 'cursed is everyone who hangs on a tree'" (Galatians 3:13).[62]

There are no reasons to believe Jesus' crucifixion was any different from the crucifixion of thousands of other criminals, belonging to the lowest rank of society. Both religious and worldly leaders believed Christ to be a real threat to the peace in Jerusalem during the Passover. The fact that Christ was arrested at night, and that Pilate even bothered to crucify him, indicates that Christ had significant support among the crowd. In order for us to understand the shame and disillusion Jesus' followers were experiencing at the scene of the crucifixion, we need to take into account the terrible mode of execution the cross was back in the first century.[63]

Mel Gibson's movie *The Passion of the Christ* (2004) is a contemporary interpretation of the passion and death of Jesus Christ, with a focus on the horror and violence of Christ's crucifixion. The radical difference Gibson makes between the treatment of Christ and that of the other two crucified with him has no historical support. Gibson's depiction of Christ's suffering and pain is in many ways a classic example of what has been called a *glorification of suffering*. In his movie, violence is not only justified as being the will of God, but it is also a necessary prerequisite for the good that is expected to come out of it. In other words, violence is desirable, and suffering is valuable in itself, regardless of its historical context.[64]

This is why Gibson's movie is not necessarily any closer to being "historically accurate" than earlier Jesus films. In movies such as *The King of Kings* (1927), *Greatest Story Ever Told* (1965), and Pasolini's *The Gospel According to Matthew* (1964), we see the opposite to what is true for Gibson's movie, in which Jesus is more or less able to escape the suffering and pain that was unavoidable for the victims of this horrific method of execution.[65]

Because of the experience of the cruel use of crucifixion, the early Christians tried to avoid the sign of the cross by all means. It was only after Emperor Constantine had outlawed crucifixions in the fourth century that the cross became "the dominant cultural icon of power" instead of "a symbol of shame." And eventually "brutality of the method of execution faded from memory."[66] Moltmann describes the radical difference between the historical cross of Christ and the victorious symbol of the emperor in the following way:

> At the beginning of Christianity there are two crosses: One is a real cross, the other a symbol. One is a murderous gallows of terror and oppression, the other a dream-cross of an emperor. One is for victims of violence, the other for violent conquerors. The one is full of blood and tears, the other empty. The first stands on Golgotha, and Jesus hangs on it, the other is the victorious dream of the Emperor Constantine in the year 312 C.E. What has the second to do with the first? How could the memory of a victim of injustice and violence be changed into a symbol of victorious injustice and violence?[67]

In Paul's letter to the young church community in Corinth, we read about Christians who were tempted to shy away from the bleak picture of Golgotha. The problem of the cross has always been tightly connected with the question of God's ability to suffer. Can God remain God and still be affected by the suffering and death of Jesus on the cross? For the early Christians, the flip side of this question was whether Jesus would remain truly human if his "divinity" was in any way affected by his "human experience," including his suffering and death. The importance of the question of the immutability of God became acute in relation to the christological question of the unity of the divine and human natures in the person of Jesus Christ. If Jesus suffered only as a human being, then the relationship between Jesus, the human being, and Christ, the Son of God, became only a matter of conjunction of wills, and the reality of the incarnation became implausible.

Those who found the idea of a suffering God hard to accept had difficulties with Cyril's theory of the radical unity of the two natures, proposed against Nestorius in the fifth century. Luther's debate with Zwingli in many ways resembles the debate that took place between Cyril and Nestorius about the relationship between the human and divine nature of Jesus Christ and whether Mary was rightfully named *theotokos*. Patricia Wilson-Kastner has suggested that despite the fact that Nestorius's understanding was denounced at the Council in Ephesus in 431, eventually his interpretation, and not Cyril's, came out stronger in the Chalcedonian agreement, put together at the fourth ecumenical council in 451. Wilson-Kastner argues that dualism (a strong emphasis on the distinction between the human and the divine) and a more negative view of human nature was characteristic for Nestorius's understanding of Christ, while Cyril's emphasis on the union rested on a very positive apprehension of the human being and its intrinsic capacity to know and be like God. Hence, Wilson-Kastner maintains, "the evolution in popular piety in the West is not best explained as the prevalence of a popular Monophysitism but as the loss of Christ's humanity and the exclusive dominance of divinity." Despite some efforts being made to revive the focus on Christ's true humanity without losing his divinity, Wilson-Kastner concludes "a genuine union in the Incarnation between divine and human was seldom present in theology or devotion."[68] Luther, however, found in Cyril's theory a helpful way to understand the person and work of Christ. In Luther's theology, the radical consequences of the unity of the two natures (*communicatio idiomatum*) became apparent. Thus, Luther argued, because of the unity, it is God who is crucified and killed on the cross, but at the same time it is God who is worshiped in the human being, Jesus Christ.

Luther's theology of the cross is rooted in the idea of the finite being capable of sharing in the nature of the infinite (*finitum capax infiniti*). This particular idea is what made it possible for Luther to claim the real presence of Christ's humanity in the sacrament, as well as God's participation in Christ's suffering and death. The true meaning of incarnation was for Luther nowhere as clear as in the nativity story. Here is an example from a Christmas sermon he preached to his congregation:

> There in a stable, without man or maid, lay the Creator of all the world. And there was the maid of fifteen years bringing forth her first-born without water, fire, light, or pan, a sight for tears! What Mary and Joseph did next, nobody knows. The scholars say they

adored. They must have marveled that this Child was the Son of God. He was also a real human being. Those who say that Mary was not a real mother lose all the joy. He was a true Baby, with flesh, blood, hands and legs. He slept, cried, and did everything else that a baby does only without sin.[69]

The strong belief in the human capacity to share in the attributes of the divine is apparent in Luther's sermon, in which he draws the picture of God, being nursed and taken care of by his mother, as any other helpless infant. Luther's emphasis on the "true historicity of God's revelation"[70] shows his positive attitude to the "finite," including the body. Furthermore, his insistence on the finite being capable of sharing the nature of the infinite has the potential to support the feminist criticism of the body/spirit dualism that has dominated Western thought for centuries and has often been used as an argument in support of women's inferiority.

In Luther's Christology, the idea of the communication of the attributes (l. *communicatio idiomatum*), based on the unity of the two natures argued for in the Chalcedonian agreement, is taken to the extreme. Luther maintains that the unity of the two natures becomes apparent on the cross, where not only it is the human part of Christ that suffers but also, in the person of the Son, it really is God "who suffered, was crucified, was dead, and rose again."[71] Contemporary trinitarian theology, responding to the nineteenth-century debate regarding the relationship between the historical Jesus and the kerygmatic Christ, picks up an important aspect of Luther's argument. Trinitarian theologians emphasize the unity of the two natures by featuring "the trinitarian story of Jesus."[72] Based on the Father-Son relationship between Jesus and the "Abba-God," the focus is on the relational character of God's own self. This is particularly important for a Christology embracing a feminist perspective, as it "encourages one to focus on interrelationship as the core of divine reality, rather than on a single personal reality, almost always imagined as male."[73]

In a remarkable theological reflection on reproductive loss, the feminist theologian Serene Jones writes about her experience of searching for comfort and help dealing with her own, as well as her friend's, excruciating pain following a miscarriage. In her writing, Jones uses powerful imagery of the communitarian character of the Trinity in order to shed light on her understanding of God's compassion and care for herself and her friend in the midst of their suffering and pain. Jones ponders upon the similarities between their experiences of miscarriage and what happens to the Trinity when the Son of God dies on the cross. She writes: "There, on the cross, the

Trinity is ruptured, haemorrhaged, a blood-flow that will not stop. And in its wake, pieces of humanity's enfleshed hope lie scattered across space and time, sewerbound, muddied."[74] By thinking of what happened to God on the cross in terms of her own experience of miscarriage, Jones realized that God had been there, with her and her friend, Wendy, when they buried the remnants of the miscarried fetus in the backyard of Wendy's house. In Jones's words:

> The most haunting, troubled specter of all, however, is not just this bloodied dying but also the terrifying reality that the God who bears this death inside does not die, but lives to grieve another day. God is bereft of life and yet alive. This is the God who came to me in that dark descending vision, the God I supposedly could not fathom. There she was, in the garden, curled around Wendy, holding her. There she was.[75]

Jones's account is a striking example of how women's experience of God's loving presence in the midst of their suffering and pain can bring forth new and innovative interpretations of the cross-event.

"The Cross in Our Context"

It became the task of the leading theologians of the early church to put into dogmas what had already been articulated concerning Jesus from Nazareth in the liturgy of the church. Although there were important political reasons for the forming of the creeds at the first ecumenical councils, it is also certain that they do reflect widely accepted baptismal formulas of the church. Like the creeds of the early church, contemporary Christology needs to respond to our own particular situation in its interpretation of the person of Jesus Christ.[76]

The importance of the historical context has in fact to do with the significance of the historical conditioning of all theological discourse. In his book *The Cross in our Context* (2003), Douglas John Hall stresses the importance of the context (referring to both the time and place we live in) for the different theological disciplines, something he claims systematic theology has been slow to learn, unlike, for example, ethics and pastoral theology.[77] "Contexts alter meaning," Hall argues, therefore, it is always a "give and take" relationship between the text and the context.[78] At this point it is still important to be mindful of the human tendency to look for something comparable from our experiences when anything new (like Jesus himself) surprises and disturbs us. This is why there is an ever-present danger that the picture of Jesus Christ, which we form in accordance with our own ideas, will eventually turn out to be "less like him than like us."[79] While we search the Gospels for answers to the question of Jesus' identity, the framework for our interpretation and the language we use in our talk about Christ will always reflect our experience and our worldview. Women's experience of the abuse of the cross, discussed earlier in this chapter, reveals the patriarchal distortion of Christ, which is a good example of the need for dialogue between the Gospel stories and our experience. Thus I will argue that one of the main challenges of contemporary Christology is to allow for a critical correlation between the scriptural witness and our experience (the text and our context), between the Jesus we meet in the Gospels and our images and interpretations of him.

An important component of the *contextualization* of the Gospel stories is the question of how Jesus is best represented in our context. Here the question of Jesus' race and class is significant, as well as his gender. In the article "A Female Christ Child in the Manger and a Woman on the Cross, Or: The Historicity of the Jesus Event and the Inculturation of the Gospel," Teresa Berger challenges her reader to think about

> why we have become so accustomed to a Black Christ figure or a
> Campesino on the cross or a Chinese Holy Family as legitimate
> forms of the inculturation of the Gospel—while a female Christ child
> in the manger or a woman on the cross appear to many of us as
> incomprehensible or unacceptable.[80]

Berger maintains that while there is a general agreement on the contextualization of Jesus' race and class, the issue of gender remains a controversial one. It is true that the question of contextualization has certainly nothing to do with the historical particularities of Jesus' humanity, but rather our interpretations of the Christ-event today. Christology today has to dare to be open to the feminist critique, and its disclosure of a malebias and a one-sidedness in the more traditional interpretation of the person of Jesus Christ.

Following the example of the *Woman's Bible* in the end of the nineteenth century, feminist theologians have rightly argued that the Christian tradition has neglected the texts that talk about women, about Jesus and women, and what women have said about Jesus. Furthermore, feminist theologians maintain that Christ's liberating message of the full humanity of both women and men has been undercut by the patriarchal bias of its interpreters. Theology of the cross supports the feminist critique in disclosing patriarchal distortion of traditional Christology through the abuse of power as well as in revealing lost dimensions in the person and work of Jesus Christ. As the cross becomes the locus of our knowledge of God, we are reminded that the embracing of those who suffer is at the center of Jesus' mission and identity. In the Gospels, we see how Jesus identified with the outcast of his society: the poor, the sick, the ritually unclean, and the morally derelict. In Jesus' society, women were the "oppressed of the oppressed," carrying the "double burden of low class and low gender status."[81] By identifying with the Samaritan woman, the widow, the woman with the flow of blood, and the prostitute, Jesus revealed the true nature of the Reign of God, in which the last will be first and finally all injustice and suffering will be overcome.

In order to open up new aspects of the christological discourse, especially with regard to the significance of Jesus' historical sex, Eleanor McLaughlin, has suggested the image of Jesus as a *transvestite* or a *cross-dresser*. McLaughlin introduces this unsettling image in order to help address what she considers the most important contemporary christological topic, namely, the gender question.[82] By introducing the concept of a transvestite, McLaughlin insists she is not suggesting "that Jesus is a 'feminine' or androgynous man":

> Rather, Jesus who was and is both "historical fact" and symbol,
> a man, is like a "cross-dresser," one not "caught" by the categories. . .
> the man whose life displays "women's ways" of love, sacrifice,
> and forgiveness, but who was never enclosed by the world's
> categories. . . .[83]

In other words, McLaughlin's notion of Jesus as a transvestite, a *gender-bender*, is meant to loosen the stranglehold that Jesus' masculinity has had on our understanding of Christ.[84] The practical implications of her argument relate specifically to the theological significance that is attributed to Jesus' maleness, a key issue in the ongoing debate about women's ordination.[85] Because Jesus was not a traditional man, we need to break up the gender categories within our christological discourse. This is where the idea of a transvestite emerges. McLaughlin explains:

> Jesus is the Trickster who peels us open to new depths of humanity,
> divinity, femaleness, and maleness. There might be no telling what
> boundaries and categories could be dis-mantled as male gender
> hegemony is disrobed. That is what the Gospel is about, the piercing
> of categories in the womb/by the dart of Love. A merely male Jesus has
> been and continues to be a violation of the scandal and transgression
> that is the Gospel.[86]

McLaughlin contends that Jesus' role as a *Trickster* is to introduce new dimensions to our fixed understanding of what it means to be human, divine, female, and male. If we are fixed on a *a merely male Jesus*, McLaughlin believes we have limited the richness of the good news and therefore not remained faithful to the message brought to us through the Gospels[87]

Christa—A Crucified Woman

Since the mid-seventies, a number of images of a crucified female Christ (often referred to as *Christa*) have stimulated interesting discussions about contemporary interpretations of the passion story. At times the Christa-figures have called for strong reactions. While some have considered a female Christ-figure on the cross a powerful symbol of God's identification with suffering women today, others have thought it was nothing less than a gross misinterpretation, even a violation of the historical event as well as the symbolic meaning of the cross of Christ. Christa-figures have pushed for important discussions about the meaning of the contextualization of the Christ-event, especially the gender question. In those debates it has become clear how differently people tend to think about the issue of gender, when it comes to interpreting the story of Jesus Christ in a new (or changed) historical context, compared to other historical particularities such as race and class.[88] Without doubt Christa-figures have made significant contributions to the christological discourse during the past decades.

One of the early female Christa-figures was a bronze sculpture made by Edwina Sandys in 1974 for the *United Nations Decade for Women: Equality, Development and Peace*, from 1976 to 1985. Sandys's *Christa* "portrays a slumped female nude wearing a crown of thorns with arms outstretched depicting the cross."[89] When the sculpture was exhibited at the side of the main altar in the Episcopal Cathedral of St. John the Divine in New York City during Holy Week in April of 1984, it caused strong reactions, which eventually called for its removal from the cathedral after being there for less than two weeks.[90] Another representation of a crucified female Christ, created by Almuth Lutkenhaus-Lackey, was originally placed in the chancel of Bloor Street United Church in Toronto during Lent and Eastertide of 1979 but was later moved to the grounds of Emmanuel College in Toronto.[91] Lutkenhaus-Lackey's sculpture stimulated strong reactions, recounted in Doris Jean Dyke's book entitled, as the sculpture itself, *Crucified Woman* (1991). Still another Christa-figure was made by Margaret Argyle, and was used in "Coming Out of the Shadows: Women Against Violence," an ecumenical service celebrating the midpoint of the World Council of Churches Decade for Churches in Solidarity with Women (1988–98) at the Anglican Cathedral in Manchester, England, on 24 October 1993.[92] Argyle's Christa, entitled *Bosnian Christa*, was created as the artist's reaction to the horrible treatment of women in former Yugoslavia, when women were systematically raped and impregnated during the war in the early nineties.

Despite very strong negative reactions by some, the Christa-figures have become powerful symbols of hope and healing for many women, particularly for those who have suffered from sexual or domestic violence. Mary Grey stresses the twofold role of the crucified woman, as it not only expresses God's solidarity with women in their suffering, but also encourages them to stand up and resist the sources of their oppression. This is why it did not come as a surprise to Grey when Edwina Sandys's *Christa* was embraced by many women as a symbol of hope in the midst of their suffering. Grey explains:

> Christ as Christa liberates not by condoning the suffering of abused women, or proclaiming that there is an innate redemptive quality in it; but by being present with and sharing in the brokenness, identifying this as the priority for God's healing love, Christ gives hope, empowers and enables the process of resistance.[93]

Regardless of the original intentions of the artists, the strong connotation to the cross of Christ was unavoidable. Lutkenhaus-Lackey, for example, hesitated to lend her *Crucified Woman* to a church because she intended it merely as "a portrayal of human suffering." She eventually changed her mind when asked if she could see Christ in a Chinese man, a black man, or a woman and was "deeply touched" by all the women who told her "that for the first time they had felt close to Christ, seeing suffering expressed in a female body."[94] The *Bosnian Christa*, which was, however, intended as a religious reflection on women's suffering, helped the sculptor reevaluate her conception of the cross and its role as a religious symbol. In her own words:

> Previously I had not been able to use the cross in my work at all because I had thought it was a terribly overused symbol which had become almost meaningless to me. . . . But the cross now has a meaning for me. It's about a God who is in the world and present wherever anyone suffers. That was an enormous revelation for me. I had never associated God with women and their suffering before. . . .[95]

In the responses to the Christa-figure, one can see reactions akin to the "Trickster" effect of the "gender-bender" images introduced by Eleanor McLaughlin. The shock and the scandal of a tortured women-body hanging on the cross can truly help open up our eyes to the "symbolic power of the crucifix," while it also reminds us of the sheer cruelty of "the original event," which we so easily forget.[96] As such, the Christa-figures have been significant as they have helped instigate the much-needed feminist critique of a male-biased tradition. I am convinced that Christa-figures can continue to be important dialogue partners if we allow them to help us understand better the meaning of the cross-event in contexts dominated by forces of injustice and oppression.

A Feminist Theology of the Cross: A Proposal

The following testimony was written by a victim of domestic violence who desperately sought courage and strength from God in order to deal with the violent situation in her own home. Confronted with her husband's abuse, she suffered from anguish and feared for her own life, as well as the well-being of her two young children. She searched for a way out and wondered why God didn't hear her cry for help:

> Where was God when, one month after our wedding, my husband
> first blackened my eyes? Where was God when he punched me in the
> stomach when I was pregnant? Where was God when my husband
> threw me off a kitchen chair because I had talked to a priest? Where
> was God when he broke my nose because I wanted to see my family?
> And what did God expect of me, a wife who had vowed at the altar to
> love and cherish my husband through good times and bad?[97]

Through prayer and reading the Bible, she looked for guidance and help, but she heard no answer:

> But God was silent. For many months, I heard no answer, no clear
> path to follow. Where was the God who had promised to be with us?
> No one was with me! My only companions were my two sweet
> children, and I refused to burden them, at their tender age, with my
> inner struggle. Was it God's will that I suffer? I thought of Jesus on
> the cross; was crucifixion God's will for me? If God had not spared
> his Son, why should he spare me?

At last, she found God, in the midst of her suffering and pain:

> Then one day something happened in my thinking. I was sitting in
> prayer, meditating on Jesus hanging on the cross. Suddenly, the cross
> seemed to move! Instead of being in front of me, it shifted over to my
> side, as if Jesus was hanging on his cross *beside* me. I was crucified and
> finally knew where God was: God was hanging beside me, crucified
> also! I was not alone; God was with me in agony also. When I hurt, God
> hurt; when I was hit, God was hit; when I was bruised, God was
> bruised; when I could not bear the pain anymore, neither could God.
> Now this was *not* the God I had hoped for; I was looking for the knight-
> in-shining armor God, the God who would gallop in on a white charger,
> waving a magic wand and save me! But this rescuer-God had been
> silent; this savior-God was dead. The God I found, the God in agony, the

> God with me in my pain, became my new God. This God understood
> my predicament; this God knew what it was to be crucified.[98]

This woman's experience of God beside her in her sufferings changed her understanding of God. The God who was hanging beside her was very different from the God she had known before. She no longer felt God's silence or absence. Her experience of God's presence in her suffering transformed her life by giving her courage to resist her oppression and no longer remain a passive victim of her husband's violence. Thus, God's presence was not simply an act of passive solidarity, but an *active compassion*, which empowered her to get out of her oppressive situation.

In traditional interpretations of the cross, characteristics such as obedience, submission, self-sacrifice, and freely chosen suffering have been pervasive.[99] Women have often been encouraged to sacrifice themselves for the sake of others. They have also been encouraged to endure their suffering because of its Christ-like character. In the book *Woman-battering* (1994), Carol J. Adams talks about the role of the Christian community and its responsibility toward women who suffer abuse by their husbands. Women who are victims of domestic violence often struggle to understand their suffering in light of their faith. While clergy frequently encourage battered women to return to their abuser and offer the model of Christ's suffering, "some battered women themselves interpret their suffering as redemptive because they think they are helping their husband whom they see as suffering."[100]

In my discussion about the role of women's experience within feminist theological discourse, in the beginning of this book, there were ample examples from the long tradition of silencing women's experience, particularly their experience of oppression and abuse. Churches and other faith communities have been slow in responding to the danger many women are faced with, due to violence and abusive behavior. Initiatives by large church communities have signaled an increasing awareness of the problem. As a follow-up to *Ecumenical Decade: Churches in Solidarity with Women 1988–1998*, the World Council of Churches (WCC) decided to confront the challenge of violence directly, by establishing *Decade to Overcome Violence: Churches Seeking Reconciliation and Peace* (2001–2010).[101] While the WCC focuses on manifold expressions of violence, violence perpetrated against women and children is among their target concerns. Margot Kässmann, the bishop of Evangelical Lutheran Church in Hanover, Germany, and a member of the Central Committee of the WCC, states in the book *Overcoming Violence: The Challenge to the Churches in All Places*: "The inability of churches to deal with domestic violence is one of clearest indicator of the urgency of a *Decade to Overcome Violence* for the churches."[102]

Following the WCC's initiative, the Lutheran World Federation (LWF), in its document *Churches Say "NO" to Violence against Women: Action Plan for the Churches* from 2002, called its member churches to act on behalf of violated women. By offering this contribution to the WCC's decade against violence, LWF sought to direct the focus of the international church community to the effect violence is having on women in their home as well as in the church and the society at large. In the foreword to the document, the general secretary of LWF, Ishmael Noko, depicts violence against women as a theological problem and not simply a social one. Noko writes: "When those who are victimized suffer, so does God. Let us work together to overcome all forms of violence that are an offense against God and humanity."[103]

It is absolutely necessary that church communities as well as theologians within academic settings make serious attempts to address people in their suffering situations.[104] It is particularly important that they respond to women's experience of suffering related to domestic or sexual violence, not only because it has been silenced for so long, but also because it has often been justified on theological grounds. I agree with those who maintain that "the abuse does not abolish the use."[105] I also believe a theology of the cross provides an important tool for those who want to be able to talk about God in the context of women's suffering and pain.[106] Therefore, I will argue for a feminist version of a theology of the cross, which agrees with the basic presumption that God is deeply affected by Jesus' suffering and death, along with all human suffering and death. Such a theology of the cross presupposes the incarnation of God, as the cross cannot be understood outside the context of Jesus' life and resurrection. Only if the one hanging on the cross is God incarnated (is God among us), and not just another martyr sacrificing his life for a good cause, can the cross of Christ bring hope into hopeless situations. But the story cannot end at Golgotha. Good Friday without Easter Sunday truly supports a theology without the cross. Only in light of the resurrection is the tragic story of the victory of evil and death turned upside down. Like the disciples who fled the dreadful site at Golgotha, whoever comes to the cross without knowing the story of Easter loses hope or will be convinced of the meaninglessness of this cruel death. By all means it should be avoided that the resurrection becomes an appendix to the theology of the cross (as is the case, for example, in Gibson's *The Passion of the Christ*). The cross and the resurrection have to be understood in light of each other.[107] Without the resurrection, death has the final victory. Hence, without Easter, the story of Jesus becomes a story of a good person who dedicated his life to the elimination of suffering and evil but, like many other good people, ended up defeated by the powers against which he spent his life in struggle. Seen together with the resurrection, the cross becomes a testimony to God's true identification with the human condition, including suffering and death, while the resurrection shows us that there is more to the cross than God's solidarity with the suffering and the oppressed. From the perspective of the resurrection (*a posteriori* perspective), we see God vindicating the life and death of Christ by turning evil into good, by transforming death into life. It is indeed God's identification (the *passive* aspect of the cross), together with God's active transformation of suffering and death (the *active* aspect of the cross), that sustains a feminist theology of the cross. While the passive aspect of the cross reassures women of God's presence in the midst of their suffering, the active aspect of the cross gives them courage to stand up and resist. It also gives them hope of liberation from their suffering, when God, who sustains them, eventually transforms their suffering and eliminates the forces of evil.

It is important that women in violent situations are *heard into speech* and their experience of God's presence in those situations is taken seriously. This is why we need to listen to women—like the battered woman in the story earlier in this chapter—who have experienced God's solidarity as well as active compassion, that is, courage and strength to stand up and resist in the middle of their suffering. In an interesting study of battered women living in a shelter, Carol L. Winkelmann offers a rhetorical analysis of survivors' personal theologies. Winkelmann maintains that faith in God, particularly a "suffering God," plays an important role for battered women, regardless of race and class, as they find hope in God, who not only helps them cope with their suffering, but also gives them what it takes to get out of their abusive situations. Responding to the prevalent criticism of feminist theologians toward the cross, Winkelmann argues that feminist theologians need to take the experience of battered women seriously, not only by listening to them, but also by giving them voice.[108] In line with Winkelmann, I think women's experience of abuse helps us understand that even if the cross has been abused, it does not mean that all theological interpretations of the cross are abusive. It is indeed fundamentally different to state that theology is abusive in essence and to assert that a theology is used for abusive purposes. In other words, there is a basic difference between the abuse of a theology of the cross in order to justify or excuse abusive behavior and the claim that every theological interpretation that gives positive meaning to the cross has to be guilty of justifying and/or excusing violent and abusive treatment of, for example, women and children. In addition to this distinction between *abuse of* and *abusive* theology of the cross, we need to learn to differentiate between *abusive* and *useful* interpretations of the cross. When it comes to the second distinction, the feminist critique of the patriarchal bias of scripture and the Christian tradition

(introduced in chapter 1) helps us recognize the significant role of the hermeneutic of suspicion.

The Problem with Imitatio Christi

The concepts of (self-)sacrifice and servanthood have been prevalent in traditional understanding of the Christian life, while they have been frequently
used to justify women's suppression.[109] In an article on the possibility of an
imitation of Christ in the twentieth century, Margaret R. Miles points out a
real difference in the way women and men have been encouraged to imitate
Christ in the past. Miles claims that women have been "consistently directed
to emulate, not Christ's qualities of intransient self-possession, but his obedience, gentleness, and compassion for others."[110] In line with Valerie Saiv-
ing's and Judith Plaskow's critique of traditional understanding of sin,[111]
Miles argues that as long as imitation of Christ is understood as self-sacrificial
concern for others, it remains a highly problematic model for women. Miles
still thinks imitation of Christ can possibly be "a useful corrective for men,
socialized to vigorous competition in societies that encourage male
aggression."[112] Hence, she maintains, in order for women to find the imitation of Christ helpful,

> it has to be on the basis of the characteristics of Christ's life that
> confront and challenge women's social conditioning rather than
> those that sustain and reinforce it. Christ's anger at injustice, Christ's
> practices of self-remembering and centering, Christ's rejection of the
> social-role expectations of his day, and the creativity with which
> Christ met difficult situations and answered awkward questions
> about himself and his ministry; any or all of these could be useful to
> women in the twentieth century.[113]

This criticism of the precarious interpretation of self-sacrifice and servanthood,
and its common exclusive assignment to women, is indeed essential for a feminist retrieval of the cross. The fact that the cross of Christ has been used to justify, or even glorify, suffering as a consequence of self-sacrifice, obedience, and
passive submission to any form of abusive behavior should never be forgotten.[114] Given the experience of abusive interpretations of the cross, it is obvious
how ambiguous Mercy Amba Oduyoye's use of self-sacrifice as a model for the
church—introduced earlier in this chapter—can be. Absolutely crucial for
Oduyoye's model is her distinction between voluntary and involuntary sacrifice,
a distinction that is, by the way, not always so clear, as Delores Williams points
out in the case of African American women.

It is certainly true that "love understood as self-sacrifice can lead women to abdicate their public responsibility to use their God-given gifts on behalf of the greater community and for the common good."[115] Nevertheless, history is full of examples of women who have not hesitated to participate in active resistance to injustice even if it has caused them suffering and pain.[116] Borrowing Kathryn Tanner's definition of the modern idea of sacrifice as being primarily a "non-cultic act involving self-renunciation for others,"[117] I agree with those who think self-sacrifice on behalf of women can be good, and even necessary at times.[118] Motherhood is an important example. In a recent article, in which she suggests the idea of *maternal sacrifice* as a "hermeneutic of the cross," Mary J. Streufert argues that even if "maternal" does not ordinarily mean "mortal sacrifice," as it used to, "women who choose to be mothers are nevertheless actively sacrificing."[119] Streufert maintains that women are indeed active, and not passive, in the "drama" of motherhood and quotes the feminist scholar Catherine MacKinnon to support her argument. MacKinnon makes an important explication on the contemporary understanding of motherhood, as she writes: "To treat motherhood as something that just happens denies a woman's participation in conception, her decision to carry a child to term, her nurturing and sacrifice for months, and the labor of birthing."[120] Even if McKinnon focuses on the experience of pregnancy and birth, it should go without saying that the idea of motherhood as active "maternal sacrifice" qualifies for the experience of child-rearing as well.

Fully recognizing the experience of both harmful and helpful use of the idea of self-sacrifice for women, Brita Gill-Austern has suggested a helpful distinction between *self-sacrifice* and *self-giving*. She writes:

> A complex web of social forces compels women to sacrifice themselves in ways that can do great damage to their lives and the lives of the people they touch. Nevertheless, women need to resist the increasingly wide-spread tendency to condemn all forms of self-giving. Self-sacrifice is not pernicious by definition; it is not always a manifestation of codependency. Self-sacrifice can be an essential element of authentic, faithful love—the self-fulfilling self-transcendence to which Jesus calls us.[121]

I think Gill-Austern is right when she argues that even if self-sacrifice has often turned out to be harmful to women, it does not mean it necessarily has to be so. It is not only unrealistic to think that we can do away with self-sacrificing, in the sense of self-*giving*, behavior, but also, and more important, not desirable. But only if the person has the freedom to decide for oneself. I agree with JoAnne Marie Terrell when she claims that self-sacrifice can become a meaningful and constructive deed only when the subject is free to choose. Terrell explains: "Sacrifice understood as the surrender or destruction of something prized or desirable for the sake of something considered as having a higher or more pressing claim is not genuinely that unless it involves one's own agency. . . ."[122]

The issue of agency cannot be stressed enough, as it makes the difference between a forced and self-chosen act of sacrifice. To use an example from film, I maintain that in Tim Robbins's film *Dead Man Walking*, Sister Helen

> becomes an *imitatio Christi* by using her skills and means, to bring out the best in other people without destroying herself. By serving as the mediator of God's transforming love, Sister Helen becomes, in Luther's words, *a Christ* to her neighbor. This female figure is a powerful agent, who is willing, but also has the freedom to choose to go the extra mile in order to actualize her calling.[123]

On the contrary, Bess, in Lars von Trier's *Breaking the Waves*, lacks agency as she "symbolizes and reinforces the stereotypical understanding of a woman, who finds meaning in life through fulfilling the needs and desires of others, regardless of the consequences to herself."[124]

What to Make of Suffering?

Closely connected to the differentiation between voluntary and involuntary (self-)sacrifice is the distinction of voluntary and involuntary suffering. Marie Fortune has made, what I consider, a valuable distinction between a *voluntary* and *involuntary suffering*, in which she defines voluntary suffering as "a painful experience which a person chooses in order to accomplish a greater good. It is optional and is a part of a particular strategy toward a particular end."[125] For voluntary suffering, Fortune uses examples of the acts of civil disobedience by civil rights workers in the United States in the 1960s, which resulted in "police brutality, imprisonment, and sometimes death" for the activists.[126] What distinguishes voluntary suffering from involuntary suffering is that the latter one is "not chosen and never serves a greater good." Characteristic for sexual and domestic violence, involuntary suffering "is inflicted by a person(s) upon another against their will and results only in pain and destruction."[127]

When it comes to interpreting the meaning and role of suffering, it is absolutely crucial to refrain from the understanding of suffering being good and desirable in itself. Within the Christian tradition, the image of the suffering servant has been a powerful one and "has reinforced for some, the belief that suffering is good per se, rather than what happens when love is committed at all costs."[128] Thus, by choosing the suffering servant as a hermeneutical key for his interpretation of the cross, Mel Gibson, in his movie *The Passion of the Christ*, follows a long and widely accepted tradition of interpreting Christ's passion in light of this powerful figure from Deutero-Isaiah.[129] The critical question is what kind of message such interpretation sends women, who have usually been the ones playing the role of the suffering servant in family and society at large?[130]

Gibson sees the amount of Christ's suffering as a clear sign of Christ's love, namely, "more pain, more gain."[131] This interpretation of Christ's passion can be seen as a classic example of a *glorification of suffering*, in which violence is not only justified as being the will of God but it is also a necessary prerequisite for the good that is expected to come out of it. In other words, violence is desirable, and suffering is valuable in itself, regardless. This interpretation of the passion story certainly raises questions in the beginning of the twenty-first century, during which violence is increasingly evaluated according to its entertaining qualities as well as marketing values. I think Gibson's movie prods very important questions about our understanding of Christ's death on the cross and the role of violence, suffering, sacrifice, obedience, and submission to authorities within a context of violence, abuse, and oppression.[132] But we also have to ask about the underlying image of God. In other words, what does Gibson's interpretation of violence and unjustifiable suffering and pain tell us about God? Whether it regards questions of Christ's suffering and death, or our understanding of God, I think Gibson's interpretation of the passion story helps us understand the important relationship between theory and practice. In other words, we should never disregard the practical implications of our theological interpretations.

In the article "The Transformation of Suffering," Marie Fortune claims that a victim of personal violence, such as domestic and sexual violence, has two options to choose from. The victim can either choose to endure and accept continued suffering, meaning to remain a *victim*, or seek for the transformation of one's suffering, thus becoming a *survivor*.[133] In the story about the woman who looked for help from God in order to survive the violent treatment she suffered from her husband, we see an example of somebody who was transformed from a victim into a survivor. What made the difference for her was when she realized that God was right there, suffering with her? Her experience of God's presence helped her not only endure her situation but also become a survivor.

God's Compassion

What the woman in the story in the beginning of this chapter experienced was "divine compassion" (l. *com-passio*), God suffering with her. Responding to basic questions of theodicy, Wendy Farley has suggested that instead of interpreting the power of God as dominion or coercion, we should understand *God's power as compassion*. Farley insists that even if this is "a different *kind* of power,"[134] it is still a real power, "the kind of power that God exercises toward the world," and not simply a feeling or mood. Farley explains:

> The power of compassion is the most real thing in the world, the signature of ultimate reality, and the name that truth bears in its active aspect. If we understand this—not in our heads but in our very bones—we will talk about God differently, interpret our scriptures differently, and relate to victims and perpetrators of violence differently. Compassion vitiates neat divisions between theory and practice, transforming theology into a practice of compassion even as it demands that all practice be rooted in the wisdom that discerns compassion as the signature of reality.[135]

By interpreting power as compassion (as a form of love), Farley attempts to resolve the conflict between God's power and love. In the midst of suffering, the presence of God as compassion makes the difference between the dehumanizing effects of what Farley calls *radical suffering* and the restoring to wholeness of the broken human being.[136]

In her earlier writings, Farley appeals to her understanding of the cross of Christ, without working out a full-fledged feminist theology of the cross.[137] For Farley, the cross of Christ is an example of radical evil, but it also represents "the incarnation of divine compassion in the midst of rupture."[138] Hence, the stories of Jesus' birth and crucifixion "tell us something deeply important about who God is and where God chooses to appear," as it is

> in those places furthest from prosperity, fullness, beauty, honor, and power that Christians have had God revealed most distinctively to them. God, source of all reality, split the heavens to come to us in a cow shed so that God could be *with* us. And, as if the ridiculousness of being born in a manger weren't enough, God dies on a cross—as loathsome, humiliating, cruel, and helpless a death as imaginable—just in case we didn't get it. . . .[139]

By presenting the cross as the locus where God's presence amongst those who suffer is revealed in a special way, Farley affirms the importance of the cross in revealing God's participation in the suffering of the world.

Building explicitly on Farley's theology of divine compassion, Elizabeth Johnson describes God's active solidarity with those who suffer as an expression of God's "compassion poured out."[140] Key to her understanding of a "suffering God" is her discarding of the classical idea of God's impassibility, which she thinks is both "morally intolerable"[141] and "not seriously imaginable."[142] At the same time Johnson warns against assuming that God suffers because God cannot do otherwise.[143] To affirm God's ability to suffer, one has to imply the notion that God, out of freedom of love, chooses to suffer with suffering people. Such a God is "the compassionate God," a God who helps by "awakening consolation, responsible human action, and hope against hope in the world marked by radical suffering and evil."[144]

Critical to Johnson's feminist interpretation of the cross of Christ, as well as her development of the symbol of a suffering God, is to renounce any view of redemption suggesting that God required Jesus' death as a payment for sin. Johnson thinks such an idea is today "virtually inseparable from an underlying image of God as an angry, bloodthirsty, violent and sadistic father, reflecting the very worst kind of male behavior." Instead of signifying a payment required for human sinfulness, Johnson insists that Jesus' death was an "act of violence" and a result of his message and behavior, a sign of God's identification with human beings in the midst of their suffering and pain.[145] Borrowing a range of metaphors drawn from women's experience, Johnson skillfully redresses a theology of the cross in feminist terms as the cross becomes a part of "the larger mystery of pain-to-life, of that struggle for the new creation evocative of the rhythm of pregnancy, delivery, and birth so familiar to women of all times."[146] The belief in the risen Christ appears consequently as the expression of "the victory of love, both human and divine, that spins new life out of this disaster."[147] While the resurrection cannot be humanly imagined, in faith, it means that evil does not have the last word. In the resurrection, Sophia-God collects her child and prophet into new transformed life, a future for all God's creation. Here, Johnson encounters the feminist vision of wholeness, "of the preservation of the bodily integrity of each, even the most violated, and the interconnectedness of the whole—at the very core of the Christian message."[148]

Going back to Oduyoye's thesis about Jesus' example of a voluntary self-sacrifice, I still think voluntary self-sacrifice can become a helpful goal for the Christian church. But before we can promote it as a model for the church, we need to take into account critical reinterpretations of the concept of self-sacrifice. Furthermore, the model of self-sacrifice should always be presented together with other models, such as the one of resistance, which for many reasons might for now be more important for women and other marginalized people who have never had the freedom to choose to live their life in service to others.

The womanist theologian Katie Cannon reinforces the importance of the context when it comes to any talk about self-sacrifice and suffering. Cannon reminds us how radically different it is to talk about accepting suffering and making sacrifices for a principle when one is in a position to choose to suffer, as opposed to "the masses of Black people" for whom "suffering is the normal state of affairs."[149] Still, black people and other marginalized people have been willing to stand up and resist, even if it might cause them suffering. By participating in nonviolent resistance, when suffering is inevitable, people have expressed "willingness to take it on oneself rather than to inflict it on others; not retaliating to violence with violence."[150] There are numerous examples of such a resistance, for example, from the civil rights movement under the leadership of Martin Luther King, Jr. and from El Salvador under the leadership of Archishop Oscar Romero. Another example of such resistance are the mothers of Plaza de Mayo in Argentina. A group of women in 1977 started marching silently for thirty minutes every Thursday afternoon on a large public square in front of the presidential palace, in the heart of Buenos Aires, requesting fair trials for their children who disappeared during a military dictatorship, which ended in 1983.[151] What started out as a small group of fourteen mothers became an internationally recognized movement, which still works to expose what happened to the estimated thirty thousand missing children and grandchildren. Some of the women disappeared themselves as a result of their resistance. But the mothers and grandmothers kept on. Since the year 2000, they have seen more trials being held and some of the perpetrators being convicted. And their search for justice goes on.[152]

NOTES

1. LaCugna, "God in Communion with Us," 99.

2. Ramshaw, *Treasures Old and New: Images in the Lectionary*, 128.

3. Matthew 25:31–46.

4. Moltmann-Wendel, "Is There a Feminist Theology of the Cross?" 87.

5. Westhelle, *The Scandalous God: The Use and Abuse of the Cross*, 147.

6. Johnson, *She Who Is: The Mystery of God in Feminist Theological Discourse*, 160–61.

7. "The symbol of God functions" (ibid., 4).

8. Ibid., 271.

9. LW 31:368. On Luther's social ethics, Forell writes: "Unlike a medieval mystic or a saintly hermit, who enjoys his personal relationship to God and cares little if the world about him perishes, Luther's entire life was social action, i.e., a conscious attempt to influence the society of which he was a part and the orders or organisms which in his opinion made up this society" (Forell, *Faith Active in Love: An Investigation of the Principles Underlying Luther's Social Ethics*, 12–13).

10. See, for example, Hall, *Lighten Our Darkness: Toward an Indigenous Theology of the Cross*, 115.

11. 1 Corinthians 1:18.

12. Daly, *Beyond God the Father: Toward a Philosophy of Women's Liberation*, 77.

13. Daly writes: "As a uniquely masculine image and language for divinity loses credibility, so also the idea of a single divine incarnation in a human being of the male sex may give way in the religious consciousness to an increased awareness of the power of Being in all persons" (ibid., 71).

14. Brown and Parker, "For God So Loved the World?" 2.

15. Ibid., 4–26.

16. Ibid., 14.

17. Ibid.

18. Ibid., 19. Moltmann responds to this critique—he maintains originally came from Dorothee Soelle—in his autobiography, *A Broad Place: An Autobiography*, 198–200, and also in his article "The Crucified God: Yesterday and Today: 1972–2002," 136–37.

19. Brown and Parker, "For God So Loved the World?" 20.

20. Ibid., 21.

21. Ibid., 23.

22. Ibid., 25.

23. Ibid., 26.

24. Ibid., 27.

25. Ibid.

26. Brock and Parker, *Proverbs of Ashes: Violence, Redemptive Suffering, and the Search for What Saves Us*, 8.

27. Ibid., 20–21.

28. Ibid., 44.

29. Ibid., 157–58.

30. Ibid., 30–31. As an example, Parker maintains that the relationship between the Father and the Son, Moltmann describes in his book, *The Crucified God*, is an abusive relationship (ibid., 198).

31. Ibid., 156.

32. Ibid., 31.

33. Ibid., 60.

34. Ibid., 31.

35. Ibid.

36. Weaver, *The Nonviolent Atonement*, 184.

37. Osick, *Beyond Anger: On Being a Feminist in the Church*, 65.

38. See Kässmann on nonviolent resistance, *Overcoming Violence: The Challenge to the Churches in All Places*, 57–71.

39. On Moltmann's response to the critique of Dorothee Sölle and others of his image of a "sadistic God," see Moltmann, *A Broad Place*, 198–200.

40. On this issue, see for example, Bond, *Trouble with Jesus: Women, Christology, and Preaching*, 136 and Ray, *Deceiving the Devil: Atonement, Abuse, and Ransom*, 71–72.

41. Williams, *Sisters in the Wilderness: The Challenge of Womanist God-Talk*, 81.

42. Ibid., 165.

43. Ibid., 166.

44. Ibid., 164.

45. Ibid.

46. Ibid., 167.

47. Ibid., 203. Another womanist christological interpretation is presented by Kelly Brown Douglas in her book *The Black Christ* (1994).

48. See Williams, *Sisters in the Wilderness*, chapter 3, "Social-Role Surrogacy: Naming Black Women's Oppression," 60–83.

49. Grant, "The Sin of Servanthood: And the Deliverance of Discipleship," 200.

50. Grant, "Come to My Help, Lord, for I'm in Trouble," 67.

51. Terrell, "Our Mothers' Gardens: Rethinking Sacrifice," 43.

52. Chung, *Struggle to Be the Sun Again*, 54.

53. Fabella, "Christology from an Asian Woman's Perspective," 7–8.

54. Fabella, "Asian Women and Christology," 15.

55. Oduyoye, "Churchwomen and the Church's Mission," 74.

56. Ibid., 79.

57. Fabella and Park, *We Dare to Dream: Doing Theology as Asian Women*, 7–8.

58. Thornton, *Broken Yet Beloved: A Pastoral Theology of the Cross*, 19–20.

59. See an interesting "Bible study" on "Peter's confession and Martha's confession," written by Moltmann-Wendel and Moltmann, in their book, *God—His Hers*, 39–56.

60. See ibid., 91; Suchocki, *God, Christ, Church: A Practical Guide to Process Theology*, 103–11; and Carr, *Transforming Grace: Christian Tradition and Women's Experience*, 153.

61. Hengel, *Crucifixion*, 86–88.

62. On the sign of the cross in the Old Testament, see Ramshaw, *Treasures Old and New*, 122.

63. Ibid., 124.

64. Guðmundsdóttir, "More Pain, More Gain! On Mel Gibson's Film, *The Passion of the Christ*," 128–29.

65. Ibid., 127.

66. Ramshaw, *Treasures Old and New*, 124.

67. Moltmann, "The Cross as Military Symbol for Sacrifice," 259.

68. Wilson-Kastner, *Faith, Feminism and the Christ*, 83–84. This is all the more interesting since Wilson-Kastner herself has been accused, by other feminist theologians, of sacrificing Jesus' humanity for the idea of a cosmic Christ. See Hampson, *Theology and Feminism*, 59–62; and Brock, *Journeys by Heart: A Christology of Erotic Power*, 58–61.

69. Luther, *The Martin Luther Christmas Book*, 39.

70. Althaus, *The Theology of Martin Luther*, 397.

71. LW 38:254.

72. Moltmann-Wendel and Moltmann, *Humanity in God*, 70.

73. Wilson-Kaster, *Faith, Feminism, and the Christ*, 122. See also LaCugna, "Baptism, Feminists, and Trinitarian Theology," 65.

74. Jones, "Rupture," 62–63.

75. Ibid., 63.

76. About the contextual conditioning of the Chalcedonian agreement, see: Hall *The Cross in our Context: Jesus and the Suffering World*, 125. For interesting examples of the contextualization of Christ by artists in the twentieth century, see *Christ for All People: Celebrating a World of Christian Art*, edited by Ron O'Grady. In this book, Christ's identification with people of various racial and cultural background is expressed by portraying Christ as black or oriental, in places as different as the southern shores of Lake Victoria or downtown Chicago. Still the question of sex is not raised in the artwork chosen for this book, as Christ is portrayed as male in every single one.

77. Hall, *The Cross in our Context*, 45.

78. Ibid., 59, 65.

79. Moltmann-Wendel and Moltmann, *God—His & Hers*, 42. This is indeed in accordance with Albert Schweitzer's conclusion in his classical work, *The Quest for the Historical Jesus*.

80. Berger, "A Female Christ Child in the Manger and a Woman on the Cross, Or: The Historicity of the Jesus Event and the Inculturation of the Gospel," 33.

81. Ruether, *Sexism and God-Talk: Toward a Feminist Theology*, 136–37.

82. McLaughlin contends: "Today, in the church and in the culture, it is not the divine/human dichotomy but gender which is the paradigm of crisis" (McLaughlin, "Feminist Christologies: Re-Dressing the Tradition," 142).

83. Ibid., 141–42.

84. The Danish director Carl Theodor Dreyer introduces a most interesting representation of a female Christ-figure, who is also a transvestite, in his film about the passion of Joan of Arc (1928) See Guðmundsdóttir, "Female Christ-figures in Films: A Feminist Critical Analysis of *Breaking the Waves* and *Dead Man Walking*," 31.

85. See, for example, *Ordinatio Sacerdotalis. Apostolic Letter on Reserving Priestly Ordination to Men Alone*, by Pope John Paul II, from 22 May 1994.

86. McLaughlin, "Feminist Christologies," 142.

87. On Female Christ-figures in films and how they can contribute to the discourse about Christ's identity and about women's ability to represent Christ, see Guðmundsdóttir, "Female Christ-figures in Films."

88. It is interesting to note that the literal meaning of the latin noun *traditio* is "that which has been handed down or over" or "the act of handing down or over" (McGrath, *Christian Theology: An Introduction*, 14).

89. Clague, "The Christa: Symbolizing My Humanity and My Pain," 84–85. See also http://www.yorku.ca/finearts/news/edwinasandys.htm and http://www.time.com/time/magazine/article/0,9171,954312,00.html.

90. Clague, "The Christa," 87.

91. Ibid., 87–90.

92. Ibid., 95.

93. Quoted by Clague, in ibid., 106.

94. Dyke, *Crucified Woman*, 3.

95. Clague, "The Christa," 97.

96. Ibid., 107.

97. Lee, "Witness to Christ, Witness to Pain: One Woman's Journey through Wife Battering," 11.

98. Ibid., 14–15.

99. We see this, for example, in the classical theories of Anselm and Abelard from the eleventh century. Interesting *reevalutions* of these theories are found in Ray, *Deceiving the Devil*; and Weaver, *The Nonviolent Atonement*.

100. Adams, *Woman-battering*, 108.

101. See http://overcomingviolence.org/.

102. Kässmann, *Overcoming Violence*, 45.

103. *Churches Say "No" to Violence against Women: Action Plan for the Churches*, 5.

104. An important example is Gutiérrez's book *On Job: God-Talk and the Suffering of the Innocent*.

105. Westhelle, *The Scandalous God*, 147.

106. See also Ray, *Deceiving the Devil*, 83.

107. See, for example, Thornton, *Broken yet Beloved*, 14–15.

108. Winkelmann, *The Language of Battered Women: A Rhetorical Analysis of Personal Theologies*, 139–41.

109. Farley, "New Patterns of Relationship: Beginnings of a Moral Revolution," 58.

110. Miles, "Imitation of Christ: Is It Possible in the Twentieth Century?," 20.

111. See chapter 1 in this book, on the role and meaning of experience.

112. Miles, "Imitation of Christ: Is It Possible in the Twentieth Century?" 20.

113. Ibid., 20–21.

114. Copeland, "The Wounds of Jesus, the Wounds of My People," 35.

115. Gill-Austern, "Love Understood as Self-Sacrifice and Self-Denial: What Does It Do to Women?" 313.

116. Johnson, *She Who Is*, 256.

117. Tanner, "Incarnation, Cross, and Sacrifice: A Feminist-Inspired Reappraisal," 50.

118. Ray, *Deceiving the Devil*, 60.

119. Streufert, "Maternal Sacrifice as a Hermeneutics of the Cross," 72.

120. Quoted by Streufert, in ibid., 72.

121. Gill-Austern, "Love Understood as Self-Sacrifice and Self-Denial," 315. See also Ramsey, "Preaching to Survivors of Child Sexual Abuse," who writes: "Sacrificial love voluntarily chosen for a period of time is put in its proper place as a means toward restoring mutual love and care . . ." (68).

122. Terrell, "Our Mothers' Gardens," 45.

123. Guðmundsdóttir, "Female Christ-figures in Films," 38.

124. Ibid.

125. Fortune, "The Transformation of Suffering: A Biblical and Theological Perspective," 87.

126. Ibid., 87.

127. Ibid., 87–88.

128. Gil-Austern, "Love Understood as Self-Sacrifice and Self-Denial," 308.

129. The citation that appears on the screen at the beginning of Gibson's movie is taken from the fifty-third chapter of the book of Isaiah, verse five, which reads like the following in its full length: "But he was wounded for our transgressions, crushed for our iniquities; upon him was the punishment that made us whole, and by his bruises we are healed" (Guðmundsdóttir, "More Pain, More Gain!" 128).

130. Gill-Austern, "Love Understood as Self-Sacrifice and Self-Denial," 308.

131. Guðmundsdóttir, "More Pain, More Gain!" 127.

132. Ray, *Deceiving the Devil*, 21.

133. Fortune, "The Transformation of Suffering," 90.

134. Farley, *Tragic Vision and Divine Compassion: A Contemporary Theodicy*, 86.

135. Farley, "Evil, Violence, and the Practice of Theodicy," 15.

136. Farley defines "radical suffering" as a suffering that is destructive of the human spirit and can never be understood as something deserved. With her category of radical suffering, Farley rejects the necessary correlation between suffering and punishment, suggested in the story of Adam and Eve in Eden (Farley, *Tragic Vision and Divine Compassion*, 53–65).

137. In her most recent work, Farley has developed further her position on Christ and the meaning of his suffering and death. See Farley, *The Wounding and Healing of Desire: Weaving Heaven and Earth*.

138. Farley, *Tragic Vision and Divine Compassion*, 132.

139. Farley, "Evil, Violence, and the Practice of Theodicy," 15.

140. Johnson, *She Who Is*, 246.

141. Ibid., 249.

142. Ibid., 253.

143. Ibid., 253–54.

144. Ibid., 269.

145. Johnson, "Redeeming the Name of Christ—Christology," 115–37, here p. 124.

146. Johnson, *She Who Is*, 159.

147. Johnson, "Redeeming the Name of Christ—Christology," 124.

148. Ibid., 125. On the cross as an important symbol of the *kenosis* of patriarchy, see Johnson, *She Who Is*, 160–61.

149. Quoted by Weaver, *The Nonviolent Atonement*, 159.

150. Kässmann, *Overcoming Violence*, 60.

151. Hunt, "Dead but Still Missing: Mothers of Plaza de Mayo Transform Argentina," 89–96.

152. See http://www.thejakartapost.com/news/2009/04/26/mothers-plaza-de-mayo-justice-disappeared-loved-ones one-step-a-long-time.html.

Conclusion: The Cross of Christ as a Symbol of Hope

As we need to take notice of the situation of the people we are addressing, the context of Jesus' cross should never be overlooked. Far from being a passive victim, Jesus fought against injustice, challenged authorities, and objected to expected social roles. Thus, his cross was the result of the kind of life he lived. Jesus chose his way of life and was ready to pay the price. Given the historical context of Jesus' life, in which crucifixion was the mode of execution for the lowest of the low, his cross becomes a testimony of God's identification with the poor, the sick, and the oppressed.[1] If the cross is to become a meaningful symbol for suffering people, it cannot remain a symbol of passive victimization but has to become a sign of hope that encourages them to stand up and resist, even if the resistance might cause them suffering. Thus, if Bonhoeffer was right, if "only a suffering God can help,"[2] it has to be kept in mind that the suffering God is not a powerless God who is suffering helplessly because she cannot do otherwise. Only a suffering God who out of love chooses to suffer with suffering people brings hope for those who suffer. Such a God is "the compassionate God," a God who helps by "awakening consolation, responsible human action, and hope against hope in the world marked by radical suffering and evil."[3] To keep in mind this double edge, the passive (in the form of solidarity) and the active (in the form of empowerment) role of the cross is a key to any meaningful reclaiming, recovering, and reappropriation of the cross.

Women's experience of exclusion and oppression truly intensifies the ethical and the political dimension of a feminist theology of the cross. As the good tree bears good fruit, so Christians are called to let their faith become active in their lives. Without simply reducing Christ's significance to that of a moral example, it is important that his disciples allow his example to encourage them to follow in his footsteps. By stressing the close connection between theology and ethics, we find support in Luther's understanding of Christians being called to be "Christ to one another."[4] In his treatise *The Freedom of a Christian*, Luther writes:

> This is what makes caring for the body a Christian work, that
> through its health and comfort we may be able to work, to acquire,
> and lay by funds with which to aid those who are in need, that in this
> way the strong member may serve the weaker, and we may be sons
> of God, each caring for and working for the other, bearing one
> another's burdens and so fulfilling the law of Christ [Galatians 6:2].
> This is a truly Christian life. Here faith is truly active through love
> [Galatians 5:6], that is, it finds expression in works of the freest
> service, cheerfully and lovingly done, with which a man willingly
> serves another without hope of reward; and for himself he is satisfied
> with the fullness and wealth of his faith.[5]

Hence, Christian praxis is understood as a continuation of the incarnation, in which God becomes truly involved in the human condition. While Jesus' message of the Reign of God points not only toward its coming in the future but also to its active role in the present time, Christ's followers are called to stand up and resist any kind of injustice, including injustice based on the abuse of power, from which women so often suffer. As we learn to take seriously our calling to become Christ to one another, God's compassion continues to be present and active today, pointing forward in hope to a future when God's will for her creation will be fulfilled.

NOTES

1. Sundermeier, "Contextualizing Luther's Theology of the Cross," 102.
2. Bonhoeffer writes: "Here is the decisive difference between Christianity and all religions. Man's religiosity makes him look in his distress to the power of God in the world: God is the *deus ex machina*. The Bible directs man to God's powerlessness and suffering; only the suffering God can help" (Bonhoeffer, *Letters & Papers from Prison*, 361).
3. Johnson, *She Who Is: The Mystery of God in Feminist Theological Discourse*, 269.
4. LW 31:368.
5. LW 31:365.

Bibliography

Adams, Carol J. *Woman-battering*. Minneapolis: Fortress, 1994.

Adams, Carol J., and Marie M. Fortune, eds. *Violence against Women and Children: A Christian Theological Sourcebook*. New York: Continuum, 1995.

Against Machismo. *Interviews by Elsa Tamez*. Edited and translated by John Eagleson. Oak Park, IL: Meyer Stone Books, 1987.

Aldredge-Clanton, Jann. *In Search of the Christ-Sophia: An Inclusive Christology for Liberating Christians*. Mystic, CT: Twenty-Third Publications, 1995.

Allen, Christine. "Christ our Mother in Julian of Norwich." *Studies in Religion* 10, no. 4 (1981): 421–28.

Althaus, Paul. *The Theology of Martin Luther*. Translated by Robert C. Schultz. Philadelphia: Fortress, 1966.

Altmann, Walter. "A Latin American Perspective on the Cross and Suffering." In *The Scandal of a Crucified World: Perspectives on the Cross and Suffering*, edited by Yacob Tesfai, 75–86. Maryknoll, NY: Orbis, 1994.

———. *Luther and Liberation: A Latin American Perspective*, trans. Mary M. Solberg. Minneapolis: Fortress, 1992.

Aquino, Maria Pilar. *Our Cry for Life: Feminist Theology from Latin America*. Translated by Dinah Livingstone. Maryknoll, NY: Orbis, 1993.

Berger, Theresa. "A Female Christ Child in the Manger and a Woman on the Cross, Or: The Historicity of the Jesus Event and the Inculturation of the Gospel." *Feminist Theology* 11 (January 1996): 32–45.

Book of Concord: The Confessions of the Evangelical Lutheran Church. Edited and translated by Theodore G. Tappert, in collaboration with Jaroslav Pelikan, Robert H. Fischer, and Arthur C. Piepkorn. Philadelphia: Fortress, 1959.

Bond, Susan L. *Trouble with Jesus: Women, Christology, and Preaching*. St. Louis, MO: Chalice Press, 1999.

Bonhoeffer, Dietrich. *Letters & Papers from Prison*. Edited by Eberhard Bethge. New York: Collier Books, Macmillan, First Paperback Edition, 1972.

Boys, Mary C. "The Cross: Should a Symbol Betrayed Be Reclaimed?" *Cross Currents* (Spring 1994): 5–27.

Braaten, Carl E. "A Trinitarian Theology of the Cross." *The Journal of Religion* 56 (January 1976): 113–21.

Braaten, Carl E., and Robert W. Jenson, eds. *Christian Dogmatics*. 2 vols. Philadelphia: Fortress, 1984.

Briere, Elizabeth. "'Rejoice, Sceptre of Orthodoxy': Christology and the Mother of God." *Sobornost* 7, no. 1 (1985): 15–24.

Brock, Rita Nakashima. "A Feminist Consciousness Looks at Christology." *Encounter* 41 (1980): 321–31.

———. *Journeys by Heart: A Christology of Erotic Power*. New York: Crossroad, 1991.

Brock, Rita Nakashima, and Rebecca Ann Parker. *Proverbs of Ashes: Violence, Redemptive Suffering, and the Search for What Saves Us*. Boston: Beacon, 2001.

Brown, Alexandra. *The Cross & Human Transformation: Paul's Apocalyptic Word in 1 Corinthians*. Minneapolis: Fortress, 1995.

Brown, Joanne Carlson, and Carole R. Bohn, eds. *Christianity, Patriarchy, and Abuse: A Feminist Critique*. New York: Pilgrim, 1989.

Brown, Joanne Carlson, and Rebecca Parker. "For God So Loved the World?" In *Christianity, Patriarchy, and Abuse: A Feminist Critique*, edited by Joanne Carlson Brown and Carole R. Bohn, 1–30. New York: Pilgrim, 1989.

Brown, Kelly Delaine. "God Is as Christ Does: Toward a Womanist Theology." *Journal of Religious Thought* 46 (Summer-Fall 1989): 7–16.

Bynum, Caroline Walker. *Fragmentation and Redemption: Essays on Gender and the Human Body in Medieval Religion*. New York: Zone Books, 1992.

———. *Jesus as Mother: Studies in the Spirituality of the High Middle Ages*. Berkeley and Los Angeles: University of California Press, 1984.

Cannon, Katie Geneva. "The Emergence of Black Feminist Consciousness." In *Feminist Interpretation of the Bible*, edited by Letty Russell, 30–40. Philadelphia: Westminster, 1985.

———. "'The Wounds of Jesus': Justification of Goodness in the Face of Manifold Evil." In *A Troubling in My Soul: Womanist Perspectives on Evil and Suffering*, edited by Emilie M. Townes, 219–31. Maryknoll, NY: Orbis, 1993.

Carr, Anne E. *Transforming Grace: Christian Tradition and Women's Experience*. San Francisco: Harper & Row, 1988.

Chopp, Rebecca S. *The Praxis of Suffering: An Interpretation of Liberation and Political Theologies*. Maryknoll, NY: Orbis, 1986.

Christ, Carol P., and Judith Plaskow, eds. *Womanspirit Rising: A Feminist Reader in Religion*. San Francisco: Harper & Row, 1979.

Chung, Hyun Kyung. *Struggle to Be the Sun Again*. Maryknoll, NY: Orbis, 1990.

Churches Say "No" to Violence against Women: Action Plan for the Churches. Geneva: The Lutheran World Federation, 2002.

Clague, Julie. "The Christa: Symbolizing My Humanity and My Pain," *Feminist Theology* 14, no. 1 (2005): 83–108. Available: http://fth.sagepub.com/cgi/reprint/14/1/83.

Concordia Triglotta: The Symbolical Books of the Evangelical Lutheran Church. Published as a Memorial of the Quadricentenary Jubilee of the Reformation anno Domini 1917 by resolution of the Evangelical Lutheran Synod of Missouri, Ohio, and Other States. St. Louis, MO: Concordia Publishing House, 1921. Reprint, Milwaukee: Northwestern Publishing House, 1988.

Cone, James H. "An African-American Perspective on the Cross and Suffering." In *The Scandal of a Crucified World: Perspectives on the Cross and Suffering*, edited by Yacob Tesfai, 48–60. Maryknoll, NY: Orbis, 1994.

Copeland, M. Shawn. "To Live at the Disposal of the Cross: Mystical-Political Discipleship as Christological Locus." In *Christology: Memory, Inquiry, Practice*, edited by Anne M. Clifford and Anthony J. Godzieba, 177–96. Maryknoll, NY: Orbis, 2003.

———. "'Wading through Many Sorrows': Toward a Theology of Suffering in Womanist Perspective." In *A Troubling in My Soul: Womanist Perspectives on Evil and Suffering*, edited by Emilie M. Townes, 109–29. Maryknoll, NY: Orbis, 1993.

———. "The Wounds of Jesus, the Wounds of My People." In *Telling the Truth: Preaching about Sexual and Domestic Violence*, edited by John S. McClure and Nancy J. Ramsay, 34–46. Cleveland, OH: United Church Press, 1998.

Cousar, Charles. In *A Theology of the Cross: The Death of Jesus in the Pauline Letters.* Minneapolis: Fortress, 1990.

Daly, Mary. *Beyond God the Father: Toward a Philosophy of Women's Liberation.* Reprint, Boston: Beacon, 1985.

Davis, Leo Donald, S.J. *The First Seven Ecumenical Councils (325–787): Their History and Theology.* Collegeville, MN: Liturgical, 1983.

Dillenberger, John, ed. *Martin Luther: Selections from His Writings.* Garden City, NY: Anchor Books, Doubleday, 1961.

Douglas, Kelly Brown. *The Black Christ.* Maryknoll, NY: Orbis, 1994.

Douglass, Jane Dempsey. *Women, Freedom, and Calvin.* Philadelphia: Westminster, 1985.

Dyke, Doris Jean. *Crucified Woman.* Toronto, ON: The United Church Publishing House, 1991.

Edwards, Sarah. "Christology and the Cross." In *Christology in Dialogue*, edited by Robert F. Berkey and Sarah A. Edwards, 157–72. Cleveland, OH: Pilgrim, 1993.

Eriksson, Anne-Louise. *The Meaning of Gender in Theology: Problems and Possibilities.* Uppsala, Sweden: Acta Universitatis Upsaliensis, 1995.

Evans, Bernadette. "Suffering and the African Diaspora." *Journal of Women and Religion* 9–10 (1990–91): 63–71.

Fabella, Virginia M.M. "Asian Women and Christology." *In God's Image* (September 1987): 14–20.

———. "Christology from an Asian Woman's Perspective." In *We Dare to Dream: Doing Theology as Asian Women*, edited by Virginia M.M. Fabella and Sun Ai Lee Park, 3–14. Maryknoll, NY: Orbis, 1990.

———. "Mission of Women in the Church in Asia: Role and Position." In *New Eyes for Reading: Biblical and Theological Reflections by Women from the Third World*, edited by John S. Pobee and Bärbel von Wartenberg-Potter, 81–89. Geneva: World Council of Churches. Meyer Stone, 1986.

Fabella, Virginia M.M., and Mercy Amba Oduyoye, eds. *With Passion and Compassion: Third World Women Doing Theology.* Maryknoll, NY: Orbis, 1988.

Fabella, Virginia M.M., and Sun Ai Lee Park, eds. *We Dare to Dream: Doing Theology as Asian Women.* Maryknoll, NY: Orbis, 1989.

Farley, Margaret A., R.S.M. "New Patterns of Relationship: Beginnings of a Moral Revolution." In *Woman: New Dimensions*, edited by Walter Burkhardt, S.J., 51–70. New York: Paulist, 1975.

Farley, Wendy. "Evil, Violence, and the Practice of Theodicy." In *Telling the Truth: Preaching about Sexual and Domestic Violence*, edited by John S. McClure and Nancy J. Ramsay, 11–20. Cleveland, OH: United Church Press, 1998.

———. "The Practice of Theodicy." In *Pain Seeking Understanding. Suffering, Medicine, and Faith*, edited by Margaret E. Mohrmann and Mark J. Hanson, 103–14. Cleveland, OH: Pilgrim, 1999.

———. *Tragic Vision and Divine Compassion: A Contemporary Theodicy.* Louisville, KY: Westminster/John Knox, 1990.

———. *The Wounding and Healing of Desire: Weaving Heaven and Earth.* Louisville, KY: Westminster/John Knox, 2005.

Forell, George W. *Faith Active in Love: An Investigation of the Principles Underlying Luther's Social Ethics.* Minneapolis, MN: Augsburg, 1954.

Fortune, Marie M. "Preaching Forgiveness?" In *Telling the Truth: Preaching about Sexual and Domestic Violence*, edited by John S. McClure and Nancy J. Ramsay, 49–57. Cleveland, OH: United Church Press, 1998.

———. "The Transformation of Suffering: A Biblical and Theological Perspective." In *Violence against Women and Children: A Christian Theological Sourcebook*, edited by Carol J. Adams and Marie M. Fortune, 85–91. New York: Continuum, 1995.

Gill-Austen, L. Brita. "Love Understood as Self-Sacrifice and Self-Denial: What Does It Do to Women?" In *Through the Eyes of Women: Insights for Pastoral Care*, edited by Jeanne Stevenson Moessner, 304–21. Minneapolis: Fortress, 1996.

Graff, Ann O'Hara. "The Struggle to Name Women's Experience: Assessment and Implications for Theological Construction." *Horizons* 20, no. 2 (1993): 215–33.

Grant, Jacquelyn. "'Come to My Help, Lord, for I'm in Trouble': Womanist Jesus and the Mutual Struggle for Liberation." In *Reconstructing the Christ Symbol: Essays in Feminist Christology*, edited by Maryanne Stevens, 54–71. New York/Mahwah: Paulist, 1993.

———. "Jesus and the Task of Redemption." In *We Belong Together: Churches in Solidarity with Women*, edited by Sarah Cunnigham, 30–42. New York: Friendship, 1992.

———. "The Sin of Servanthood: And the Deliverance of Discipleship." In *A Troubling in My Soul: Womanist Perspectives on Evil and Suffering*, edited by Emilie M. Townes, 199–218. Maryknoll, NY: Orbis, 1993.

———. *White Women's Christ and Black Women's Jesus: Feminist Christology and Womanist Response*. Atlanta: Scholars, 1989.

Grillmeier, Alois, S.J. *Christ in Christian Tradition. Vol.One. From the Apostolic Age to Chalcedon (451)*. 2nd revised ed., trans. John Bowden. Atlanta: John Knox Press, 1975.

Guðmundsdóttir, Arnfríður. "Abusive or Abused? Theology of the Cross from Feminist Critical Perspective." *Journal of the European Society of Women in Theological Research* 15 (2007): 37–54.

———. "Female Christ-figures in Films: A Feminist Critical Analysis of *Breaking the Waves* and *Dead Man Walking*." *Studia Theologica* 56 (2002): 27–43.

———. "More Pain, More Gain! On Mel Gibson's Film, *The Passion of the Christ*." In *Recent Releases: The Bible in Contemporary Cinema*, edited by Geert Hallbäck and Annika Hvithamar, 115–32. Sheffield: Sheffield Phoenix, 2008.

Gutiérrez, Gustavo. *On Job: God-Talk and the Suffering of the Innocent*. Translated by Matthew J. O'Connell. Maryknoll, NY: Orbis, 1987.

Hall, Douglas John. *The Cross in Our Context: Jesus and the Suffering World*. Minneapolis: Fortress, 2003.

———. *God & Human Suffering: An Exercise in the Theology of the Cross*. Minneapolis: Augsburg, 1986.

———. *Lighten Our Darkness: Toward an Indigenous Theology of the Cross*. Philadelphia: Westminster, 1976.

———. "Theology of the Cross: Challenge and Opportunity for the Post-Christendom Church." *Cross Examinations. Readings on the Meaning of the Cross Today*, edited by Marit Trelstad, 252–58. Minneapolis: Augsburg Fortress, 2006.

Hampson. *After Christianity*. London: S.C.M., 1996.

———. *Christian Contradictions: The Structures of Lutheran and Catholic Thought* Cambridge: Cambridge University Press, 2001.

———. Daphne. *Theology and Feminism*. Oxford: Basil Blackwell, 1990.

———, ed. *Swallowing a Fishbone: Feminist Theologians Debate Christianity*. London: SPCK 1996.

Hegel, G. W. F. *Lectures on the Philosophy of Religion*, edited by Peter C. Hodgson, translated R. F. Brown et. al. Berkeley: University of California Press, 1988.

Hellwig, Monika K. *Jesus. The Compassion of God*. Wilmington, DE: Michael Glazier, 1983.

———. *Whose Experience Counts in Theological Reflection?* Milwaukee: Marquette University Press, 1982.

Hengel, Martin. *Crucifixion*. Translated by John Bowden. Philadelphia: Fortress, 1977.

Heyward, Carter. *Our Passion for Justice: Images of Power, Sexuality and Liberation*. New York: Pilgrim, 1984.

———. *The Redemption of God: A Theology of Mutual Relation*. New York: University Press of America, 1982.

————. "Ruether and Daly: Theologians Speaking and Sparking, Building and Burning." *Christianity and Crisis: A Christian Journal of Opinion* 39, no. 5 (April 2, 1979): 66–72.

————. *Speaking of Christ: A Lesbian Feminist Voice.* New York: Pilgrim, 1989.

————. "Suffering, Redemption, and Christ: Shifting the Grounds of Feminist Christology." *Christianity and Crisis: A Christian Journal of Opinion* 49 (December 11, 1989): 381–86.

————. *Touching Our Strength: The Erotic as Power and the Love of God.* San Francisco: Harper & Row, 1989.

Hilkert, Mary Catherine. "Feminist Theology: A Review of Literature." *Theological Studies* 56, no. 2 (June 1995): 327–52.

Hodgson, Peter. *The Formation of Historical Theology: A Study of Ferdinand Christian Baur.* New York: Harper & Row, 1966.

Holy Bible. New Revised Standard Version. New York: Oxford University Press, 1989.

Hunt, Mary E. "Dead but Still Missing: Mothers of Plaza de Mayo Transform Argentina." In *Concilium* 1993/3, 89–96. Maryknoll: Orbis, 1993.

Japinga, Lynn. *Feminism and Christianity: An Essential Guide.* Nashville: Abingdon, 1999.

Johnson, Elizabeth A. *Consider Jesus: Waves of Renewal in Christology.* New York: Crossroad, 1990.

————. *Friends of God and Prophets: A Feminist Theological Reading of the Communion of Saints.* New York: Continuum, 1998.

————. "The Incomprehensibility of God and the Image of God Male and Female." *Theological Studies* 45 (1984): 441–65.

————. "Jesus the Wisdom of God. A Biblical Basis for Non-androcentric Christology." *Ephemerides Theologicae Lovaniensis* 61, no. 4 (1985): 261–94.

————. "The Maleness of Christ." *The Special Nature of Women? Concilium* 6, edited by Anne Carr and Elisabeth Schüssler Fiorenza, 108–16. Philadelphia: Trinity, 1991.

————. *Quest for the Living God: Mapping Frontiers in the Theology of God.* New York: Continuum, 2008.

————. "Redeeming the Name of Christ—Christology." *Freeing Theology: The Essentials of Theology in Feminist Perspective,* edited by Catherine Mowry LaCugna, 115–37. San Francisco: Harper San Francisco, 1993.

————. *She Who Is: The Mystery of God in Feminist Theological Discourse.* New York: Crossroad, 1992.

————. *Truly Our Sister: A Theology of Mary in the Communion of Saints.* New York: Continuum, 2003.

————. "Wisdom Was Made Flesh and Pitched Her Tent Among Us." In *Reconstructing the Christ Symbol: Essays in Feminist Christology,* edited by Maryanne Stevens, 95–117. New York/Mahwah: Paulist, 1993.

Jones, Serene. "Rupture." In *Hope Deferred: Heart-Healing Reflections on Reproductive Loss,* edited by Nadine Pence Frantz and Mary T. Stimming, 47–65. Cleveland, OH: Pilgrim, 2005.

Kähler, Martin. *The So-Called Historical Jesus and the Historic Biblical Christ.* Translated, edited, and introduction by Carl E. Braaten. Philadelphia: Fortress, 1964.

Kant, Immanuel. *Religion within the Limits of Reason Alone.* Translated and introduction by T. Greene and H. Hudson. New York: Harper Torchbooks, Harper & Row, 1960.

Käsemann, Ernst. *Essays on New Testament Themes.* Philadelphia: Fortress, 1982.

———. "The Saving Significance of the Death of Jesus in Paul." In *Perspectives on Paul,* translated by Margaret Kohl, 32–59. Philadelphia: Fortress, 1971.

Kässmann, Margot. *Overcoming Violence: The Challenge to the Churches in All Places.* Geneva: WCC, 1998.

Kopas, Jane. "Teaching Christology in Light of Feminist Issues." *Horizons* 13, no. 2 (1986): 332–43.

Kvam, Kristen E. "Comfort." In *Hope Deferred: Heart-Healing Reflections on Reproductive Loss,* edited by Nadine Pence Frantz and Mary T. Stimming, 71–84. Cleveland, OH: Pilgrim, 2005.

Küng, Hans. *The Incarnation of God.* Translated by J. R. Stephenson. Edinburgh: T & T Clark, 1987.

LaCugna, Catherine Mowry. "Baptism, Feminists, and Trinitarian Theology." *Ecumenical Trends. Graymoor Ecumenical Institute* 17, no. 5 (May 1988): 65–68.

———, ed. *Freeing Theology: The Essentials of Theology in Feminist Perspective.* San Francisco: Harper San Francisco, 1993.

———. "God in Communion with Us." In *Freeing Theology: The Essentials of Theology in Feminist Perspective,* edited by Catherine Mowry LaCugna, 83–114. San Francisco: Harper San Francisco, 1993.

———. *God for Us: The Trinity and Christian Life.* San Francisco: Harper San Francisco, 1991.

Lee, Susan Hagood. "Witness to Christ, Witness to Pain: One Woman's Journey through Wife Battering." In *Sermons Seldom Heard: Women Proclaim Their Lives,* edited by Annie Lally Milhaven, 11–21. New York: Crossroad, 1991.

Leonard, Ellen. "Experience as a Source for Theology: A Canadian and Feminist Perspective." *Studies in Religion* 19, no. 2 (1990): 143–69.

Lerner, Gerda. *The Creation of Feminist Consciousness.* New york: Oxford University Press, 1993.

Lienhard, Marc. *Luther: Witness to Jesus Christ.* Translated by Edwin H. Robertson. Minneapolis: Augsburg, 1982.

Loads, Ann. *Searching for Lost Coins: Explorations in Christianity and Feminism.* Allison Park, PA: Pickwick, 1987.

Loewenich, Walther von. *Luther's Theology of the Cross.* Translated by Herbert J. A. Bouman. Minneapolis: Augsburg, 1976. A translation of the 5th edition of Loewenich's *Luther's Theologia Crucis* from 1967.

———. *Martin Luther: The Man and His Work.* Translated by Lawrence W. Denef. Minneapolis: Augsburg, 1986.

———. *The Theology of Martin Luther.* Translated by Robert C. Schultz. Philadelphia: Fortress, 1966.

Lohse, Bernhard. *Martin Luther: An Introduction to His Life and Work.* Translated by Robert Schultz. Philadelphia: Fortress, 1986.

Luther, Martin. *D. Martin Luthers Werke: Kritische Gesamtausgabe* [WA]. Weimar: Hermann Böhlaus Nachfolger,1912–.

————. *Luther's Works* [LW]. American Edition. Edited by Jaroslav Pelikan and Helmut T. Lehmann. Philadelphia: Fortress; St. Louis: Concordia Publishing House, 1955–86.

————. *The Martin Luther Christmas Book*. Translated and arranged by Roland H. Bainton. Philadelphia: Fortress, 1948.

————. *Martin Luther: Selections from His Writings.*Edited by John Dillenberger. Garden City, NY: Anchor Books, Doubleday, 1961.

Macquarrie, John. *Jesus Christ in Modern Thought*. Philadelphia: Trinity, 1991.

Maimela, Simon. "The Suffering of Human Divisons and the Cross." In *The Scandal of a Crucified World: Perspectives on the Cross and Suffering*, edited by Yacob Tesfai, 36–47. Maryknoll, NY: Orbis, 1994.

McDougall, Joy Ann. *Pilgrimage of Love: Moltmann on the Trinity and Christian Life*. New York: Oxford University Press, 2005.

McFague, Sallie. *Models of God: Theology for an Ecological, Nuclear Age*. Philadelphia: Fortress, 1987.

McGrath, Alister E. *Christian Theology: An Introduction*. Malden, MA: Blackwell, 2007.

————. *Luther's Theology of the Cross*. Cambridge, MA: Basil Blackwell, 1985.

————. *The Making of Modern German Christology 1750–1990*. 2nd ed. Grand Rapids, MI: Zondervan, 1994.

McLaughlin, Eleanor. "Feminist Christologies: Re-Dressing the Tradition."In *Reconstructing the Symbol of Christ: Essays in Feminist Christology*, edited by Maryanne Stevens, 118–49. New York/Mahwah: Paulist, 1993.

McWilliams, Warren. *The Passion of God: Divine Suffering in Contemporary Protestant Theology*. Macon, GA: Mercer University Press, 1985.

Miles, Margaret R. "Imitation of Christ: Is It Possible in the Twentieth Century?" *The Princeton Seminary Bulletin* 10, no. 1 (1989): 7–22.

Mollenkott, Virginia Ramey. "Who's Redeeming Whom?" *Christianity and Crisis* 43, no. 5 (April 4, 1983): 123–24.

Moltmann, Jürgen. *A Broad Place: An Autobiography*. English translation by Margaret Kohl. Minneapolis: Fortress, 2008.

————. "The Cross as Military Symbol for Sacrifice." In *Cross Examinations. Readings on the Meaning of the Cross Today*, edited by Marit Trelstad, 259–63. Minneapolis: Augsburg Fortress, 2006.

————. *The Crucified God: The Cross of Christ as the Foundation and Criticism of Christian Theology*. Translated by R. A. Wilson and John Bowden. New York: Harper & Row, 1974.

————. "The 'Crucified God': A Trinitarian Theology of the Cross." *Interpretation* 26 (July 1972): 278–329.

————. "The Crucified God: Yesterday and Today: 1972–2002." In *Cross Examinations. Readings on the Meaning of the Cross Today*, edited by Marit Trelstad, 127–38. Minneapolis: Augsburg Fortress, 2006.

————. *The Future of Creation*. Translated by Margaret Kohl. Philadelphia: Fortress, 1979.

————. *History and the Triune God: Contributions to Trinitarian Theology*. Translated by John Bowden. New York: Crossroad, 1992.

————. *Jesus Christ for Today's World*. Translated by Margaret Kohl. Minneapolis: Fortress, 1994.

————. "The Motherly Father: Is Trinitarian Patripassianism Replacing Theological Patriarchalism?" In *God as Father?* edited by Johannes-Baptist Metz and Edward Schillebeeckx, 51–56. Edinburgh: T. & T. Clark, 1981.

————. *Theology of Hope: On the Ground and the Implications of a Christian Eschatology*. Translated by James W. Leitch. Minneapolis: Fortress, 1993.

————. *The Way of Jesus Christ: Christology in Messianic Dimensions*. Translated by Margaret Kohl. San Francisco: Harper San Francisco, 1990.

Moltmann-Wendel, Elisabeth. "Christ in Context." In *A Reader in Feminist Theology*, edited by Prasanna Kumari, 67–79. Gurukul, Madras: Department of Research and Publications for Department of Women's Studies, Gurukul Lutheran Theological College and Research Institute, Madras India, 1993.

————. "Is There a Feminist Theology of the Cross?" In *The Scandal of a Crucified World: Perspectives on the Cross and Suffering*, edited by Yacob Tesfai, 87–98. Maryknoll, NY: Orbis, 1994.

————. *A Land Flowing with Milk and Honey: Perspectives on Feminist Theology*. New York: Crossroad, 1988.

————. "Toward a Wholistic Feminine Theology." *Theology Digest* 33, no. 2 (Summer 1986): 239–43.

————. *The Women Around Jesus: Reflections on Authentic Personhood*. Translated by John Bowden. London: SCM, 1982.

Moltmann-Wendel, Elisabeth, and Jürgen Moltmann. *God—His & Hers*. New York: Crossroad, 1991.

————. *Humanity in God*. New York: Pilgrim, 1983.

"Mothers of Plaza De Mayo: Justice for Disappeared Loved Ones, One Step at a (Long) Time." http://www.thejakartapost.com/news/2009/04/26/mothers-plaza-de-mayo-justice-disappeared-loved-ones-one-step-a-long-time.html. Accessed May 15, 2009.

Norris, Richard A.,Jr., trans. and ed. *The Christological Controversy*. Philadelphia: Fortress, 1980.

Oberman, Heiko A. *Luther: Man Between God and the Devil*. Translated by Eileen Walliser-Schwarzbart. New York: Image Books, Doubleday, 1992.

Oduyoye, Mercy Amba. "Churchwomen and the Church's Mission." In *New Eyes for Reading: Biblical and Theological Reflections by Women from the Third World*, edited by John S. Pobee and Bärbel von Wartenberg-Potter, 68–80. Bloomington, IN: Meyer Stone Books, 1987.

O'Grady, Ro, ed. *Christ for All People: Celebrating a World of Christian Art*. Geneva, Switzerland: WCC.

Osiek, Carolyn, RSCJ. *Beyond Anger: On Being a Feminist in the Church*. New York: Paulist, 1986.

Pannenberg, Wolfhart. "A Theology of the Cross." *Word and World: Theology for Christian Ministry* 8, no. 2 (Spring 1988): 162–72.

Pelikan, Jaroslav. *Reformation of Church and Dogma (1300–1700)*. Chicago: University of Chicago Press, 1984.

Peters, Ted. "A Book Worth Discussing: Faith, Feminism, and the Christ." *Currents in Theology and Mission* 12 (October 1985): 313–16.

Plaskow, Judith. *Sex, Sin, and Grace: Women's Experience and the Theologies of Reinhold Niebuhr and Paul Tillich.* New York: University Press of America, 1980.

Plaskow, Judith, and Carol P. Christ, eds. *Weaving the Visions: New Patterns in Feminist Spirituality.* San Francisco: Harper San Francisco, 1989.

Pobee, John S., and Bärbel von Wartenberg-Potter, eds. *New Eyes for Reading: Biblical and Theological Reflections by Women from the Third World.* Bloomington, IN: Meyer Stone Books, 1987.

Pui Lan, Kwok. "God Weeps with Our Pain." In *New Eyes for Reading: Biblical and Theological Reflections by Women from the Third World,* edited by John S. Pobee and Bärbel von Wartenberg-Potter, 90–95. Bloomington, IN: Meyer Stone Books, 1987.

Purvis, Sally B. *The Power of the Cross: Foundations for a Christian Feminist Ethic of Community.* Nashville: Abingdon, 1993.

Ramsay, Nancy J. "Preaching to Survivors of Child Sexual Abuse." In *Telling the Truth: Preaching about Sexual and Domestic Violence,* edited by John S. McClure and Nancy J. Ramsay, 58–70. Cleveland, OH: United Church Press, 1998.

Ramshaw, Gail. *Treasures Old and New: Images in the Lectionary.* Minneapolis: Fortress, 2002.

Ray, Darby Kathleen. *Deceiving the Devil: Atonement, Abuse, and Ransom.* Cleveland, OH: Pilgrim, 1998.

Rich, Adrienne. *Of Woman Born: Motherhood as Experience and Institution.* Tenth anniversary ed. New York: Norton, 1986.

Ruether, Rosemary Radford. "Feminist Interpretation: A Method of Correlation." In *Feminist Interpretation of the Bible,* edited by Letty Russell, 111–24. Philadelphia: Westminster, 1985.

———. "Is Feminism the End of Christianity? A Critique of Daphne Hampson's *Theology and Feminism.*" *Scottish Journal of Theology* 43 (August 1990): 390–400.

———. "The Liberation of Christology from Patriarchy." *The Cumberland Seminarian* 27 (Winter 1989): 65–75.

———. *Sexism and God-Talk: Toward a Feminist Theology.* Boston: Beacon, 1983.

———. "The Sexuality of Jesus: What Do the Synoptics Say?" *Christianity and Crisis* (May 29, 1978): 134–37.

———. *To Change the World: Christology and Cultural Criticism.* New York: Crossroad, 1989. Reprint.

Russell, Letty, ed. "Authority and the Challenge of Feminist Interpretation," In *Feminist Interpretation of the Bible,* edited by Letty Russell, 137-146. Philadelphia: Westminster, 1985.

———. *Feminist Interpretation of the Bible.* Philadelphia: Westminster, 1985.

———. *Household of Freedom: Authority in Feminist Theology.* Philadelphia: Westminster, 1987.

———. *Human Liberation in a Feminist Perspective—A Theology.* Philadelphia: Westminster, 1974.

Sandys, Edwina: Creating Personal and Public Art; Internationally Renowned Artist Gives Public Lecture at York University. Available: http://www.yorku.ca/finearts/news/2005/edwinasandys.htm. February 14, 2007.

Sasse, Hermann. *This Is My Body: Luther's Contention for the Real Presence in the Sacrament of the Altar*. Adelaide, South Australia: Lutheran, 1977.

Schleiermacher, Friedrich. *The Christian Faith*. Edited by H. R. MacKintosh and J. S. Stewart. Edinburgh: T. & T. Clark, 1986.

———. *On Religion: Speeches to Its Cultured Despisers*. Translated by John Oman.Introduction by Rudolf Otto. San Francisco: Harper Torchbooks; Harper & Row, 1958.

Schüssler Fiorenza, Elisabeth. *In Memory of Her: A Feminist Theological Reconstruction of Christian Origins*. New York: Crossroad, 1987.

———. *Jesus: Miriam's Child, Sophia's Prophet: Critical Issues in Feminist Christology*. New York: Continuum, 1994.

———. "To Set the Record Straight: Biblical Women's Studies." *Horizons* 10, no. 1 (Spring 1983): 111–21.

———. "The Will to Choose or to Reject: Continuing Our Critical Work." In *Feminist Interpretation of the Bible*, edited by Letty Russel, 125–36. Philadelphia: Westminster, 1985.

Schüssler Fiorenza, Elisabeth, and Anne Carr, eds. *Women, Work and Poverty, Concilium* 194 (6/1987). Edinburgh: T. & T. Clark, 1987.

Schüssler Fiorenza, Elisabeth. *Bread Not Stone: The Challenge of Feminist Biblical Interpretation*. Boston: Beacon, 1984.

Florence, Anna Carter. *Preaching as Testimony*. Louisville, KY: Westminster John Knox, 2007.

Schüssler Fiorenza, Elisabeth, and Mary Shawn Copeland, eds. *Violence Against Women, Concilium* 1994/1. Maryknoll, NY: Orbis, 1994.

Schweitzer, Albert. *The Quest of the Historical Jesus: A Critical Study of Its Progress from Reimarus to Wrede*. Translated by W. Montgomery. London: Adam & Charles Black, 1945.

Schweitzer, Don. "Jürgen Moltmann's Theology as a Theology of the Cross." *Studies in Religion/Sciences Religieuses* 24, no. 1 (1995): 95–107.

Scroggs, Robin. *Christology in Paul and John: The Reality and Revelation of God*. Philadelphia: Fortress, 1988.

Siggins, Ian Kingston. *Martin Luther's Doctrine of Christ*. New Haven: Yale University Press, 1970.

Snyder, Mary Hembrow. *The Christology of Rosemary Radford Ruether: A Critical Introduction*. Mystic, CT: Twenty-Third Publications, 1988.

Sobrino, Jon, S.J. *Christology at the Crossroads: A Latin American Approach*. Translated by John Drury. Maryknoll, NY: Orbis, 1978.

———. "A Crucified People's Faith in the Son of God." In *Jesus, Son of God? Concilium* 153, edited by E. Schillebeeckx and J. B. Metz, 23–28. New York: Seabury, 1982.

Soelle, Dorothee. *Suffering*. Translated by Everett R. Kalin. Philadelphia: Fortress, 1975.

Solberg, Mary, M. "All That Matters: What an Epistemology of the Cross Is Good For." In *Cross Examinations: Readings on the Meaning of the Cross Today*, edited by Marit Trelstad, 139–53. Minneapolis: Augsburg Fortress, 2006.

———. *Compelling Knowledge: A Feminist Proposal for an Epistemology of the Cross*. Albany: State University of New York Press, 1997.

Song, C. S. *Jesus, the Crucified People*. New York: Crossroad, 1990.

Stanton, Elizabeth Cady. *Woman's Bible*. New York: European, 1898.

Stevens, Maryanne, ed. *Reconstructing the Symbol of Christ: Essays in Feminist Christology.* New York/Mahwah: Paulist, 1993.

Strauss, David Friedrich. *The Christ of Faith and the Jesus of History: A Critique of Schleiermacher's Life of Jesus.* Translated, edited, and introduction by Leander E. Keck. Philadelphia: Fortress, 1977.

Streufert, Mary J. "Maternal Sacrifice as a Hermeneutics of the Cross." In *Cross Examinations: Readings on the Meaning of the Cross Today,* edited by Marit Trelstad, 63–75. Minneapolis: Augsburg Fortress, 2006.

Suchocki, Marjorie Hewitt. *God, Christ, Church: A Practical Guide to Process Theology.* New rev. ed. New York: Crossroad, 1989.

Sundermeier, Theo. "Contextualizing Luther's Theology of the Cross." In *The Scandal of a Crucified World: Perspectives on the Cross and Suffering,* edited by Yacob Tesfai, 99–110. Maryknoll, NY: Orbis, 1994.

Swidler, Leonard. "Jesus Was a Feminist." *Catholic World* (January 1971): 177–83.

Talvacchia, Kathleen. "Contradictions of the Cross." *Christianity and Crisis* (February 17, 1992): 28–29.

Tamez, Elsa, ed. *Through Her Eyes: Women's Theology from Latin America.* Maryknoll, NY: Orbis, 1989.

Tanner, Kathryn. "Incarnation, Cross and Sacrifice: A Feminist-Inspired Reappraisal." *Anglican Theological Review* 86, no. 1 (Winter 2004): 35–56.

Tappa, Louise. "The Christ-Event from the Viewpoint of African Women." In *With Passion and Compassion: Third World Women Doing Theology,* edited by Virginia M.M. Fabella and Mercy Amba Oduyoye, 30–34. Maryknoll, NY: Orbis, 1988.

Terrell, JoAnne Marie. "Our Mothers' Gardens: Rethinking Sacrifice." In *Cross Examinations: Readings on the Meaning of the Cross Today,* edited by Marit Trelstad, 33–49. Minneapolis: Augsburg Fortress, 2006.

Tesfai, Yacob, ed. *The Scandal of a Crucified World: Perspectives on the Cross and Suffering.* Maryknoll, NY: Orbis, 1994.

Thistlethwaite, Susan Brooks. "Every Two Minutes: Battered Women and Feminist Interpretation." In *Weaving the Visions: New Patterns in Feminist Spirituality,* edited by Judith Plaskow and Carol P. Christ, 302–13. San Francisco: Harper, 1989.

———. *Sex, Race, and God: Christian Feminism in Black and White.* New York: Crossroad, 1991.

Thistlethwaite, Susan Brooks, and Mary Potter Engel, eds. *Lift Every Voice: Constructing Christian Theologies from the Underside.* San Francisco: Harper & Row, 1990.

Thornton, Sharon G., *Broken yet Beloved: A Pastoral Theology of the Cross.* St. Louis, MO: Chalice, 2002.

Tillich, Paul. *A History of Christian Thought: From Its Judaic and Hellenistic Origins to Existentialism.* Edited by Carl E. Braaten. New York: A Touchstone Book; Simon & Schuster, 1968.

Townes, Emilie M., ed. *A Troubling in My Soul: Womanist Perspectives on Evil and Suffering.* Maryknoll, NY: Orbis, 1993.

Trelstad, Marit A., ed. *Cross Examinations: Readings on the Meaning of the Cross Today.* Minneapolis: Augsburg Fortress, 2006.

———. "'Lavish Love.' A Covenantal Ontology." In *Cross Examinations: Readings on the Meaning of the Cross Today*, edited by Marit Trelstad, 109–24. Minneapolis: Augsburg Fortress, 2006.

Trible, Phyllis. *Texts of Terror: Literary-Feminist Readings of Biblical Narratives.* Philadelphia: Fortress, 1984.

Turner, Pauline, and Bernard Cooke. "Feminist Thought and Systematic Theology." *Horizons* 11, no. 1 (1984): 125–35.

Van Dyk, Leanne. *Believing in Jesus Christ.* Louisville, KY: Geneva, 2002.

———. "How Does Jesus Make a Difference?" In *Essentials of Christian Theology*, edited by William C. Placher, 205–18. Louisville, KY: Westminster John Knox, 2003.

Vexing Christa. http://www.time.com/time/magazine/article/0,9171,954312,00.html. Accessed February 14, 2007.

Wahlberg, Rachel Conrad. *Jesus According to a Woman.* Rev. ed. New York: Paulist, 1986.

———. *Jesus and the Freed Woman.* New York: Paulist, 1978.

Weaver, J. Denny. *The Nonviolent Atonement.* Grand Rapids: Eerdmans, 2001.

——— "Violence in Christian Theology." *Cross Examinations: Readings on the Meaning of the Cross Today*, edited by Marit Trelstad, 225–39. Minneapolis: Augsburg Fortress, 2006.

Weiss, Johannes. *Jesus' Proclamation of the Kingdom of God.* Translated by R. H. Hiers and D. L. Holland. Philadelphia: Fortress, 1971.

Welch, Claude. *God and Incarnation in Mid-Nineteenth Century German Theology.* Edited and translated by Claude Welch. New York: Oxford University Press, 1965.

———. *Protestant Thought in the Nineteenth Century. Vol. 1. 1799–1870.* New Haven: Yale University Press, 1972.

———. *Protestant Thought in the Nineteenth Century. Vol. 2. 1870–1914.* New Haven: Yale University Press, 1985.

Westhelle, Vitor. *The Scandalous God: The Use and Abuse of the Cross.* Minneapolis: Fortress, 2006.

Williams, Delores. *Sisters in the Wilderness: The Challenge of Womanist God-Talk.* Maryknoll, NY: Orbis, 1995.

Wilson-Kastner, Patricia. *Faith, Feminism and the Christ.* Philadelphia: Fortress, 1983.

Winkelmann, Carol L. *The Language of Battered Women. A Rhetorical Analysis of Personal Theologies.* Albany: State University of New York Press, 2004.

WHO Multi-country Study on Women's Health and Domestic Violence against Women: Summary Report of Initial Results on Prevalence, Health Outcomes and Women's Responses. Geneva: World Health Organization, 2005.

Women and Religion: A Bibliographic Guide to Christian Feminist Liberation Theology. Compiled by Shelly Davis Finson. Toronto: University of Toronto Press, 1991.

Yeago, David S. "The New Testament and the Nicene Dogma: A Contribution to the Recovery of Theological Exegesis." *Pro Ecclesia* 3, no. 2 (1994): 152–64.

Yerkes, James. *The Christology of Hegel.* Missoula, MT: Scholars, 1978.

Young, Pamela Dickey. "Diversity in Feminist Christology." *Studies in Religion/Sciences Religieuses* 21, no. 1 (1992): 81–90.

———. *Feminist Theology/Christian Theology: In Search of Method.* Minneapolis: Fortress, 1990.

Zikmund, Barbara Brown. "The Trinity and Women's Experience." *The Christian Century* 104, no. 12 (April 15, 1987): 354–56.

Index